PowerPoi

Made Simple

PowerPoint
Made Simple

Moira Stephen

MADE SIMPLE
BOOKS

Made Simple
An imprint of Butterworth-Heinemann Ltd
Linacre House, Jordan Hill, Oxford OX2 8DP

ℛ   A member of the Reed Elsevier plc group

OXFORD   LONDON   BOSTON
MUNICH   NEW DELHI   SINGAPORE   SYDNEY
TOKYO   TORONTO   WELLINGTON

First published 1995
© Moira Stephen 1995

TRADEMARKS/REGISTERED TRADEMARKS
Computer hardware and software brand names mentioned in this book are protected
by their respective trademarks and are acknowledged.

British Library Cataloguing in Publication Data
A catalogue record for this book is available from the British Library

ISBN 0 7506 2420 5

Design and Typeset by P.K.McBride, Southampton

Archetype, Bash Casual, Cotswold and Gravity fonts from Advanced Graphics Ltd
Icons designed by Sarah Ward © 1994
Printed and bound in Great Britain by Scotprint, Musselburgh, Scotland

Contents

Preface

The computer is about as simple as a spacecraft, and who ever let an untrained spaceman loose? You pick up a manual that weighs more than your birth-weight, open it and find that its written in computerspeak. You see messages on the screen that look like code and the thing even makes noises. No wonder that you feel it's your lucky day if everything goes right. What do you do if everything goes wrong? Give up.

Training helps. Being able to type helps. Experience helps. This book helps, by providing training and assisting with experience. It can't help you if you always manage to hit the wrong keys, but it can tell you which are the right ones and what to do when you hit the wrong ones. After some time, even the dreaded manual will start to make sense, just because you know what the writers are wittering on about.

Computing is not black magic. You don't need luck or charms, just a bit of understanding. The problem is that the programs that are used nowadays look simple but aren't. Most of them are crammed with features you don't need – but how do you know what you don't need? This book shows you what is essential and guides you through it. You will know how to make an action work and why. The less essential bits can wait – and once you start to use a program with confidence you can tackle these bits for yourself.

The writers of this series have all been through it. We know your time is valuable, and you don't want to waste it. You don't buy books on computer subjects to read jokes or be told that you are a dummy. You want to find what you need and be shown how to achieve it. Here, at last, you can.

1 Getting started

What is PowerPoint?

PowerPoint is a presentation graphics package. If you have to make presentations, PowerPoint can help make your life easier by giving you the tools to produce your own presentation materials without (or with minimal) help from presentation graphics specialists.

A PowerPoint Presentation consists of:-

Slides

Slides are the individual pages of your presentation. They may contain text, graphs, clip art, tables, drawings, visuals created in other applications, shapes - and more!! PowerPoint will allow you to present your slides via a slide show on your computer, 35mm slides or overheads.

Speaker's Notes (Sections 5, 10 & 12)

A Speaker's Notes page accompanies each slide you create. Each page contains a small image of the slide plus any notes you type in. You can print your notes pages and use them to prompt you during your presentation.

Handouts (Sections 10 & 12)

Handouts consist of smaller, printed versions of your slides, printed 2, 3 or 6 slides to a page. They provide useful backup material for your audience and can easily be customised with your company name or logo.

Outline (Section 4, 10 & 12)

Your presentation Outline contains the slide titles and main text items, but not art or text typed in using the text tool. The Outline gives a useful overview of your presentation's structure.

Take note

A PowerPoint presentation is a collection of slides, with (optional, but useful) support materials – speaker's notes, handouts and your outline, all in one file.

Tip

You can use PowerPoint to produce a slide show on your computer

Getting into PowerPoint

Basic steps

1 From Program Manager, open the group that contains PowerPoint by double clicking the group icon (probably the Microsoft Office group icon)

2 Double click the PowerPoint application icon to get into PowerPoint

OR

1 If Microsoft Office is set up on your computer, click the PowerPoint tool on the Microsoft Office toolbar

Is PowerPoint installed on your computer? If it isn't, install it now (or get someone else to do it for you).

If you are already working in Windows, save any files that you want to keep, close down the application(s) you are working in and return to the Program Manager window.

If you are not working in Windows, switch on your computer (if necessary) and go into Windows.

You are now ready to start.

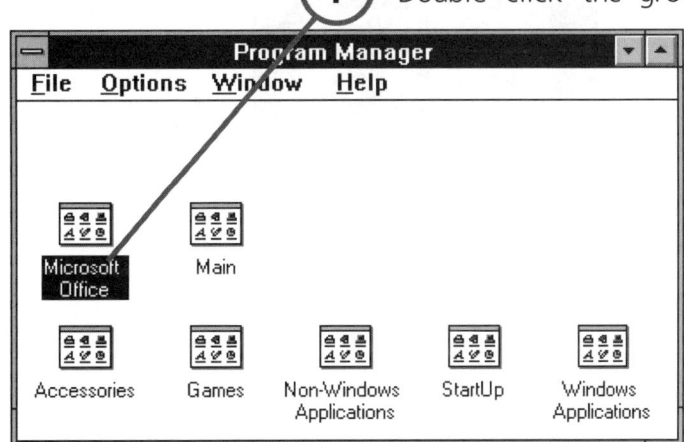

① Double click the group icon

The PowerPoint tool

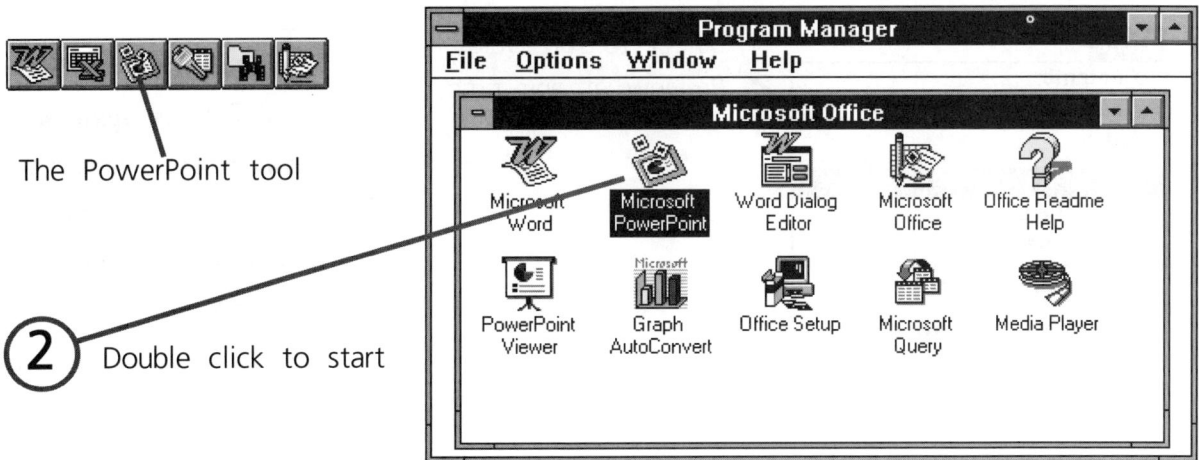

② Double click to start

Quick preview

If this is the first or second time PowerPoint has been accessed on your computer a Quick Preview runs automatically. You can follow the screen prompts to work through this if you wish (or click Quit if you find it a bit boring!).

Return to previous screen

Move on to next screen

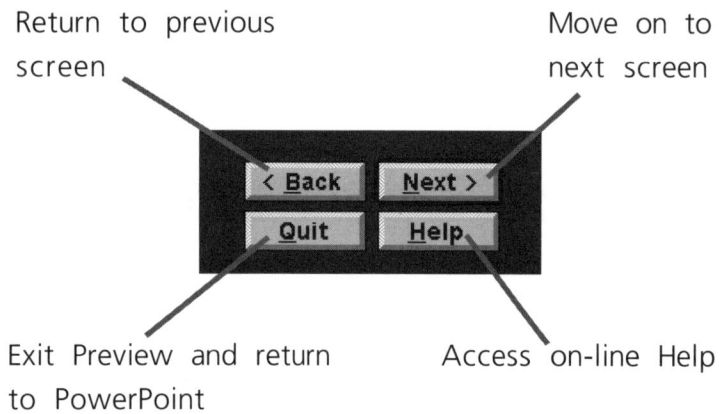

Exit Preview and return to PowerPoint

Access on-line Help

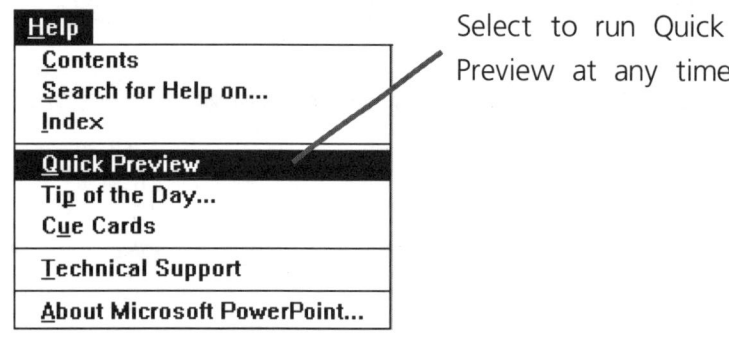

Select to run Quick Preview at any time

Tip

Work through the Quick Preview at least once – it gives you an overview of what the packages can do. And it only lasts about 5 minutes from beginning to end.

Tip

If you want to see the Quick Preview again, or show it to a colleague at a later date, you can switch it on from the Help menu in PowerPoint.

4

Tip of the day

After the Quick Preview, a Tip of the Day appears each time you go into PowerPoint. These tips can be a useful learning aid when you are getting to know the package.

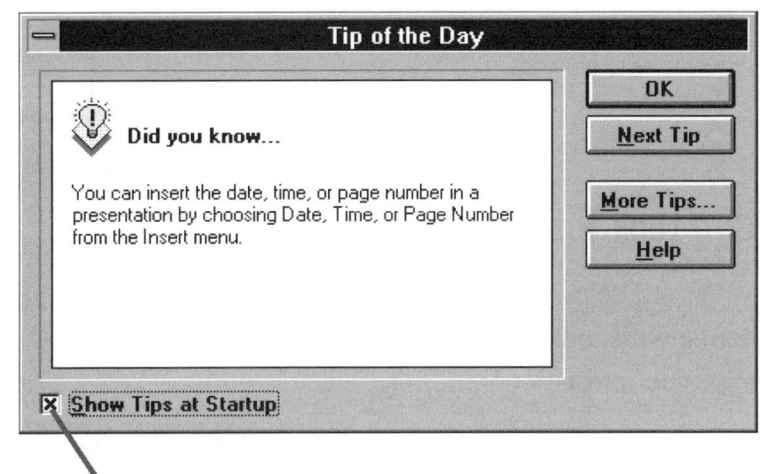

Clear the checkbox to stop the Tips

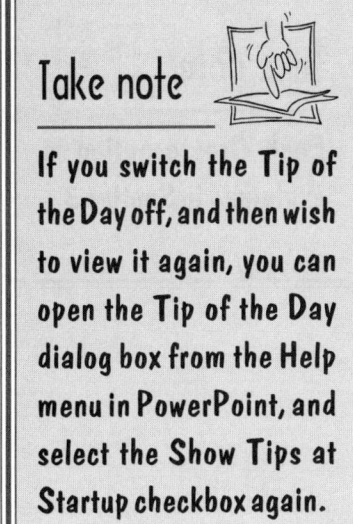

Take note

If you switch the **Tip of the Day** off, and then wish to view it again, you can open the **Tip of the Day** dialog box from the **Help** menu in PowerPoint, and select the **Show Tips at Startup** checkbox again.

Pick up a tip at any time

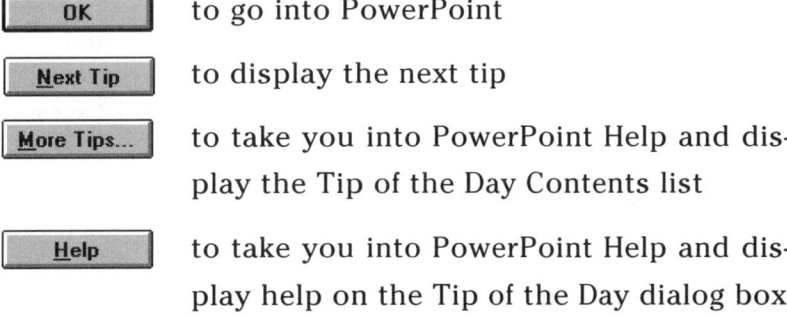

From the Tip of the Day dialog box you can choose:-

OK	to go into PowerPoint
Next Tip	to display the next tip
More Tips...	to take you into PowerPoint Help and display the Tip of the Day Contents list
Help	to take you into PowerPoint Help and display help on the Tip of the Day dialog box

You can switch the Tip of the Day off if you wish by deselecting the Show Tips at Startup checkbox in the lower left corner of the dialog box.

5

PowerPoint dialog box

After the Quick Preview or Tip of the Day, you arrive at the PowerPoint dialog box, where you start to set up your Presentation.

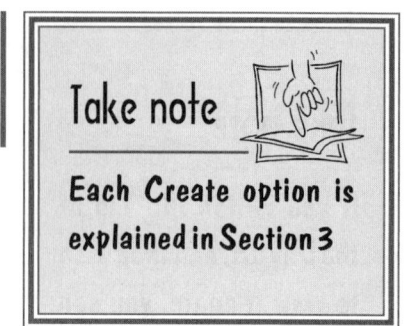

Take note

Each Create option is explained in Section 3

AutoContent Wizard

Choose this if you want to start by using a Wizard that helps you work out the content and organisation of your presentation.

Pick a Look Wizard

This Wizard helps you determine the look and feel of your presentation.

Template

This option lets you pick a presentation template with the colour scheme, fonts and other design features already set up.

Blank Presentation

If you opt for this one, you get a blank presentation with all the colour scheme, font and design features set to the default values.

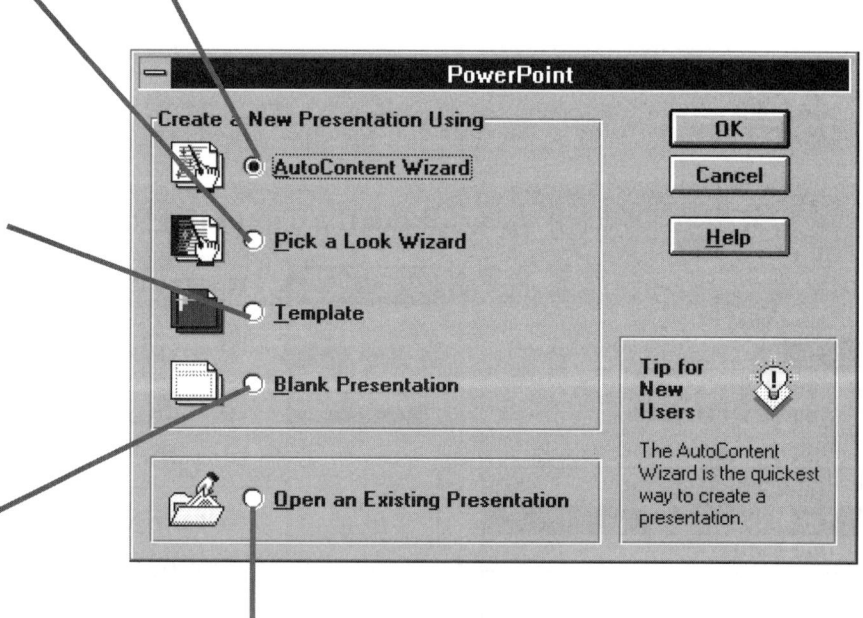

Open an Existing Presentation

This option takes you to the Open dialog box, where you can open an existing presentation.

PowerPoint window

Tip

The Toolbars can be moved around so you can arrange the screen layout to suit yourself.

The PowerPoint window is very similar to other Microsoft application windows. If you use Word, Excel or Access you will recognise some of the tools on the Toolbars.

The Standard and Formatting Toolbars usually appear along the top of the window. The Drawing Toolbar is usually down the left hand side of the window

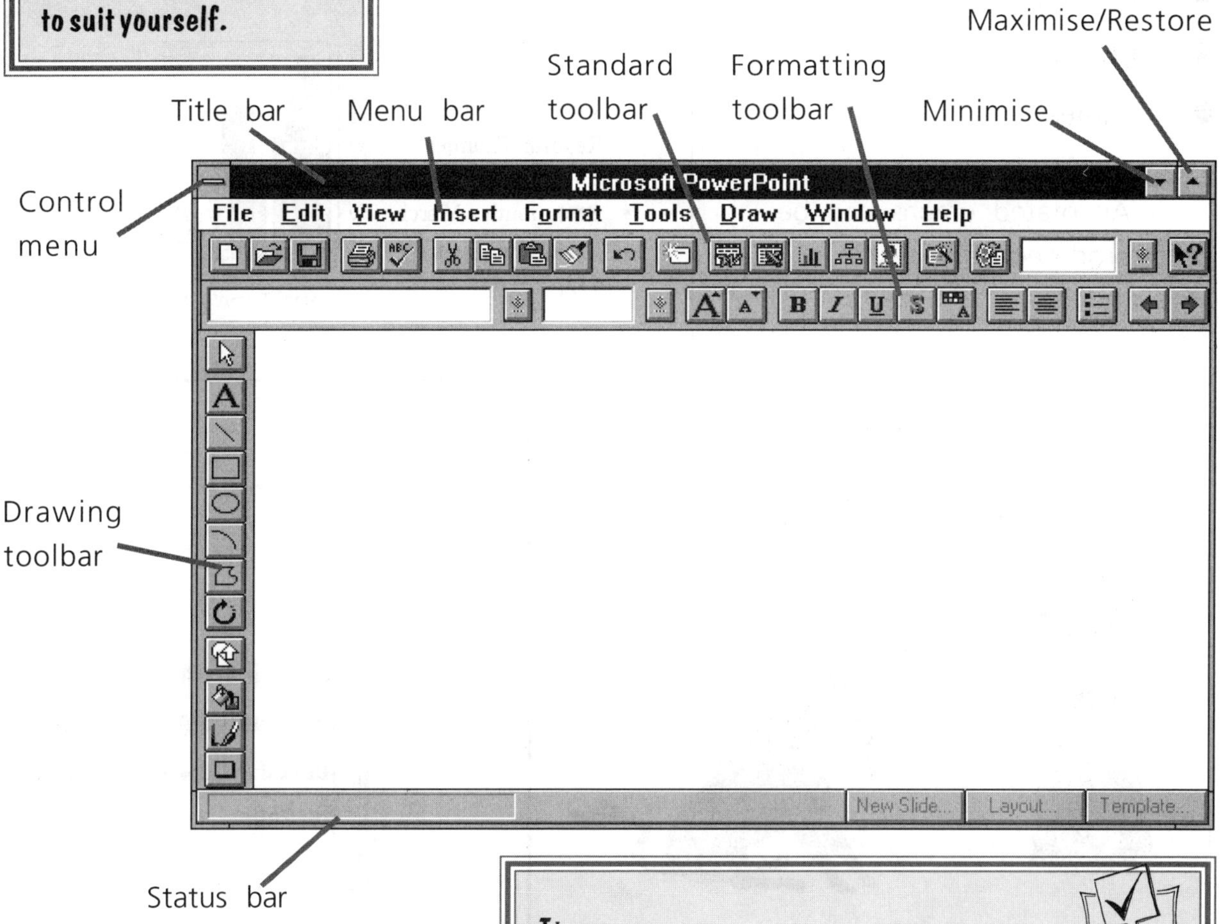

Maximise/Restore

Standard toolbar   Formatting toolbar

Title bar   Menu bar   Minimise

Control menu

Microsoft PowerPoint

File Edit View Insert Format Tools Draw Window Help

Drawing toolbar

New Slide...   Layout...   Template...

Status bar

Tip

If you need to more about Windows, try the companion volume – Windows Made Simple.

7

PowerPoint objects

When working in PowerPoint you work with PowerPoint OBJECTS. The objects may be:-

● Text

● Drawings

● Graphs

● Organisation Charts

● ClipArt or

● Tables

Annotated graphs can be produced very easily

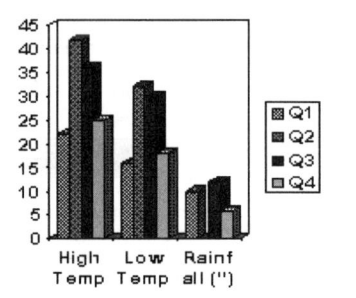

There are over 1000 ClipArt images supplied with PowerPoint

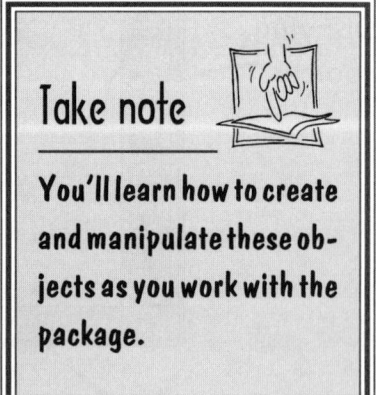

Leaving PowerPoint

Leaving PowerPoint is very easy. If you use other windows packages, the technique is very similar.

(1) Open the File menu

File	
<u>N</u>ew...	Ctrl+N
<u>O</u>pen...	Ctrl+O
<u>C</u>lose	
<u>S</u>ave	Ctrl+S
Save <u>A</u>s...	
<u>F</u>ind File...	
Summary <u>I</u>nfo...	
Slide Set<u>u</u>p...	
<u>P</u>rint...	Ctrl+P
<u>1</u> C:\MSOFFICE\POWERPNT\DEFAULT.PPT	
<u>2</u> C:\MSOFFICE\POWERPNT\MOIRA.PPT	
<u>3</u> C:\MSOFFICE\POWERPNT\MOIRA1.PPT	
E<u>x</u>it	

Closes the presentation, but leaves PowerPoint running

(2) Select Exit

Organisation charts are simple to create – once you have worked out the structure of your organisation!

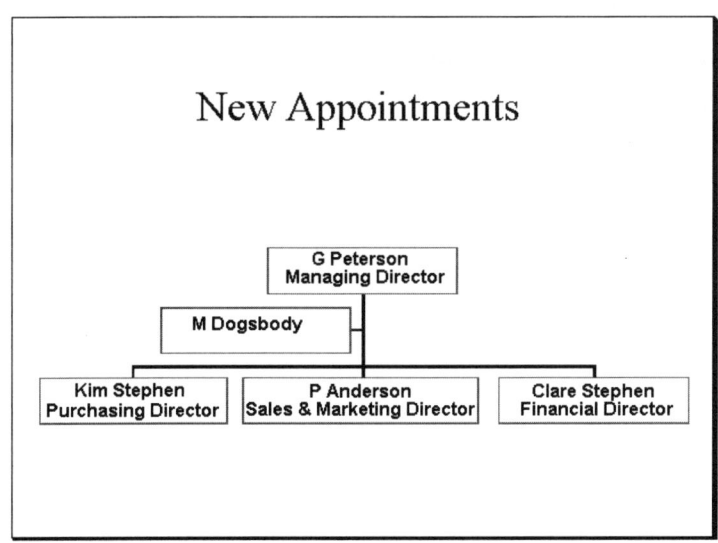

Summary

- **PowerPoint** is a powerful presentation graphics package

- To access PowerPoint, double click the **group** icon that PowerPoint is in, then double click the **PowerPoint application** icon

- If the **Microsoft Office toolbar** is displayed, click the PowerPoint tool once to access the package

- The **Quick Preview** gives you an overview of what PowerPoint is about

- The **Tip of the Day** displays a feature or shortcut you may find useful when using PowerPoint

- The PowerPoint **dialog box** gives you a range of options to get you started on your presentation

- The PowerPoint **window** displays a selection of toolbars to give you quick access to commonly used features in the package

- Text, Drawings, Graphs, Organisation Charts, Clipart and Tables are called PowerPoint **objects**

- To **exit** PowerPoint, double click the control menu button on the application's title bar

2 Help

Browsing

When working in the Windows environment there is always plenty of help available – in books, in manuals, in magazines and on-line. The trick is being able to find the help you need, when you need it. In this section, we look at the various ways you can interrogate the on-line Help when you discover you're in need of it.

There are several ways you can dip into Help, and you can choose the most suitable method, depending on what you are doing. You can:-

● **Browse** through the on-line Help to get a feel for what is available (as described below)

● **Search** for help on a specific topic once you know what you need help on

● Use **Context Sensitive** Help to get help with Menu items and Dialog boxes

● View **Cue cards** to help you work through new tasks

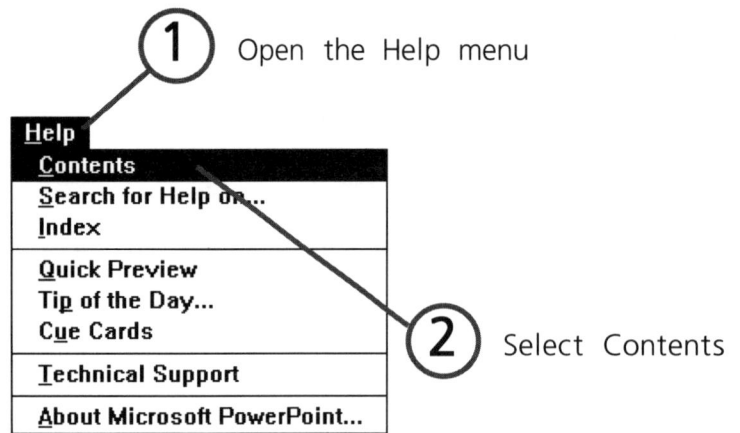

① Open the Help menu

② Select Contents

1 Open the **Help** menu

2 Choose **Contents**

3 From the Contents window, click on the green underlined topic that you are interested in, eg "Using PowerPoint"

4 From the list of options displayed, click on the green underlined topic that you are interested in eg "Creating Presentations and Slides". Continue in this way until you have found the help page that contains the information you want to read

5 Double Click the **Control Menu** Button on the Help Window title bar to close Help

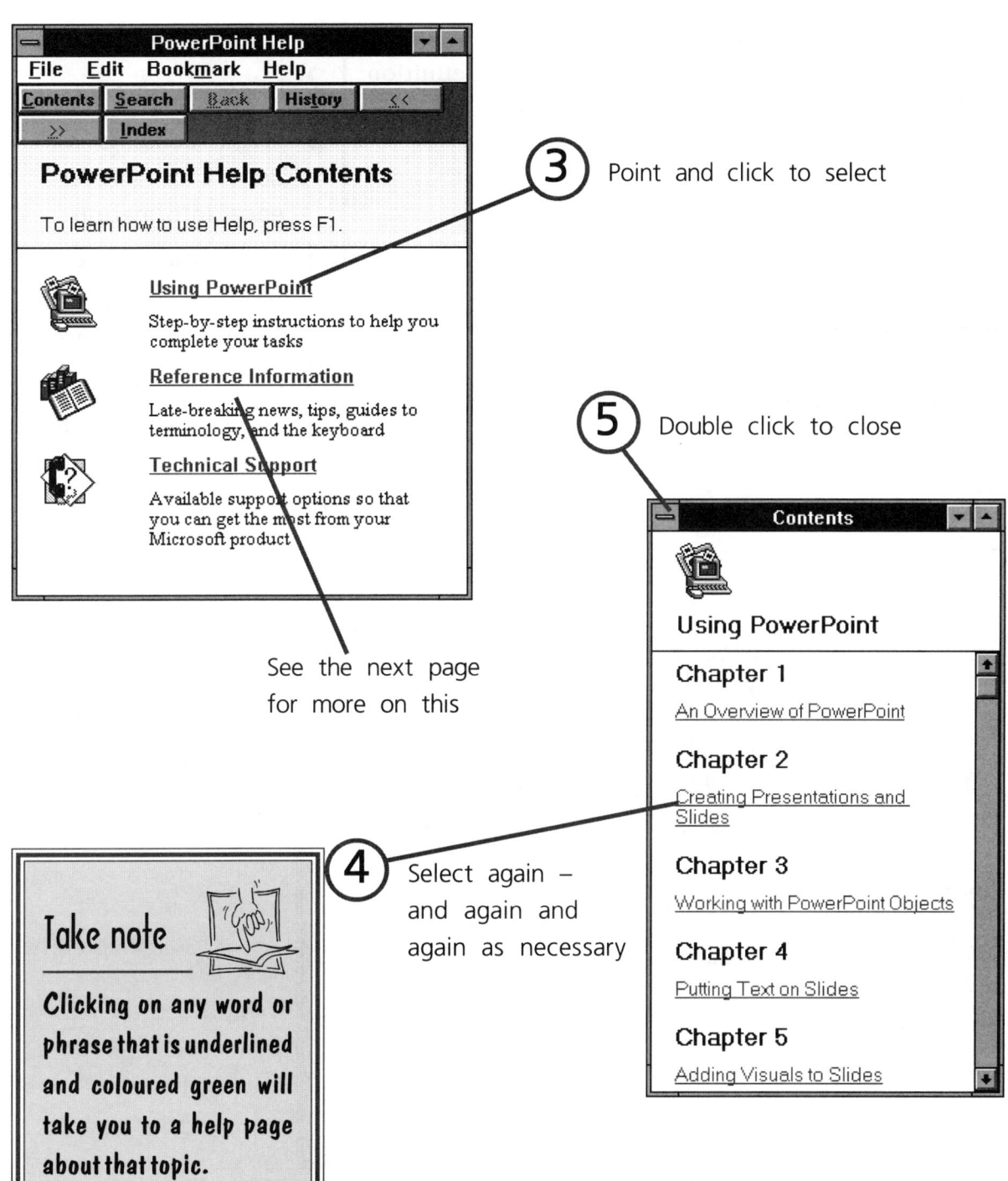

PowerPoint Help

File   Edit   Bookmark   Help

Contents | Search | Back | History | <<
>> | Index

PowerPoint Help Contents

To learn how to use Help, press F1.

Using PowerPoint
Step-by-step instructions to help you
complete your tasks

Reference Information
Late-breaking news, tips, guides to
terminology, and the keyboard

Technical Support
Available support options so that
you can get the most from your
Microsoft product

③ Point and click to select

⑤ Double click to close

Contents

Using PowerPoint

Chapter 1
An Overview of PowerPoint

Chapter 2
Creating Presentations and
Slides

Chapter 3
Working with PowerPoint Objects

Chapter 4
Putting Text on Slides

Chapter 5
Adding Visuals to Slides

See the next page
for more on this

④ Select again –
and again and
again as necessary

Take note

**Clicking on any word or
phrase that is underlined
and coloured green will
take you to a help page
about that topic.**

13

Definition of terms

If you want to see the definitions of the specialist terms you will find in PowerPoint, you can access the definition list from the Help system.

Basic steps

1 Open the **Help** menu

2 Choose **Contents**

3 In the **Contents** window, choose **Reference Information**

4 Select **Definitions** from the **PowerPoint Reference** window

5 Locate the term you are interested in, then click for the definition

6 Click anywhere on the screen to close the Definition box

Tip

On any Help page, clicking on a word with a broken underline gives you its definition.

Click a letter to jump to the set that start with that letter

④ Choose Definitions

⑤ Click on an item for its definition

Contents

PowerPoint Referenc

La**t**e-breaking
Inf**o**rmation about
Po**w**erPoint

PowerPoint Readme Help

**General Reference
Information**

Definitions

Keyboar

Getting H

Getting H
PowerP
Toolbar

Comm
Tips

What's New in Microsoft

PowerPoint Help

File   Edit   Bookmark   Help

| Contents | Search | Back | History | << |

| >> | Index |

Definitions

A B C D E F G H I J K L M N
O P Q R S T U V W X Y Z

Click the first letter of the word you want to look up, or press TAB to select the letter, and then press ENTER.

outline

Outline

The titles and main text from your slides. Pictures and other visuals don't appear in an outline. Other text you've added using the Text tool and embedded text and graphics won't show up either, since they're not part of the main text.

Basic steps

1 Open the **Help** menu and choose **Search for Help on**

2 Scroll through the list of help topics until you see the one you want, then click on it to select it

3 Choose **Show Topics** to display the titles of related Help topics

4 Select an item from the list

5 Click **Go To** to display the Help page

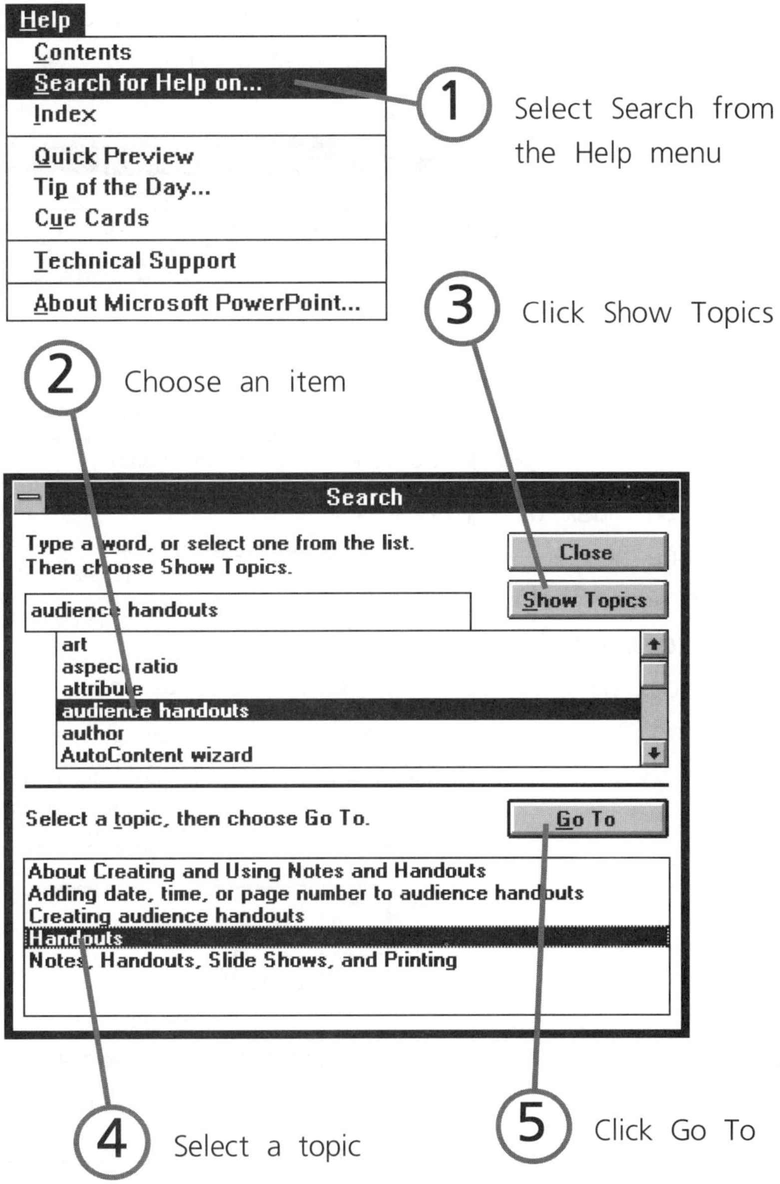

Tip

Double click the Help Tool on the Standard Toolbar to get to the Search dialog box.

Search

Browsing as described above, although interesting when you have the time, can be a time-consuming process.

If you know what you need help on, you will probably be quicker **searching** for the topic.

Help
Contents
Search for Help on...
Index
Quick Preview
Ti**p** of the Day...
C**u**e Cards
Technical Support
About Microsoft PowerPoint...

1 Select Search from the Help menu

3 Click Show Topics

2 Choose an item

Search

Type a word, or select one from the list. Then choose Show Topics.

Close

Show Topics

audience handouts

art
aspect ratio
attribute
audience handouts
author
AutoContent wizard

Select a topic, then choose Go To.   **Go To**

About Creating and Using Notes and Handouts
Adding date, time, or page number to audience handouts
Creating audience handouts
Handouts
Notes, Handouts, Slide Shows, and Printing

4 Select a topic

5 Click Go To

15

Help buttons

Within the Help window, there are several buttons to aid you on your way as you navigate through the system.

Go to the Search dialog box.

Move back through the topics you've viewed, one topic at a time.

Display a list topics you've looked at. To move to one of the topics listed, point to it and double click.

Go to the PowerPoint Contents window

Forward to the next page on the topic displayed (Dimmed if you are at the last page in a topic).

Displays an index of the on-line help. You can access help on any topic listed in the index by clicking on it.

Back to the previous page of the topic displayed (Dimmed if you are at the first page in a topic)

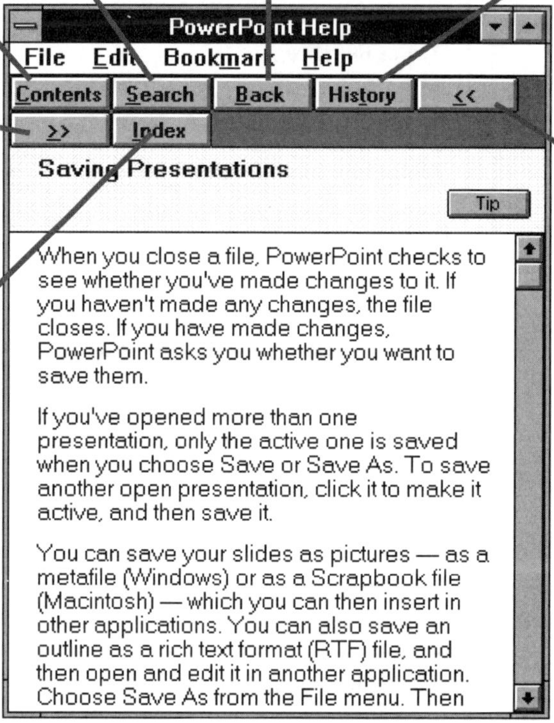

PowerPoint Help

File   Edit   Bookmark   Help

| Contents | Search | Back | History | << |
| >> | Index |

Saving Presentations

Tip

When you close a file, PowerPoint checks to see whether you've made changes to it. If you haven't made any changes, the file closes. If you have made changes, PowerPoint asks you whether you want to save them.

If you've opened more than one presentation, only the active one is saved when you choose Save or Save As. To save another open presentation, click it to make it active, and then save it.

You can save your slides as pictures — as a metafile (Windows) or as a Scrapbook file (Macintosh) — which you can then insert in other applications. You can also save an outline as a rich text format (RTF) file, and then open and edit it in another application. Choose Save As from the File menu. Then

---

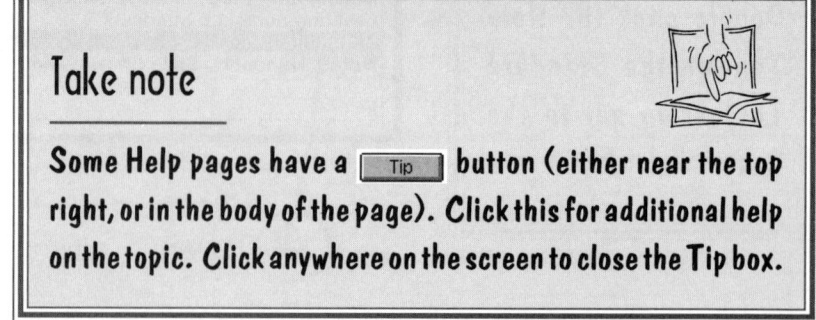

Take note

Some Help pages have a ⬚Tip⬚ button (either near the top right, or in the body of the page). Click this for additional help on the topic. Click anywhere on the screen to close the Tip box.

Basic steps

❏ **Help on the Tools or Menu items**

1 Click the **Help** Tool on the Toolbar, then

EITHER

2 Click on the Tool that interests you – this displays Help on the selected Tool

OR

2 Open a menu

3 Click on the menu item that you want Help on – you are taken to its Help Page

This is a very direct way of getting help on whatever you are working on. There are 3 main methods here -

● Tooltip and Status bar

● Help on the the Tools or Menu Items

● Help on the Dialog Boxes

Tooltip and Status bar

If you pause the mouse pointer over a Tool, you will see a **ToolTip** at the pointer and a brief description of its function on the status bar.

When you select a menu or menu option, a brief description of what it does appears on the Status Bar.

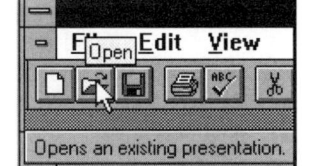

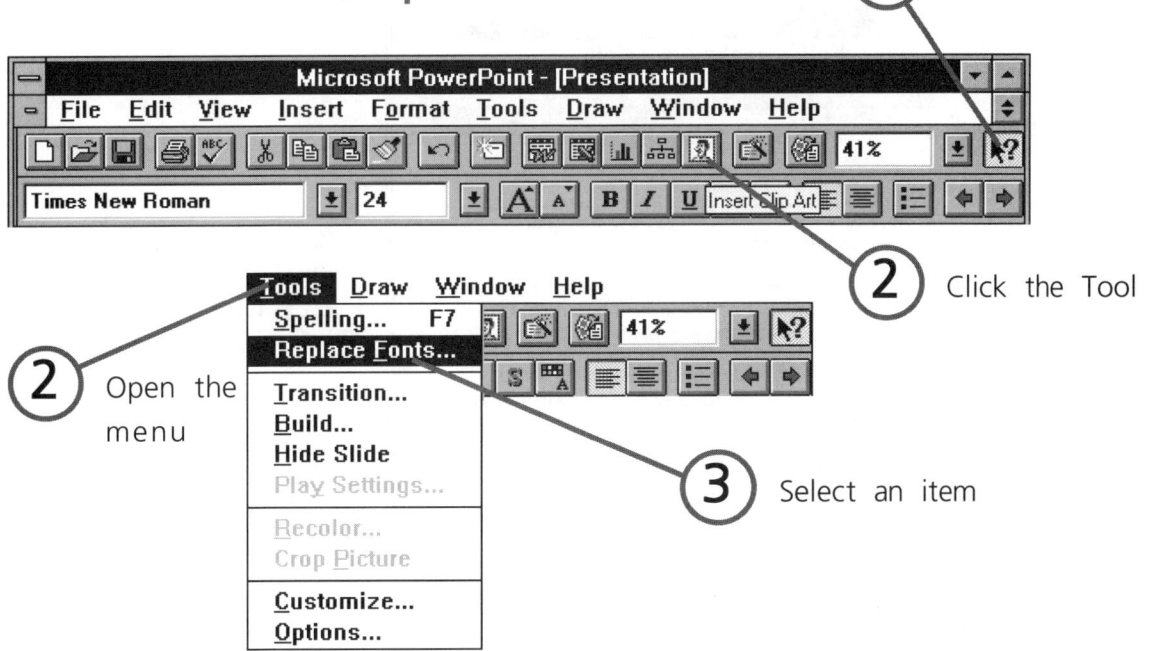

① Click the Help tool

② Click the Tool

② Open the menu

③ Select an item

Help on the Dialog Boxes

If you find yourself in a dialog box, and you need help on how to complete it, Context Sensitive Help is always available.

Basic steps

1 From the dialog box, click **Help** or press [F1]

2 Move through the on-line help until you find what you need

3 When you're finished with the Help, double click its Control Menu Button to close it

❑ You are returned to the dialog box you were in when you asked for Help

① Press [F1] or click Help

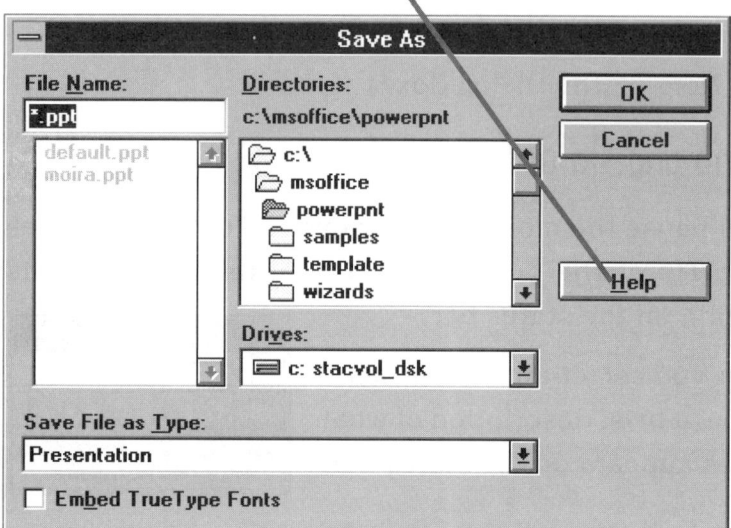

③ Double click

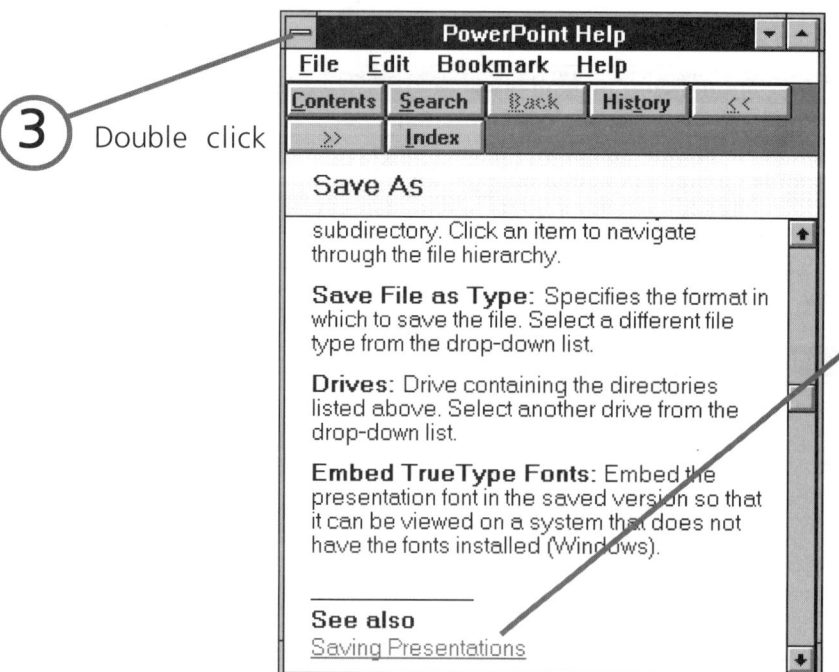

② Navigate through to find the Help you want

18

Basic steps

1 Open the **Help** menu and choose **Cue Cards**

2 Select the topic you want help with from the list provided

3 When you no longer need to view the cards, double click the Control Menu button on the title bar to close them.

If you are working on something you haven't done before, you might want to view the Cue Cards as you work. They can be displayed at the same time as your presentation, so you can keep the help you need on screen.

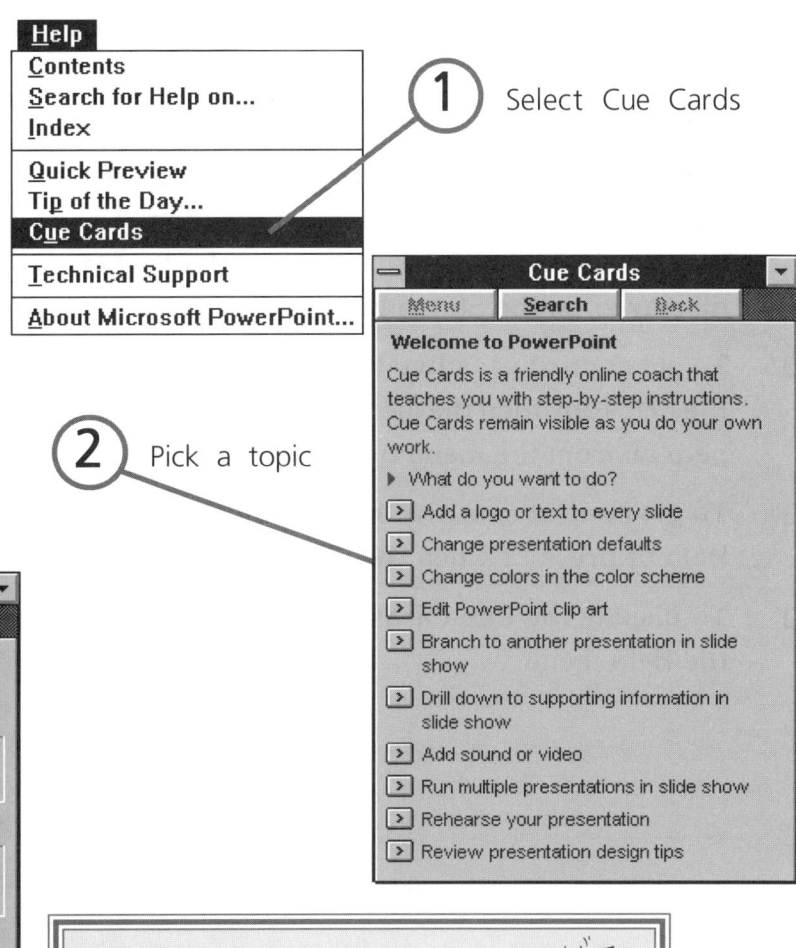

Select Cue Cards

Pick a topic

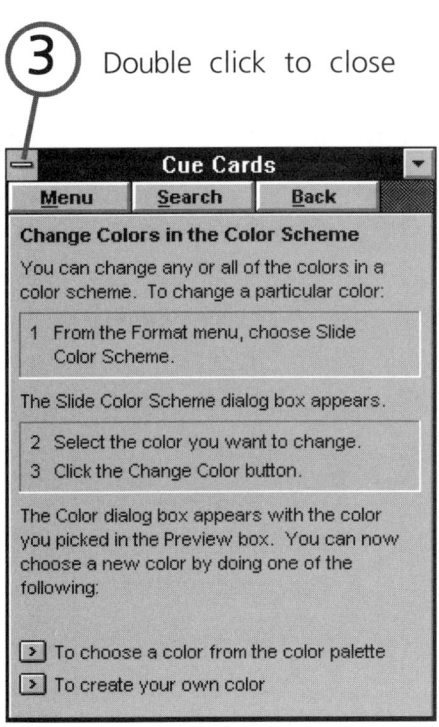

Double click to close

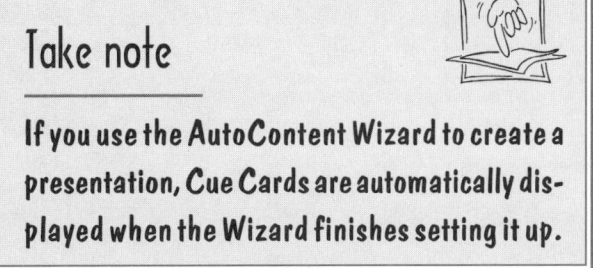

Take note

If you use the AutoContent Wizard to create a presentation, Cue Cards are automatically displayed when the Wizard finishes setting it up.

Summary

- [ ] To **Browse** through the Help pages, choose **Contents** from the Help menu, then select any topic that interests you from the list

- [ ] If you know what you are looking for, choose **Search** from the Help menu, then use the Search dialog box to locate the help pages required

- [ ] Pause over any tool on a toolbar to display the **Tooltip** that describes the tool's function in one or two words. A brief description of the tool is also displayed on the Status Bar.

- [ ] To get context sensitive help on a **menu item**, click the help tool, then the menu, then the item you want help on from the menu list

- [ ] To get context sensitive help on a **dialog box**, click Help or press F1 when the dialog box is open

- [ ] To display the **Cue Cards**, choose Cue Cards from the Help menu

3 The new Presentation

AutoContent Wizard

Creating a presentation using PowerPoint is easy. Once you are into PowerPoint, and have passed the Quick Preview or the Tip of the Day dialog box , the PowerPoint dialog box appears.

In this section we will look at the different options for creating a presentation – we will consider the content of the presentation later. Regardless of which option you select, you still end up creating slides, notes and hand-outs for your presentation. We will consider each option in this section – once you've tried them out, you can decide for yourself which method suits you best.

The easiest way to create your first presentation is to use the AutoContent Wizard. The wizard helps you set up the Title Slide (the first slide in your presentation), and gives you an outline to follow as you build up the other slides.

Basic steps

1 Start up PowerPoint and go to the **Power-Point** dialog box

OR

1 If you are already in PowerPoint, click the **New** tool 🗋 to open the **New Presentation** dialog box

❑ Both offer the same options

2 Select **AutoContent Wizard** and click **OK**

② Select how you want to create the presentation

These other ways of creating a presentation are covered in the next few pages.

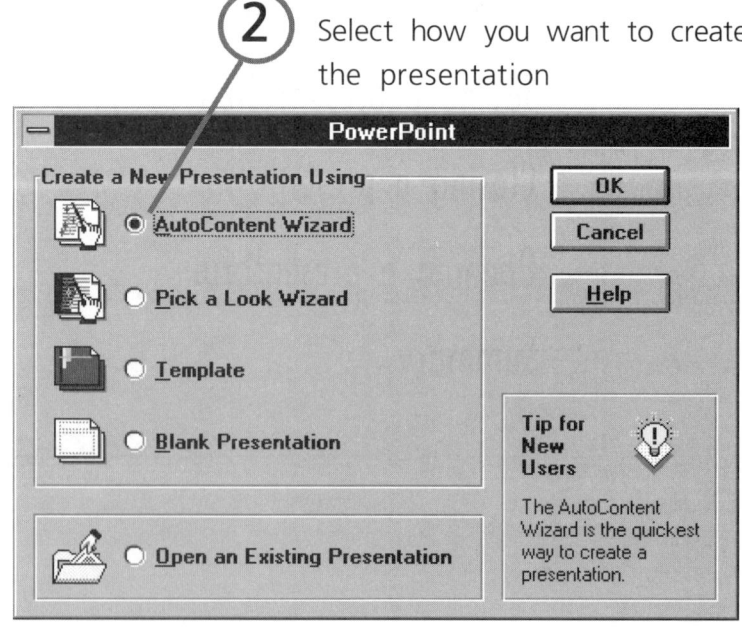

3 Wizard Step 1 simply tells you what it does. Click [Next >] to get started

4 Wizard Step 2 asks for information for the Title Slide. Complete the fields as appropriate

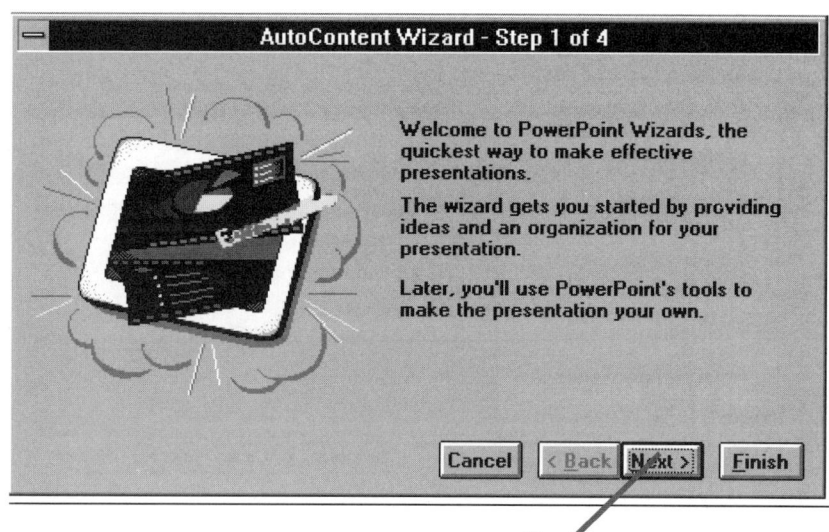

③ Click to start

④ Complete the Title Slide details

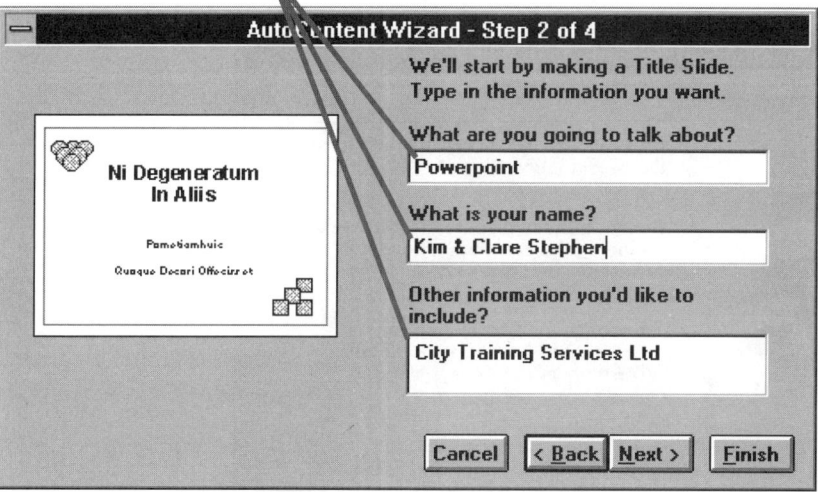

Take note

As you work through a Wizard, click [Next >] when you have completed each step and [Finish] at the chequered flag

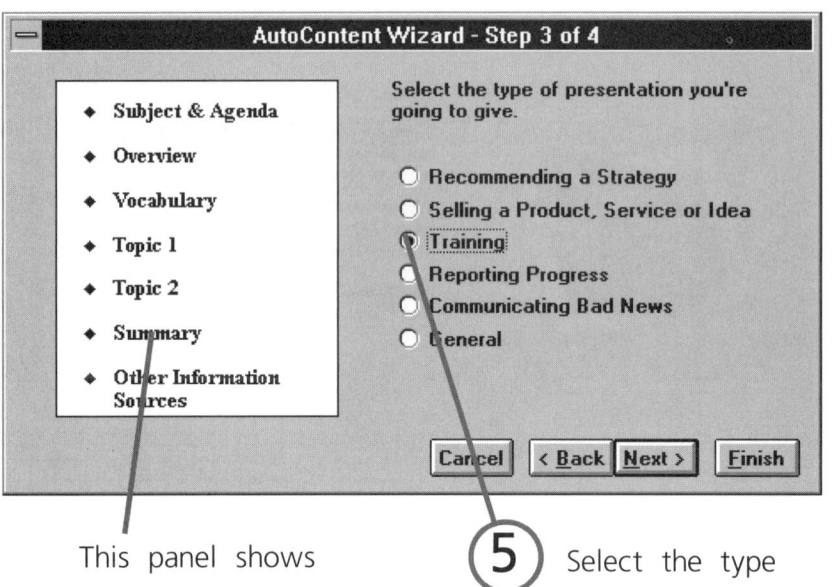

5 At Wizard Step 3, select the option that best describes the type of presentation you are going to give

6 At Wizard Step 4, click Finish and PowerPoint will set up your presentation

This panel shows the structure of the presentation

(5) Select the type

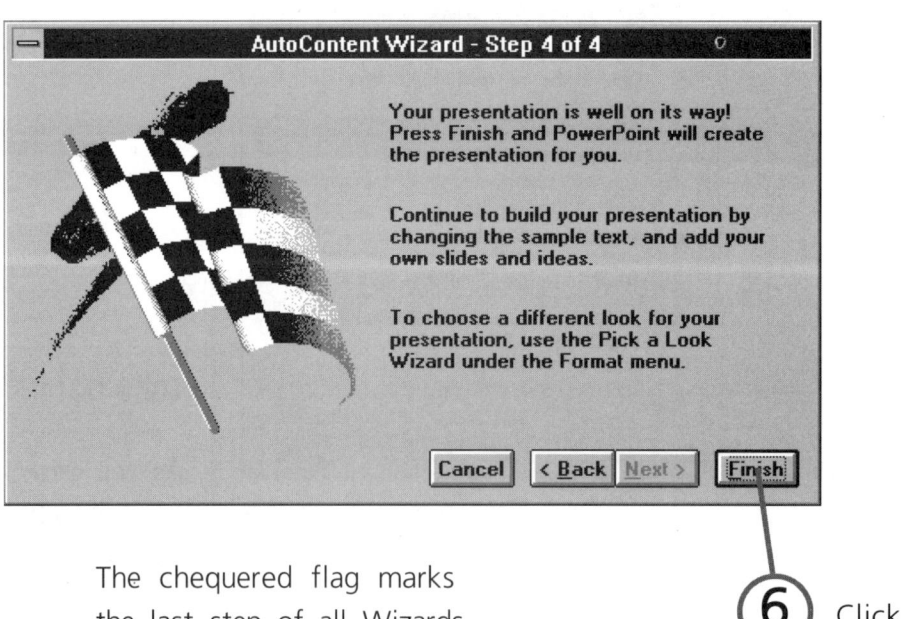

The chequered flag marks the last step of all Wizards

(6) Click Finish

Slide number   Slide icon

Title slide

Subsequent slides

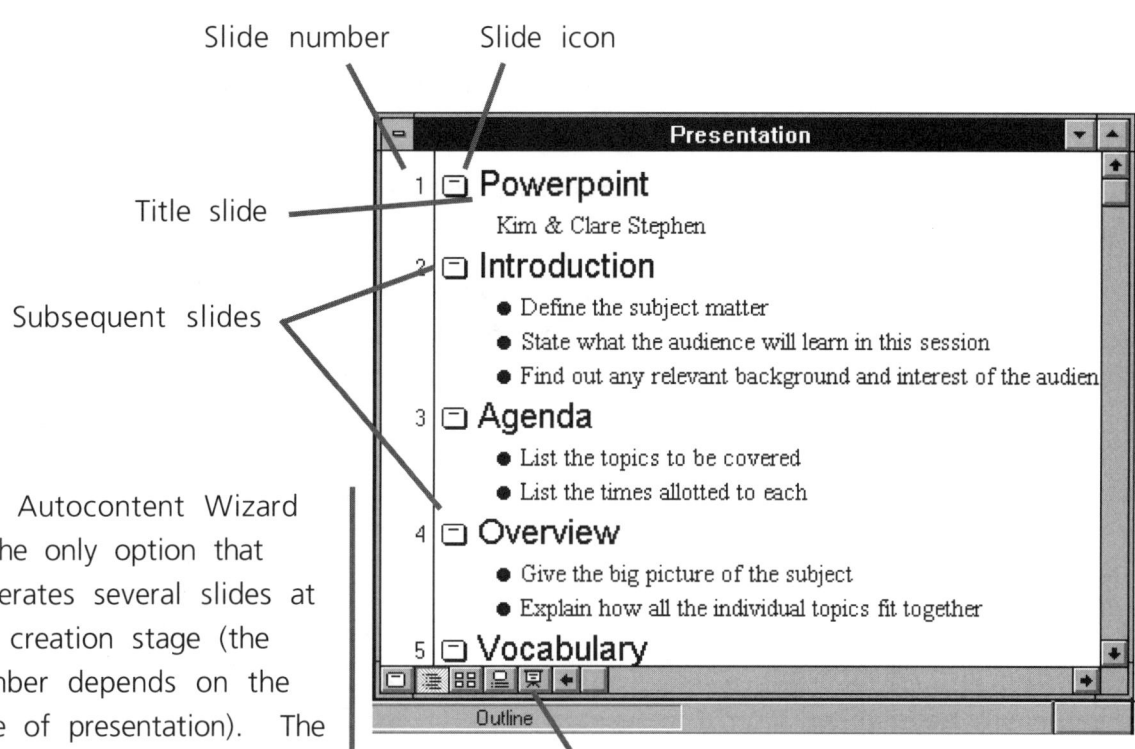

View tools

The Autocontent Wizard is the only option that generates several slides at the creation stage (the number depends on the type of presentation). The slide contents are only intended as a guide – edit them as necessary for your own presentation (see section 4).

It is also the only option that takes you directly into Outline view.

Your presentation can be displayed on the screen using different views – Slide, Outline, Slide Sorter, Notes Pages or Slide Show. You'll soon learn which view is most appropriate to the task you are doing.

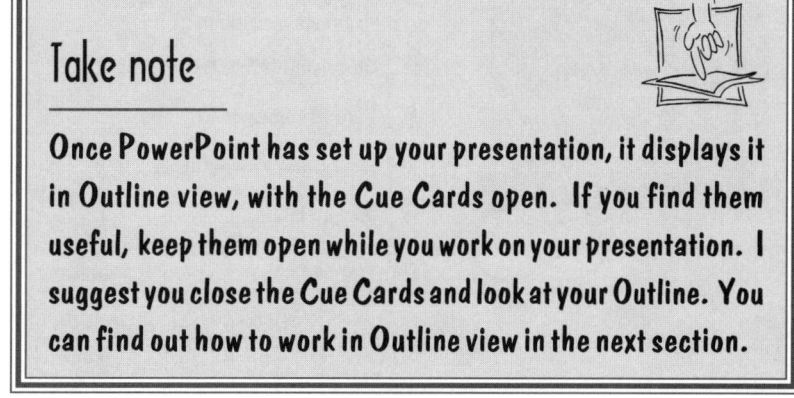

Take note

Once PowerPoint has set up your presentation, it displays it in Outline view, with the Cue Cards open. If you find them useful, keep them open while you work on your presentation. I suggest you close the Cue Cards and look at your Outline. You can find out how to work in Outline view in the next section.

Pick a Look Wizard

This is the second way of creating a presentation. Using this option you select the "look" or "style" of your presentation. This is done by specifying the:-

● Output method - Overheads, On-Screen presentation or 35 mm slides

● Template on which to base your presentation - the template determines your colour scheme, fonts and design features

● Slide options

● Notes options

● Handout options

● Outline options

The options you select while working through this Wizard can easily be changed later if necessary.

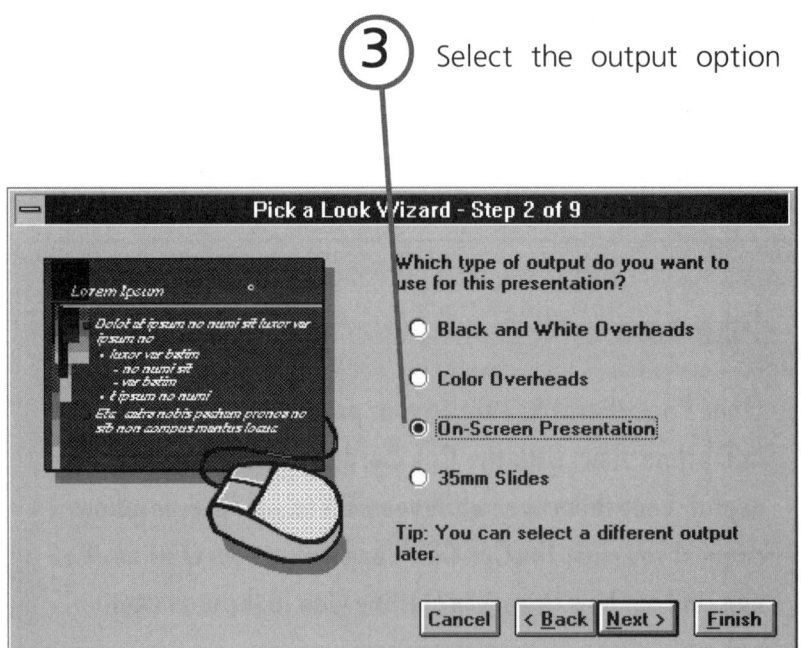

(3) Select the output option

1 At the PowerPoint dialog box or New Presentation dialog box, select the **Pick a Look Wizard**

2 Click **Next** at Wizard Step 1

3 Specify the **Output option** you required at Wizard Step 2

❑ Remember – click Next > after each step and Finish at the chequered flag

Take note

You can use the Pick A Look Wizard at any time - not just when you create a presentation. Click the tool on the Standard toolbar when you want to create or edit the "look" of your presentation and complete the steps as required.

4 Select the **Template** you want to use at Wizard Step 3

5 Choose the **Print** options required at Wizard Step 4

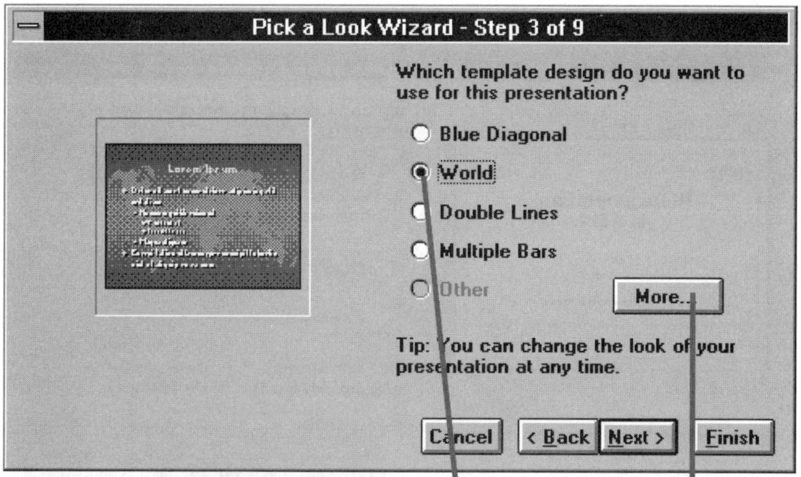

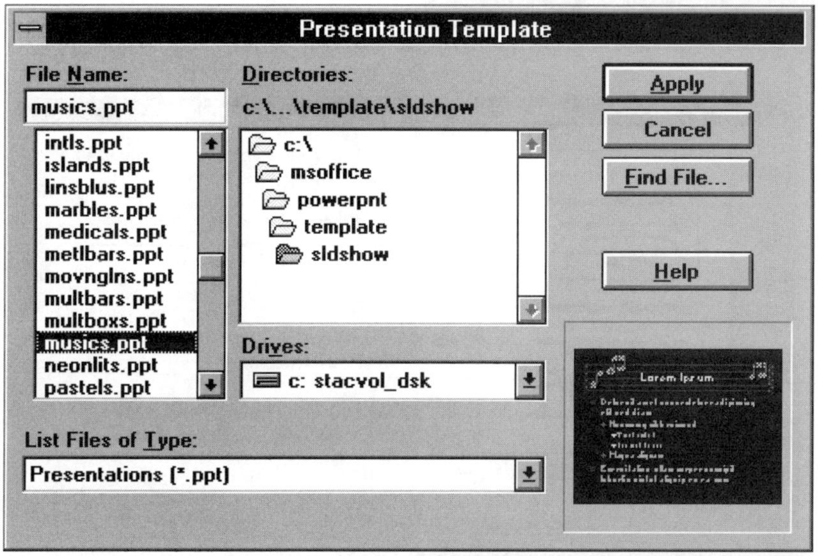

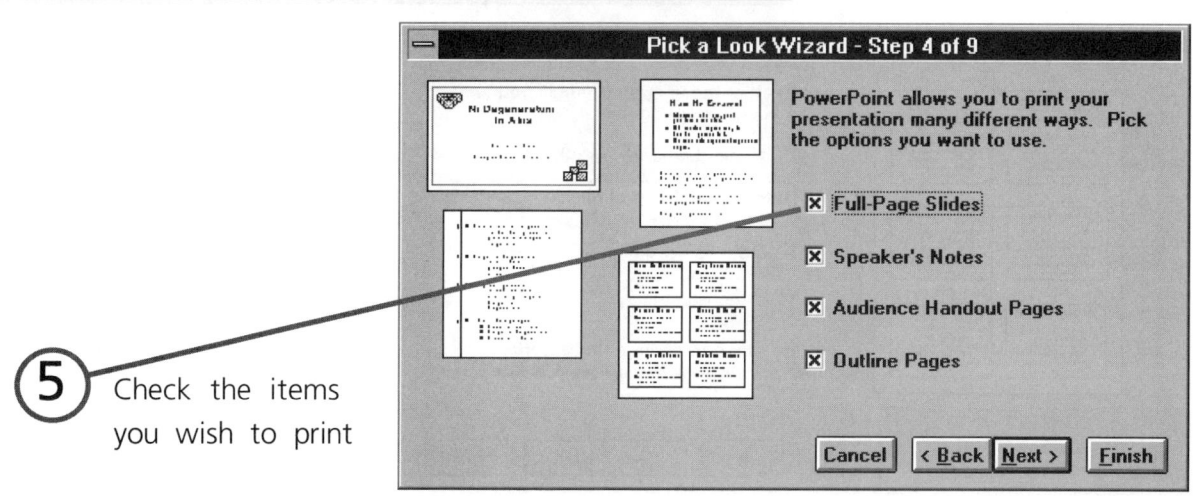

④ Choose a Template

If you click More.. it opens the Presentation Template dialog box, where you will find many more to choose from

⑤ Check the items you wish to print

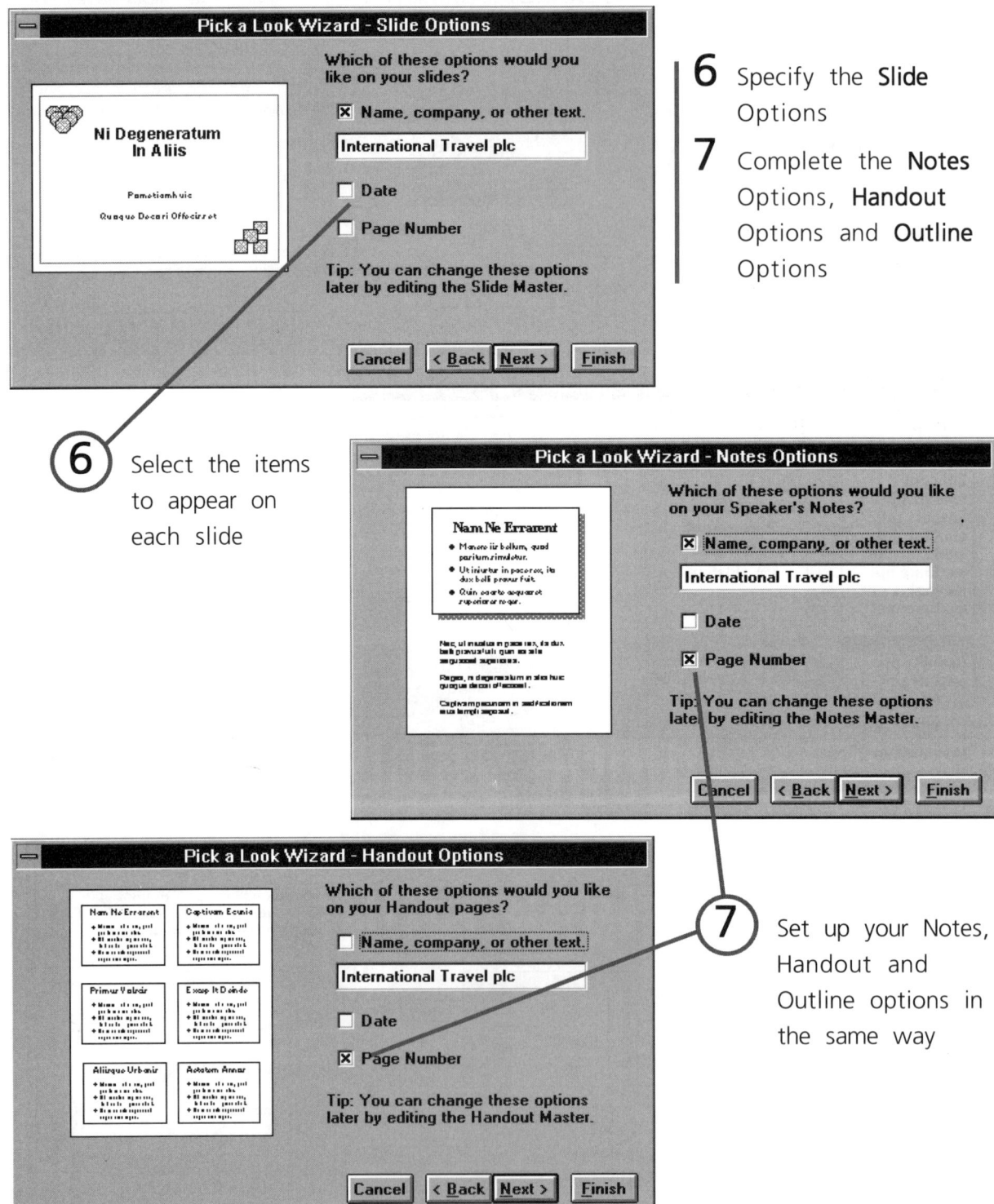

Pick a Look Wizard - Slide Options

Which of these options would you
like on your slides?

☒ Name, company, or other text.

International Travel plc

☐ Date

☐ Page Number

Tip: You can change these options
later by editing the Slide Master.

Cancel | < Back | Next > | Finish

6 Specify the **Slide**
Options

7 Complete the **Notes**
Options, **Handout**
Options and **Outline**
Options

6 Select the items
to appear on
each slide

Pick a Look Wizard - Notes Options

Which of these options would you like
on your Speaker's Notes?

☒ Name, company, or other text.

International Travel plc

☐ Date

☒ Page Number

Tip: You can change these options
later by editing the Notes Master.

Cancel | < Back | Next > | Finish

Pick a Look Wizard - Handout Options

Which of these options would you like
on your Handout pages?

☐ Name, company, or other text.

International Travel plc

☐ Date

☒ Page Number

Tip: You can change these options
later by editing the Handout Master.

Cancel | < Back | Next > | Finish

7 Set up your Notes,
Handout and
Outline options in
the same way

❑ Note that the slide, note, handout and outline option screens only appear if they are selected in the print options at Wizard Step 4 above

8 Click Finish when you see the chequered flag at Step 9

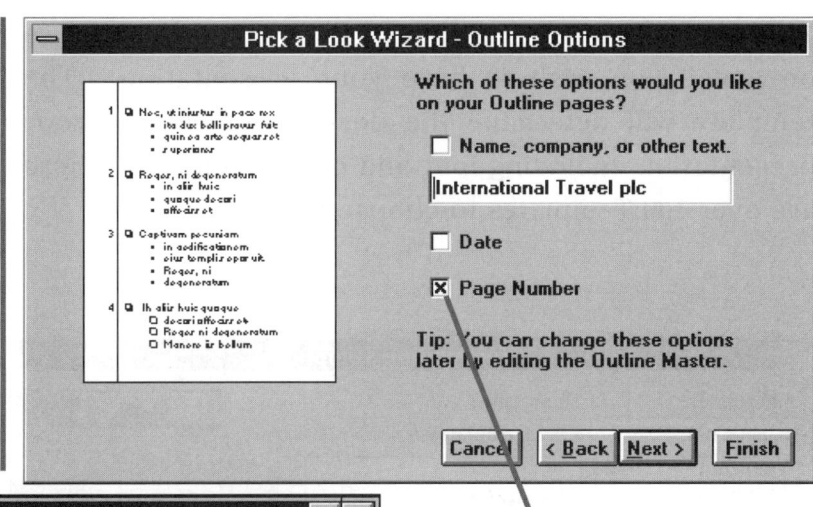

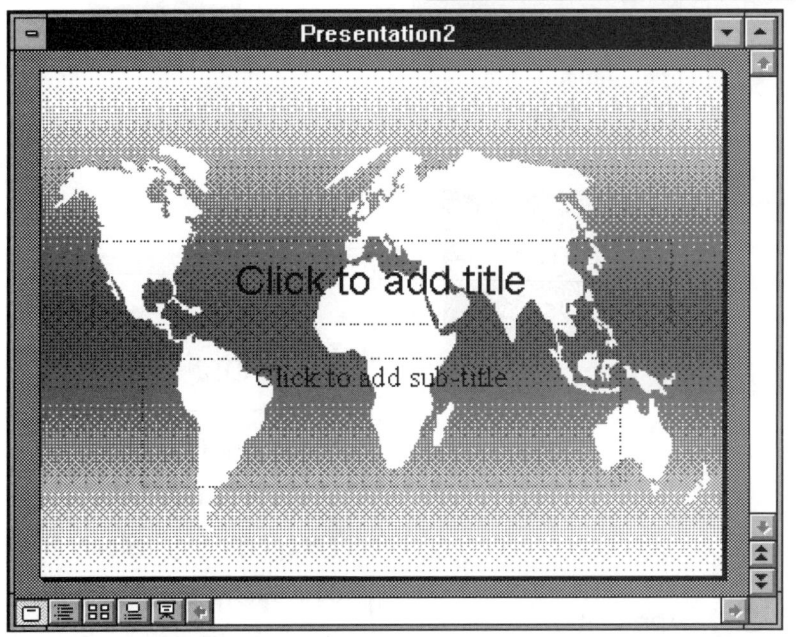

Take note

Once PowerPoint has set up your presentation, it displays the Title Slide in Slide view, ready for your input.

Take note

Only your first slide is created - find out how to add more slides in sections 4 and 5.

Template

This option lets you start out by choosing the Template on which you wish to base your presentation. The template will determine the design elements of your presentation, including font and colour scheme. There are over 100 Templates to choose from!

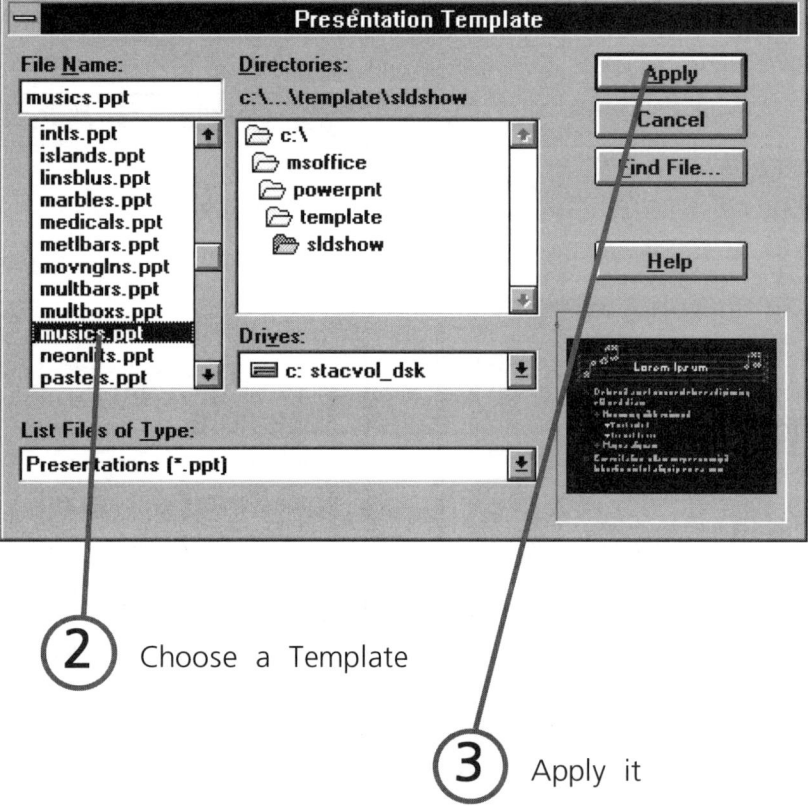

② Choose a Template

③ Apply it

1 At the PowerPoint or New Presentation dialog box, select the **Template** option

2 Choose the Presentation Template you wish to use from the **Presentation Template** dialog box

3 Click [**Apply**]

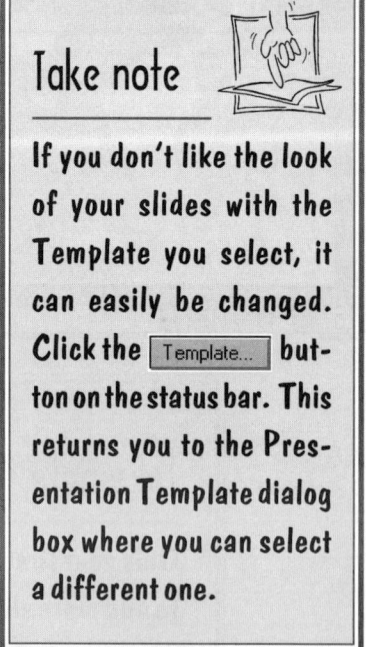

Take note

If you don't like the look of your slides with the Template you select, it can easily be changed. Click the [Template...] button on the status bar. This returns you to the Presentation Template dialog box where you can select a different one.

4 Choose a slide layout
for your first slide -
usually the Title Slide

5 Click OK

Once PowerPoint has
set up your presenta-
tion, it displays it in
Slide View. The Title
Slide is displayed,
ready for your input.

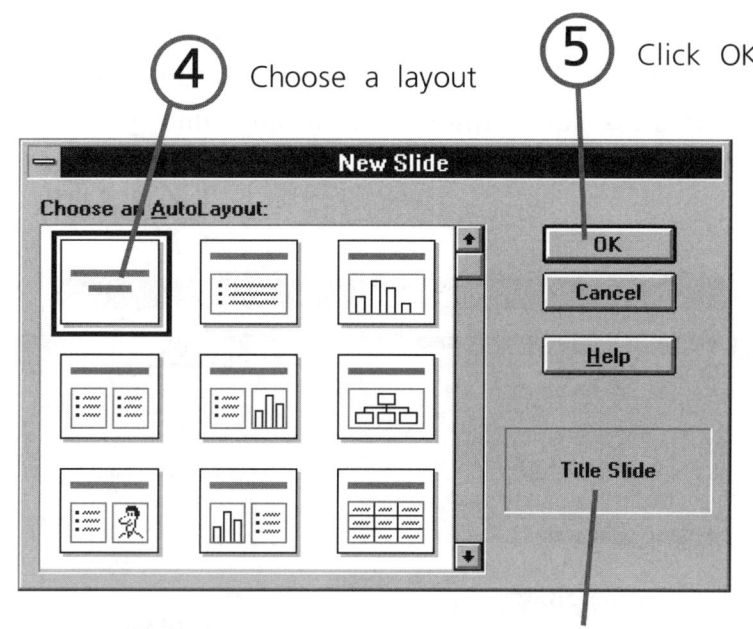

④ Choose a layout

⑤ Click OK

Slide description

Take note

Only your first slide is created using this method.
You'll find out how to add
more slides in Sections 4
and 5.

Blank Presentation

If you prefer to set up your own presentation try the Blank Presentation. The colour scheme, fonts and other design features are set to the default values when you choose this option.

② Click OK

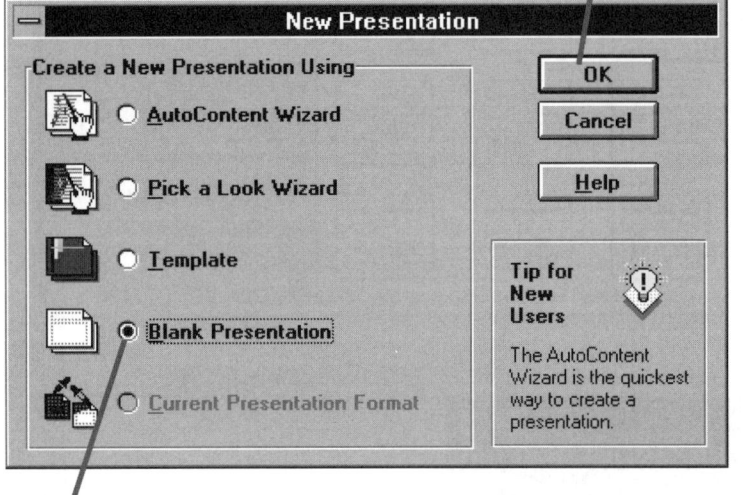

① Choose Blank Presentation

④ Click OK

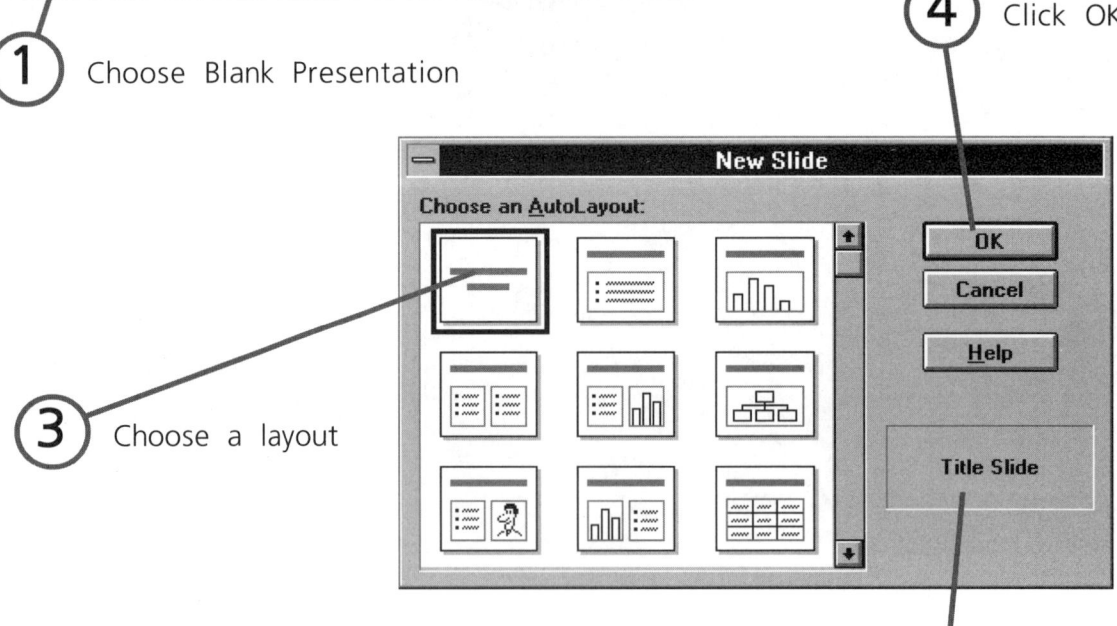

③ Choose a layout

Slide description

32

❑ Once PowerPoint has set up your presentation, it displays it in Slide View. The Title Slide (or the slide you chose at step 3) is displayed, ready for your input.

Take note

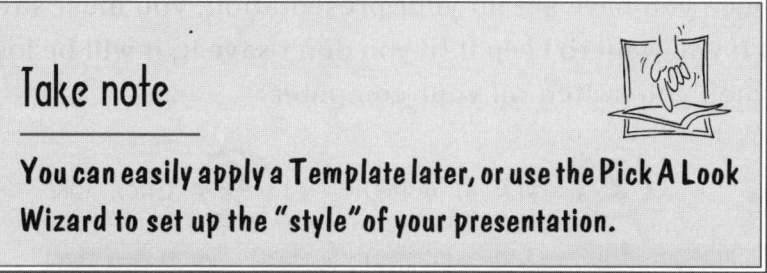

You can easily apply a Template later, or use the Pick A Look Wizard to set up the "style" of your presentation.

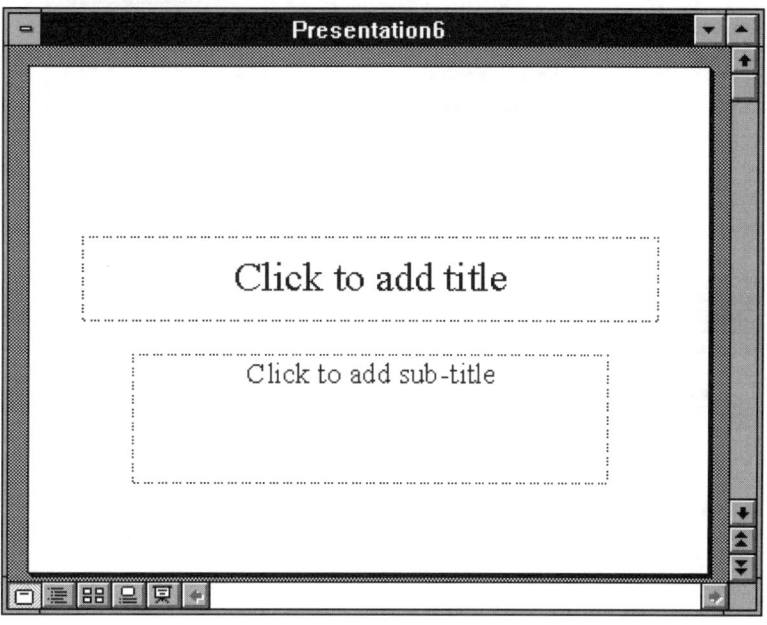

Presentation6

Click to add title

Click to add sub-title

Tip

If you don't like the structured approach of the AutoContent wizard, you may find the "clean" look of the Blank Presentation easiest to work with in the early stages of setting up your presentation. The colours, templates and patterns can all be applied later.

Take note

Find out how to add more slides in Sections 4 & 5.

Saving a presentation

Once you have set up your presentation, you must save it if you want to keep it (if you don't save it, it will be lost when you switch off your computer).

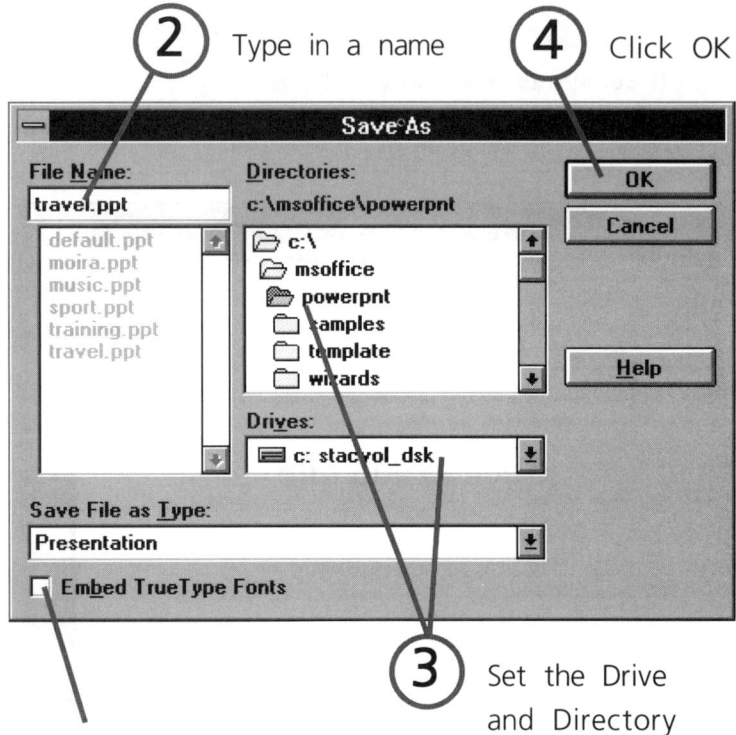

② Type in a name

④ Click OK

③ Set the Drive and Directory

Embed True Type Fonts
If you select this option, the presentation fonts will be embedded in your saved file. The presentation can then be viewed on a system that does not have the fonts installed.

1 Click the **Save** tool  on the Standard Toolbar

2 Give your presentation a name (8 character maximum, no spaces) – the .ppt extesnion is added by PowerPoint

3 Specify the **Drive** and **Directory** into which you wish to save your presentation

4 Click **OK**

5 Complete the **Summary Info** dialog box as required – it is only to remind you about the presentation

6 Click **OK**

Take note

If you need to change the Summary Info you have recorded with a presentation, you can easily edit it. When the presentation is open, choose Summary Info from the File menu to open its Summary Info dialog box.

Save vs Save As

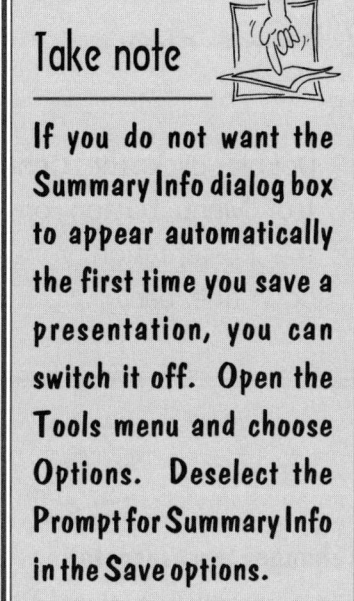

Take note

If you do not want the Summary Info dialog box to appear automatically the first time you save a presentation, you can switch it off. Open the Tools menu and choose Options. Deselect the Prompt for Summary Info in the Save options.

The first time you save a presentation, you are taken to the **Save As** dialog box so you can give your presentation a name and specify the directory and drive you want it saved on. Thereafter, any time you save the presentation using the **Save** tool on the toolbar, the old version of the file is replaced by the new, edited version. This is what you would usually want to happen.

However, if you have saved your presentation, go on to edit it, then decide you want to save the edited version as a separate file, you cannot use the Save tool.

Open the **File** menu and choose **Save As** to get to the Save As dialog box. Give your file a different name, and/or specify a different location then click OK.

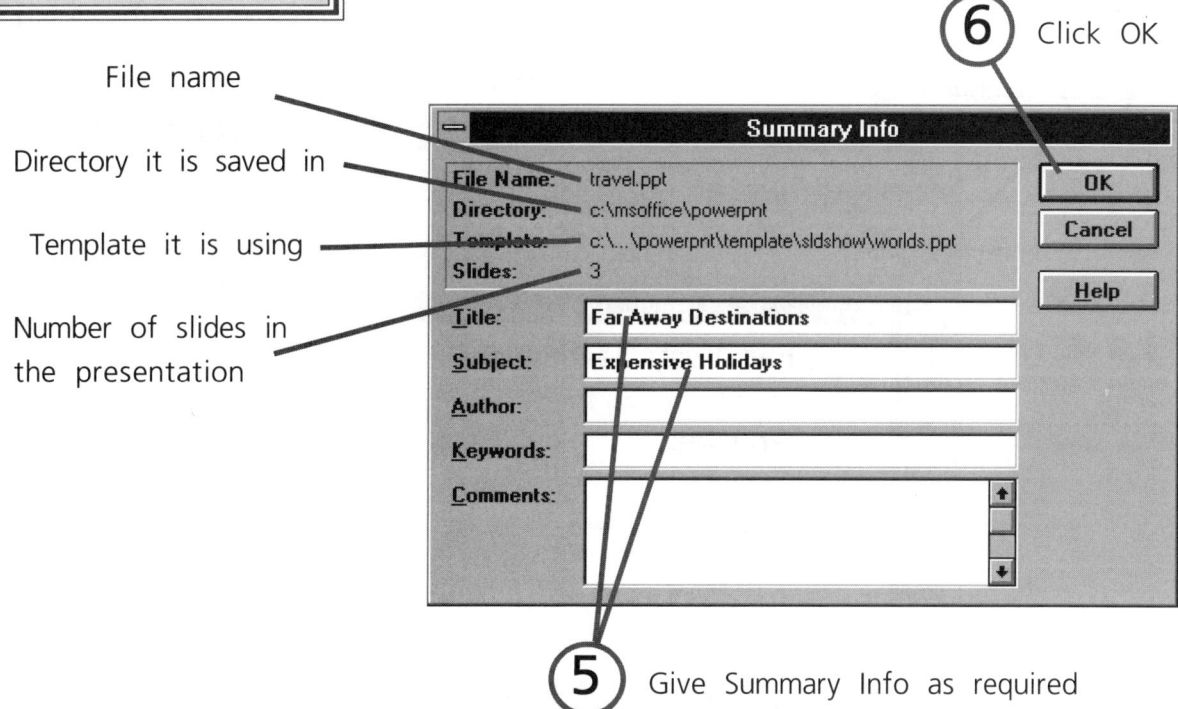

⑥ Click OK

File name

Directory it is saved in

Template it is using

Number of slides in the presentation

Summary Info

File Name: travel.ppt
Directory: c:\msoffice\powerpnt
Template: c:\...\powerpnt\template\sldshow\worlds.ppt
Slides: 3

Title: Far Away Destinations

Subject: Expensive Holidays

Author:

Keywords:

Comments:

OK
Cancel
Help

⑤ Give Summary Info as required

Closing a presentation

When you've finished working on your presentation you must save it (see above) and close it.

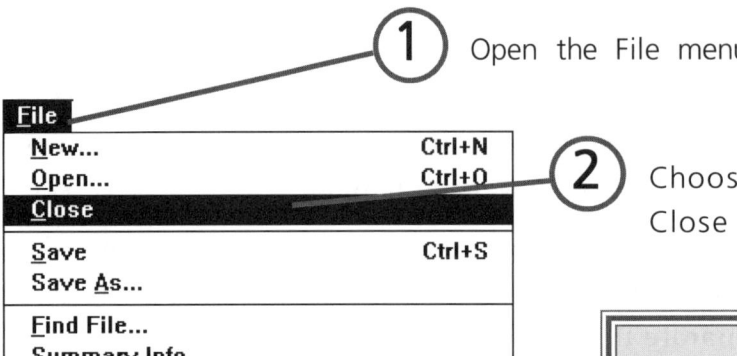
Open the File menu

Choose Close

Basic steps

1 Open the **File** menu

2 Choose **Close**

OR

1 Double click the **Control Menu** button on the Presentation window title bar

Take note

If you have made changes to a presentation since you last saved it, you will be prompted to save your changes before the file is closed.

Double click

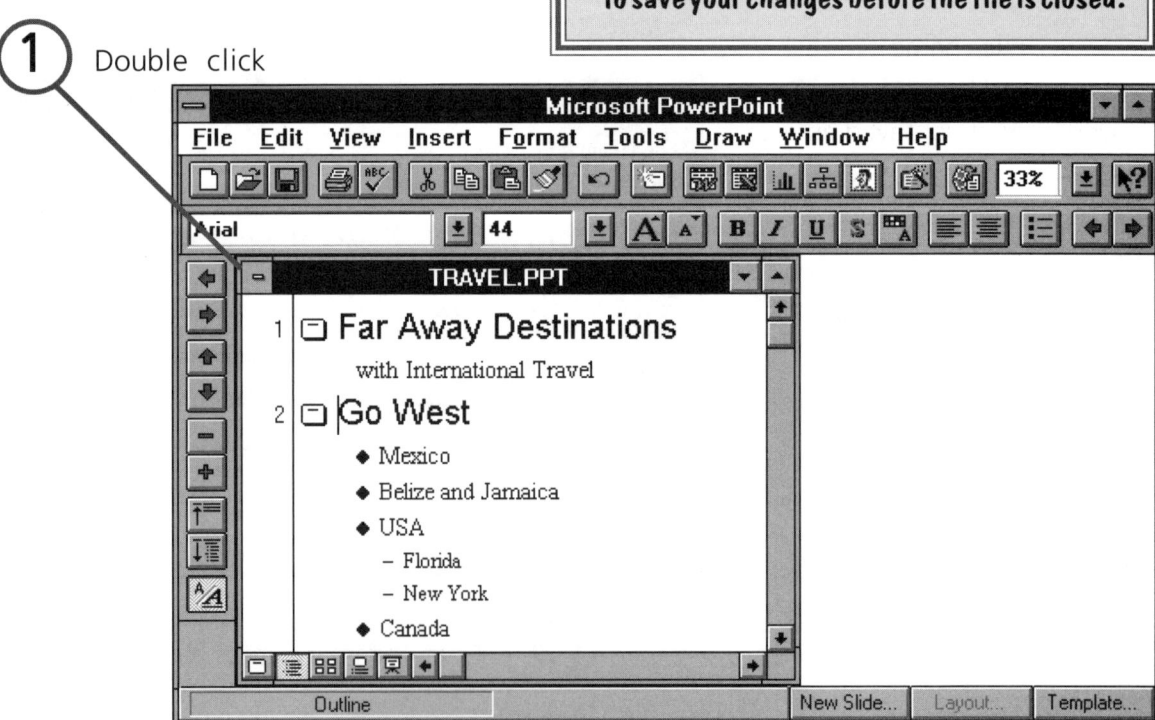

Basic steps

1 Click the **Open** tool
![open icon] on the Standard
Toolbar

OR

1 Open the **File** menu
and choose **Open**

2 Select the drive and
directory that contains
your presentation file

3 Select the presentation you want to open

4 Double click on it, or
click OK

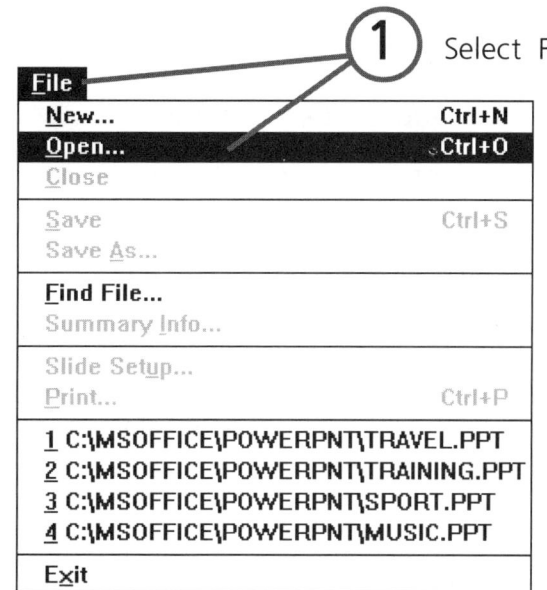

Take note

**If you choose Open an
Existing Presentation at
the PowerPoint dialog
box, which appears when
you access PowerPoint
,you are taken into the
Open dialog box.**

Opening a presentation

If you want to work on a presentation you've already
created, saved and closed, you must open it first.

Select File then Open

The last few
presentations
worked on are
listed here. Click
to open one.

Set the Drive and Directory

Select the file   Click OK

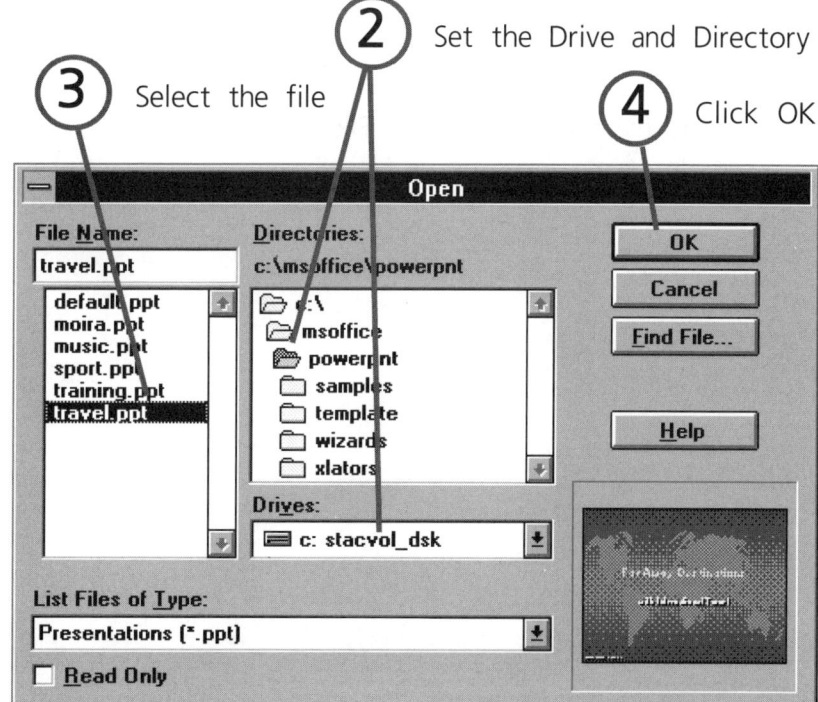

37

Summary

❑ When **creating a presentation**, you can choose your starting point – the AutoContent Wizard, the Pick a Look Wizard, a Template or a Blank Presentation

❑ The easiest/quickest option for your first presentation is probably the **AutoContent Wizard**

❑ If you use the AutoContent Wizard, you are taken into **Outline View**

❑ If you create your presentation using any other method you are take into **Slide View**

❑ Regardless of the options selected when you create your presentation, you can easily **change any option** as your presentation develops

❑ Use the **Save** tool on the Standard Toolbar to save your presentation

❑ Double click the Control Menu button on the presentation Title Bar to **close the file**

❑ Use the file name list in the **File** menu to open a recently used presentation

4 Outline view

Setting up the outline

Once you've passed the initial stages, the next step is usually to decide on the text you want to appear on your slides – the slide title, and the main points you want to cover during your presentation. You can add text to slides in either Outline view or Slide view.

In *Outline* view you can work on your text without the distraction of colour, graphics etc.

As well as deciding on the text, you can also determine the structure of each slide (main points, sub-points etc). Your points can be structured into 5 levels if necessary.

```
                Slide Title
        Level 1
          Level 2
            Level 3
              Level 4
                Level 5
```

If you create your presentation using the AutoContent Wizard, you are taken into Outline view. If you start from any of the other options you are taken into Slide view. You can easily move from one view to the other (at any time) using the tools at the bottom left of the screen.

If you do not have a presentation open at this stage, create or open one now to experiment on. If necessary, click the Outline view tool to go into Outline view.

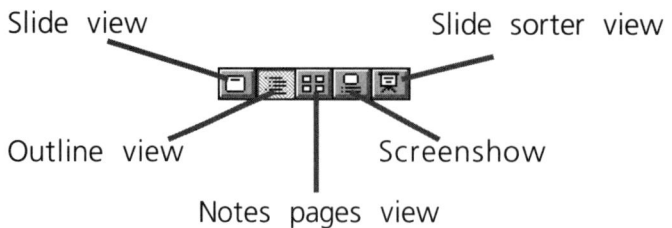

Slide view · Slide sorter view · Outline view · Screenshow · Notes pages view

The Outlining Toolbar

This is displayed down the left hand side of the screen.

- Promote
- Demote
- Move up
- Move down
- Collapse selection
- Expand selection
- Show titles
- Show all
- Show formatting

40

Basic steps

1 Select the text you want to replace

2 Key in you own text

3 Should you wish to make a list of points, simply press **[Enter]** after each point to move onto a new line.

Entering text

If you used the AutoContent Wizard it will have set up a number of slides for you (the number varies depending on the type of presentation option you selected).

Each slide has been given a Slide Title. Suggestions on the points you might want to make on each slide are also given. These suggestions must be replaced by the points *you* actually want to make. (You can also edit the Slide Title if you don't like it).

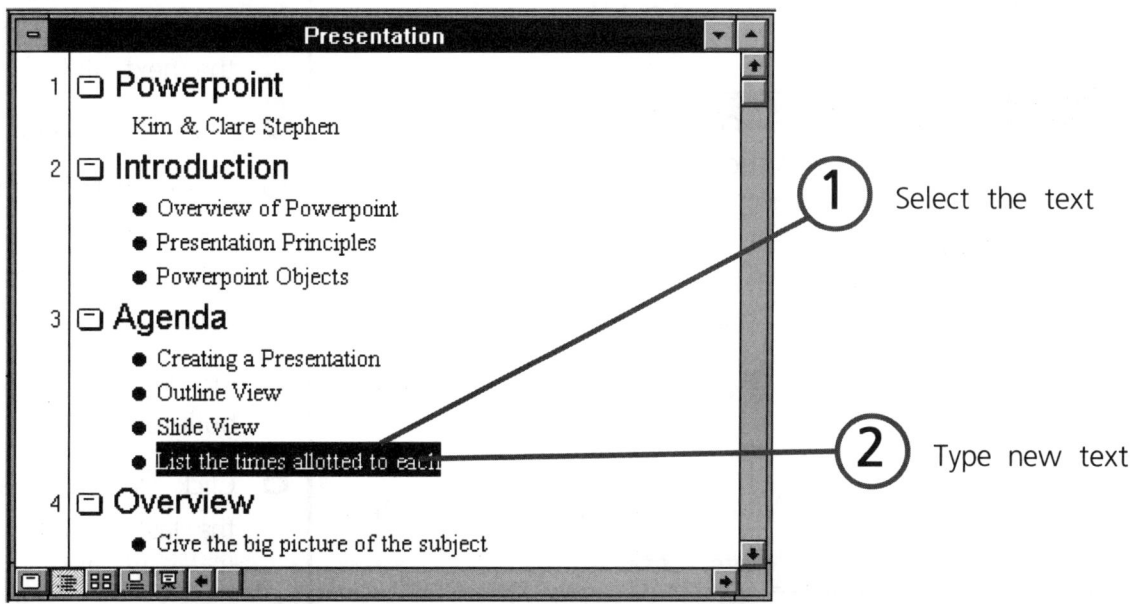

1 Select the text

2 Type new text

```
Presentation
1  Powerpoint
      Kim & Clare Stephen
2  Introduction
      ● Overview of Powerpoint
      ● Presentation Principles
      ● Powerpoint Objects
3  Agenda
      ● Creating a Presentation
      ● Outline View
      ● Slide View
      ● List the times allotted to each
4  Overview
      ● Give the big picture of the subject
```

Selecting in Outline view

● Click & Drag

● Click, Shift-Click (click to place the insertion point at one end of the text to be selected, then move the I-beam to the other end, hold down **[Shift]** and click the left button)

● Single click to the left of the point to be selected (note the 4-arrowed pointer)

● Double click to the right of the point to be selected

Text for new slides

With presentations created by other methods than AutoContent Wizard, you are taken into Slide view and the first slide is created. This slide must be completed and new slides added as required.

The Basic steps assume that the first slide in your presentation has the Title Slide layout.

● Steps 4 to 9 will add new slides to any presentation.

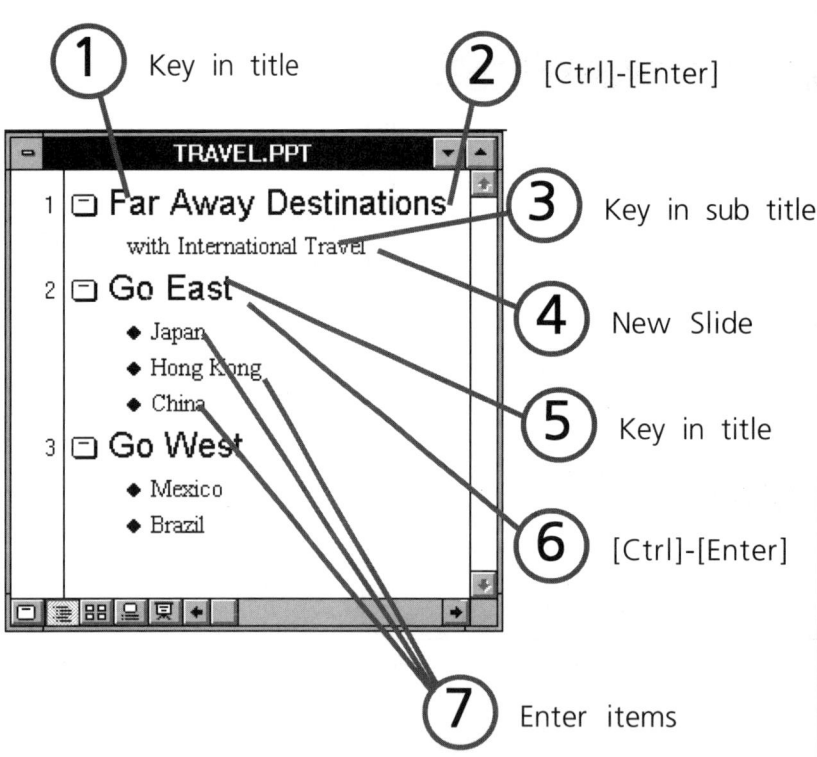

1 Key in the slide title

2 Press **[Ctrl]–[Enter]**. If you are on a Title Slide layout, you are taken to the sub-title (text with no bullet).

3 Key in your sub-title.

4 Click [New Slide...] on the status bar to create the next slide

5 Key in your slide title

6 Press **[Ctrl]–[Enter]**. This takes you to the first bulleted level on your slide.

7 Key in your list of bulleted items

8 Click [New Slide...] after the last item to create the next slide

9 Repeat steps 5-8 until all your slides have been created

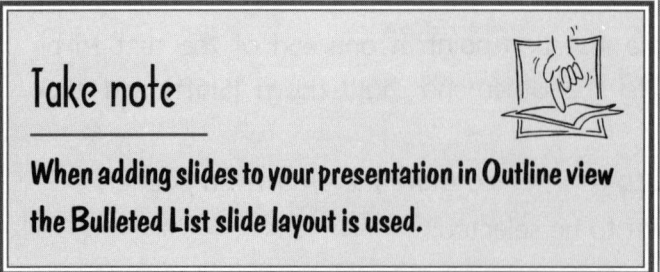

Take note

When adding slides to your presentation in Outline view the Bulleted List slide layout is used.

42

Basic steps

- **To Demote an item**

1 Place the insertion point in the item you wish to Demote

2 Click the **Demote** tool on the Outlining (or Formatting) toolbar

- **To Promote an item**

1 Place the insertion point in the item you wish to Promote

2 Click the **Promote** tool on the Outlining (or Formatting) toolbar

Take note

You can also click and drag to Demote or Promote points. Move the mouse pointer to the left of the item (note the mouse pointer changes). Drag right (to demote) or left (to promote) until you are at the required level.

The points you want to make on your slides will be structured - you will have main points (at the first bulleted level) and some of these points will have sub-points (at the second, third, fourth or even fifth level).

Initially, all points on your slide are at level 1. You can easily Demote sub items if necessary (and promote them again if you change your mind).

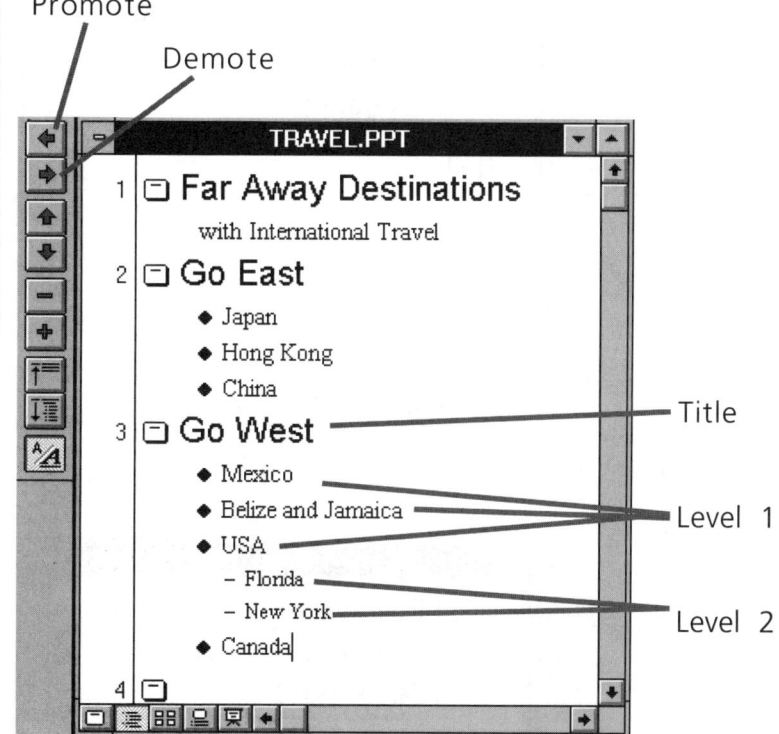

Promote

Demote

TRAVEL.PPT

1 Far Away Destinations
    with International Travel
2 Go East
    ◆ Japan
    ◆ Hong Kong
    ◆ China
3 Go West — Title
    ◆ Mexico
    ◆ Belize and Jamaica — Level 1
    ◆ USA
      – Florida
      – New York — Level 2
    ◆ Canada
4

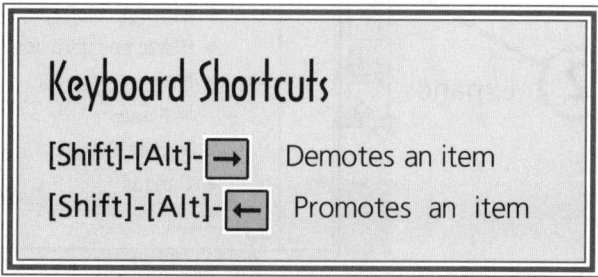

Keyboard Shortcuts

[Shift]-[Alt]-→ Demotes an item

[Shift]-[Alt]-← Promotes an item

43

Collapse the outline

If you want to get an overview of your presentation, or part of your presentation, you can collapse all (or part of) the outline down to show just the Slide Titles. The outline can then be expanded again to show the text as required.

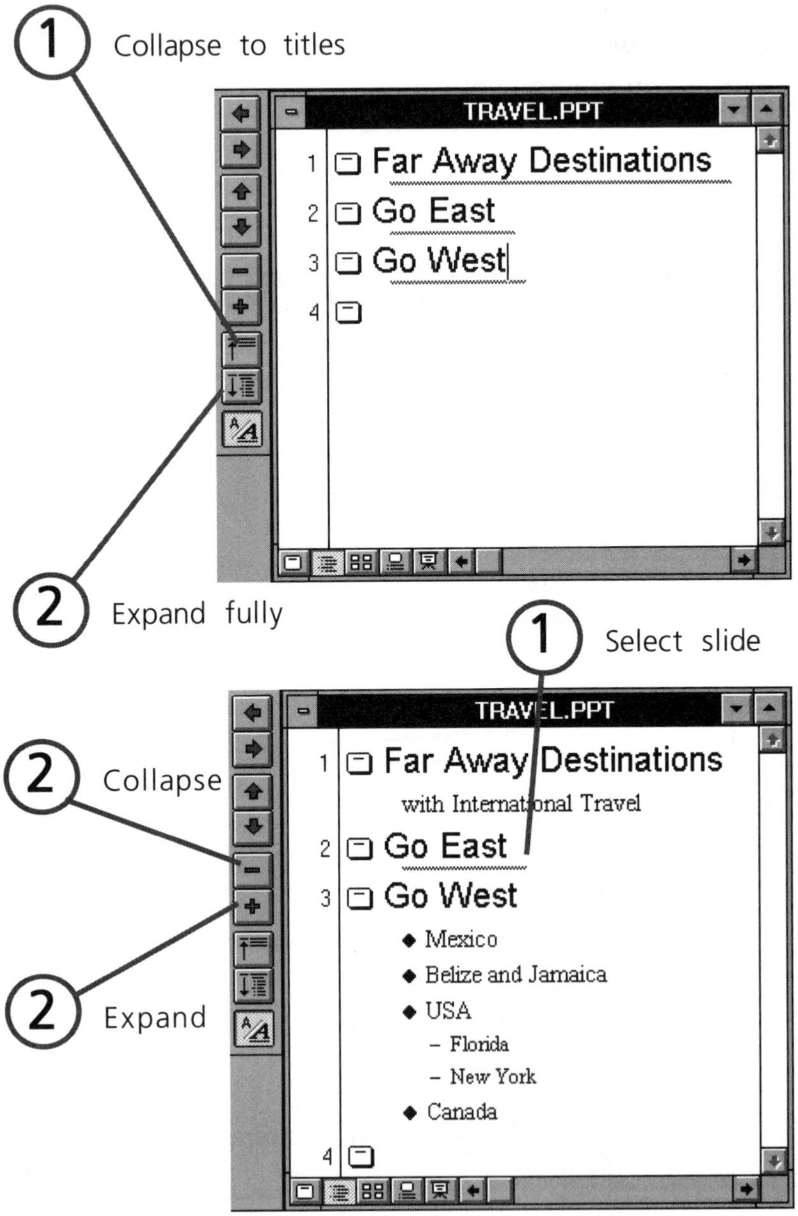

❑ **All the slides**

1 Click the **Show Titles** tool 🔲 on the Outlining toolbar

2 To expand your presentation again, click the **Show All** tool 🔲

❑ **Individual slides**

1 Place the insertion point anywhere within the slide you want to collapse

2 Click the **Collapse Selection** tool 🔲

❑ **To expand the slide again**

1 Place the insertion point anywhere in the slide title

2 Click the **Expand Selection** tool 🔲

① Collapse to titles

```
TRAVEL.PPT
1  ▢ Far Away Destinations
2  ▢ Go East
3  ▢ Go West
4  ▢
```

② Expand fully

① Select slide

② Collapse

② Expand

```
TRAVEL.PPT
1  ▢ Far Away Destinations
      with International Travel
2  ▢ Go East
3  ▢ Go West
       ◆ Mexico
       ◆ Belize and Jamaica
       ◆ USA
          – Florida
          – New York
       ◆ Canada
4  ▢
```

44

❑ **Several consecutive slides**

1 Select the slides

2 Click **Collapse Selection** ▬

OR

2 **Expand Selection** ✚ as required

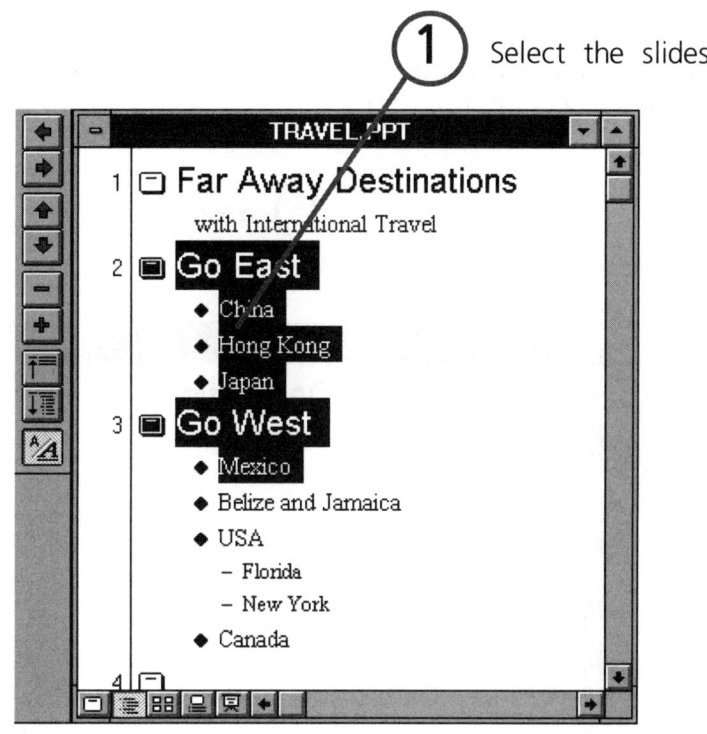

① Select the slides

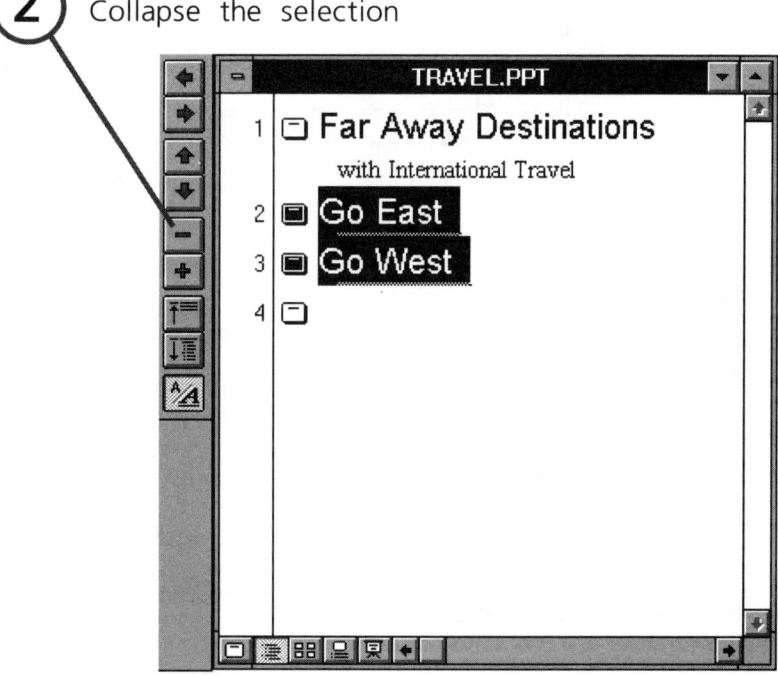

② Collapse the selection

Tip

The quickest way to select a set of consecutive slides is to drag the cursor over them, highlighting them all. For other selection techniques see page 41.

45

Rearranging an outline

If you decide that you want to change the order of the points or the order of slides, this is very easily done in Outline view.

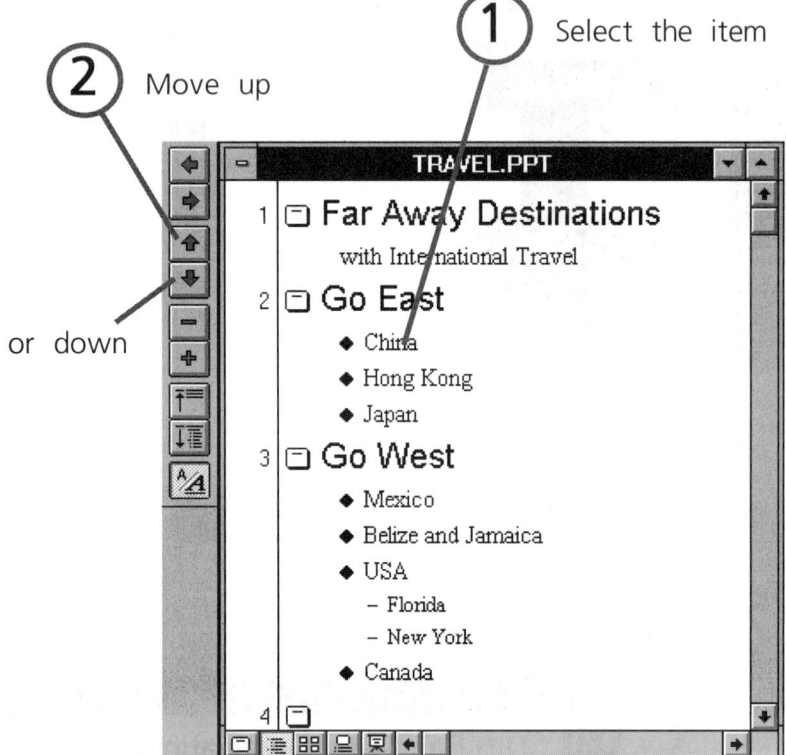

① Select the item

② Move up

or down

Basic steps

❑ **Moving items**

1 Place the insertion point in the item you wish to move

2 Click the **Move Up** tool to move it up through the slide (or slides)

OR

2 Click the **Move Down** tool to move it down through the slide (or slides)

❑ **Moving slides**

1 Click on the slide icon at the left of the one you want to move.

2 Use the tools, mouse or keyboard to move the whole slide to its new location.

Take note

You can also click and drag to rearrange points. Move the mouse pointer to the left of the item. Drag up or down until the item is in the required position.

Keyboard Shortcuts

[Shift]-[Alt]-↑ moves an item up

[Shift]-[Alt]-↓ moves an item down

Basic steps

1 Click the slide icon on the left of the title to select the slide

2 Press the Delete key on your keyboard

OR

2 Open the Edit menu

3 Choose Delete Slide

Take note

You can delete slides in Outline view, Slide view, Slide Sorter view or Notes Pages view.

Deleting slides

If you need to remove a slide it can easily be deleted in Outline view.

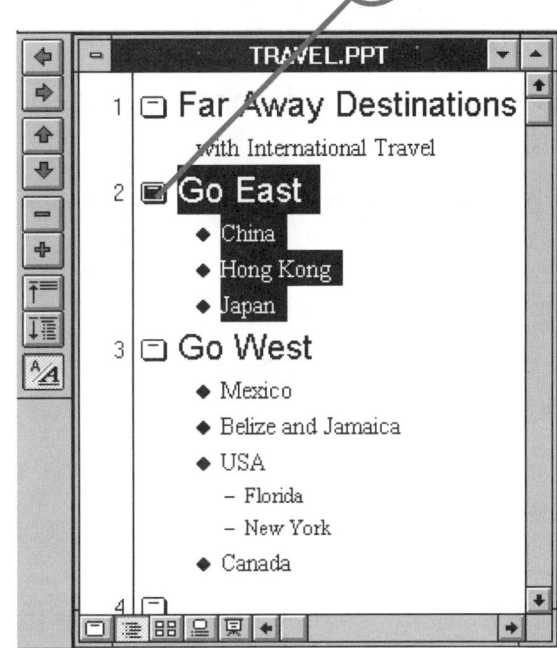

① Select the slide

Slide deleted!

② Open the Edit menu

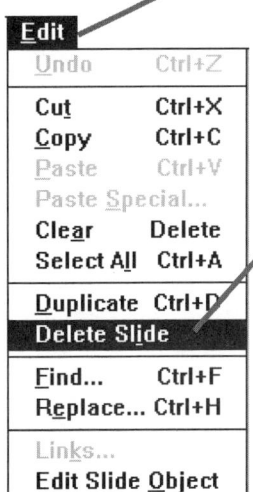

③ Select delete slide

Summary

- **Outline view** lets you concentrate on the text and structure of your presentation

- In outline view, you can specify the **slide title** and the **points** you wish to make on each slide

- Your points can contain **sub-points** if necessary (up to 5 levels)

- You can **promote** or **demote** points to change their levels

- You cannot add **pictures, charts** etc in outline view

- Using an outline, you can **collapse** and **expand** your presentation to show the slides required

- You can move between outline view and the **other views** whenever you wish

5 Working on slides

Slide view

You can move between the different views at any time – use whatever view seems most appropriate to what you are doing. Once you appreciate what you can do in the different views, you can decide for yourself which you need to use. In this section we will look at the ways you can work in Slide view. You can add text, graphics, clipart, tables and charts in Slide view. We'll stick to text for the time being.

If you are still in Outline view, change to Slide view for this section.

Basic steps

1 Place the insertion point in the slide you want to look at in Slide view

2 Click the **Slide** View tool

OR

1 Double click the **icon** beside the title of the slide you want to see in Slide view

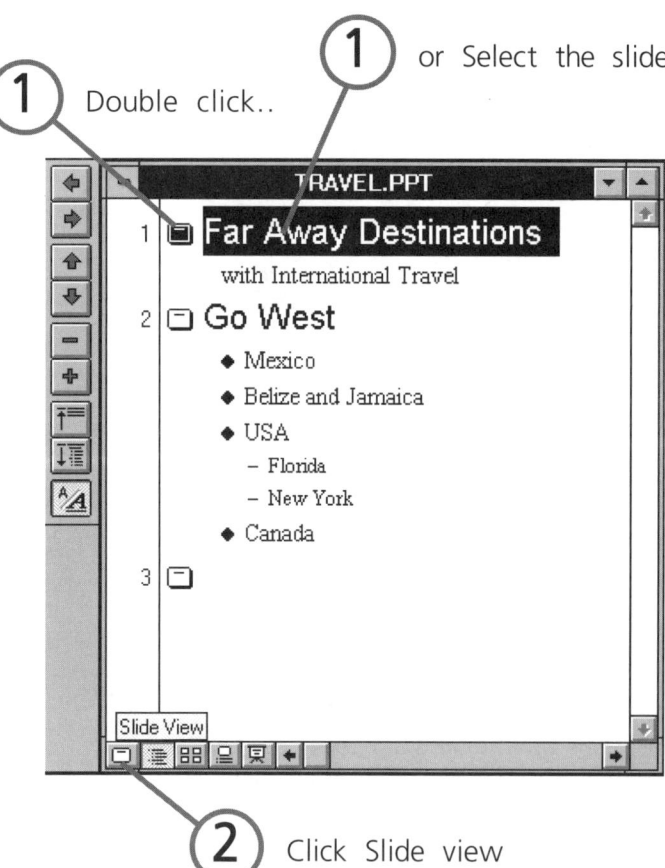

Take note

You can change from one view to another at any time.

Basic steps

1 Click the Previous Slide button ⊞ to move up

OR

2 Click the Next Slide button ⊞ to move down

OR

3 Drag the elevator up or down the scroll bar to the desired slide. Note the slide number that appears when you drag the elevator. When you let go the button, the slide number indicated appears on the screen.

Take note

You can move back to the previous slide using [PageUp], or on to the next using [PageDown].

Moving through your slides in slide view

In Slide view, you see one slide at a time on your screen. If you have several slides, you must move up or down through them to view them.

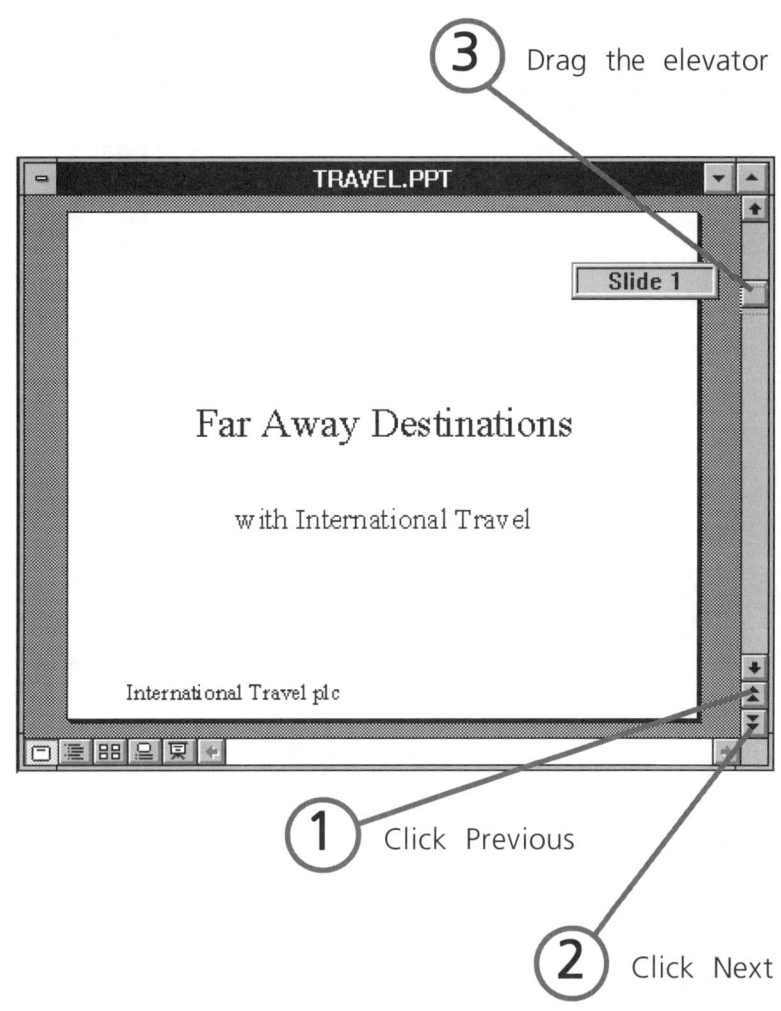

③ Drag the elevator

TRAVEL.PPT

Slide 1

Far Away Destinations

with International Travel

International Travel plc

① Click Previous

② Click Next

Adding new slides

As your presentation develops you will need to add slides to it. You can add them at any place in your presentation.

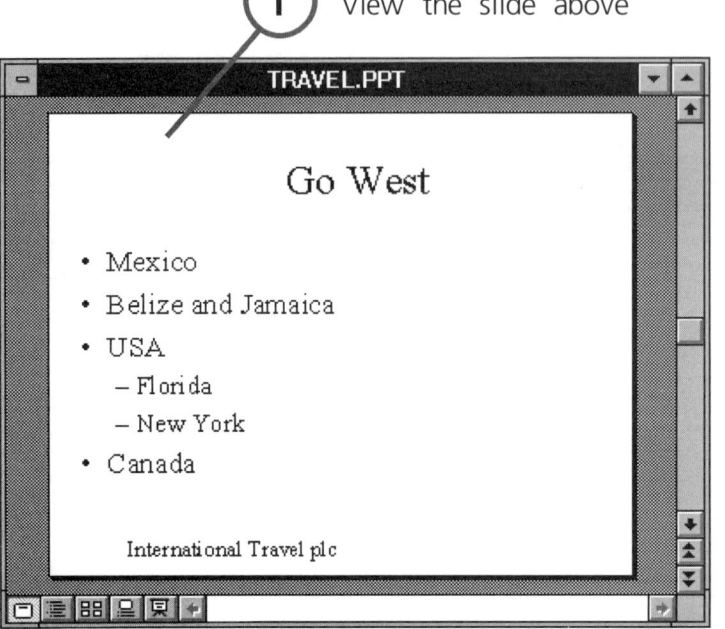

① View the slide above

② Click New Slide

Basic steps

1 View the slide that will be above your new one

2 Click New Slide...

3 Select the slide layout required from the **New Slide** dialog box

4 Click **OK**

Tip

You can add slides in Outline, Slide, Slide Sorter or Notes Pages view.

Take note

Some of the slide layouts in the New Slide dialog box have graphic, table, organisation chart and clipart objects set up on them. We will look at these later in the book.

③ Select the layout

④ Click OK

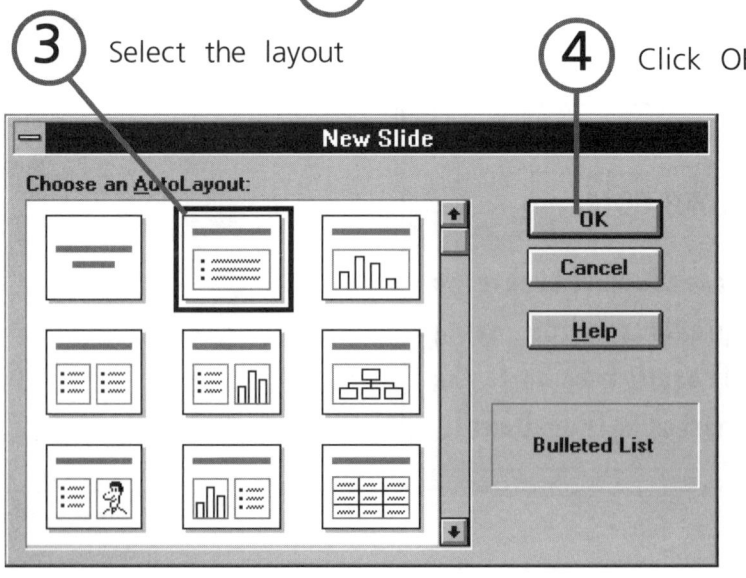

52

Basic steps

□ **Adding text**

1 Click in the Title area and key in your text

2 Click in the bulleted list area

3 Key in your text and press **[Enter]**

4 Repeat step 3 until all your points are listed

□ **Editing text**

1 Click to place the insertion point inside the text to be edited

2 Insert or delete characters as required

Tip

If you want to change the text completely, select the old text (click and drag over it) and key in the replacement text.

To enter text just follow the instructions on the slide! To edit text, use the normal Windows techniques.

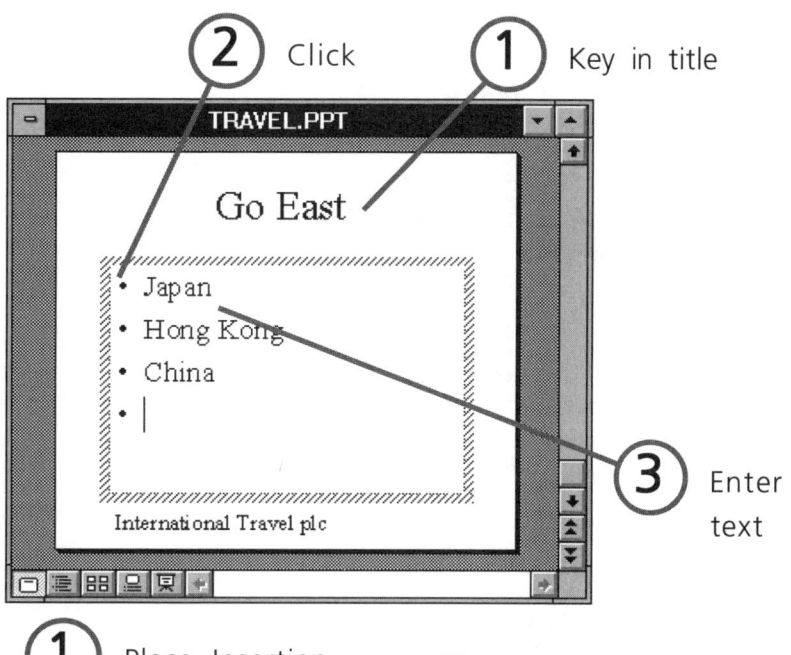

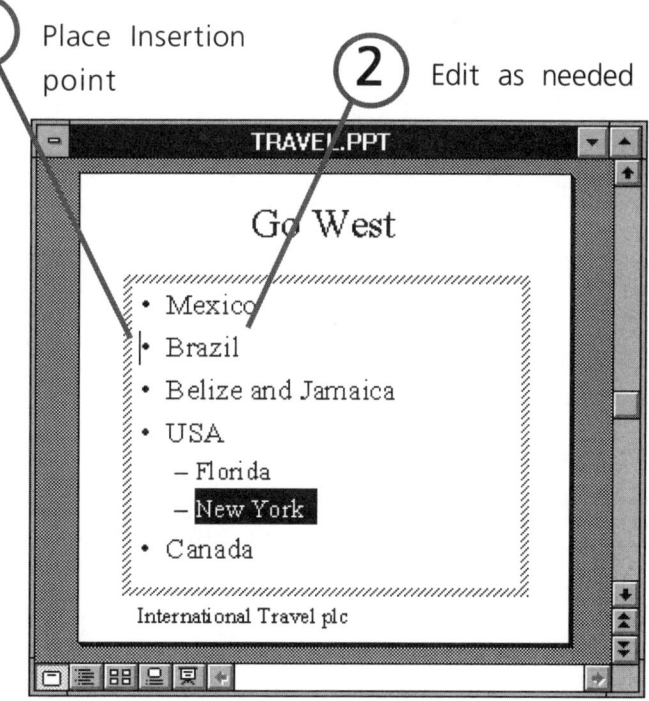

Formatting text

So far, we've accepted the font formats attributed to our text by PowerPoint. You can of course change these at any time using the formatting toolbar.

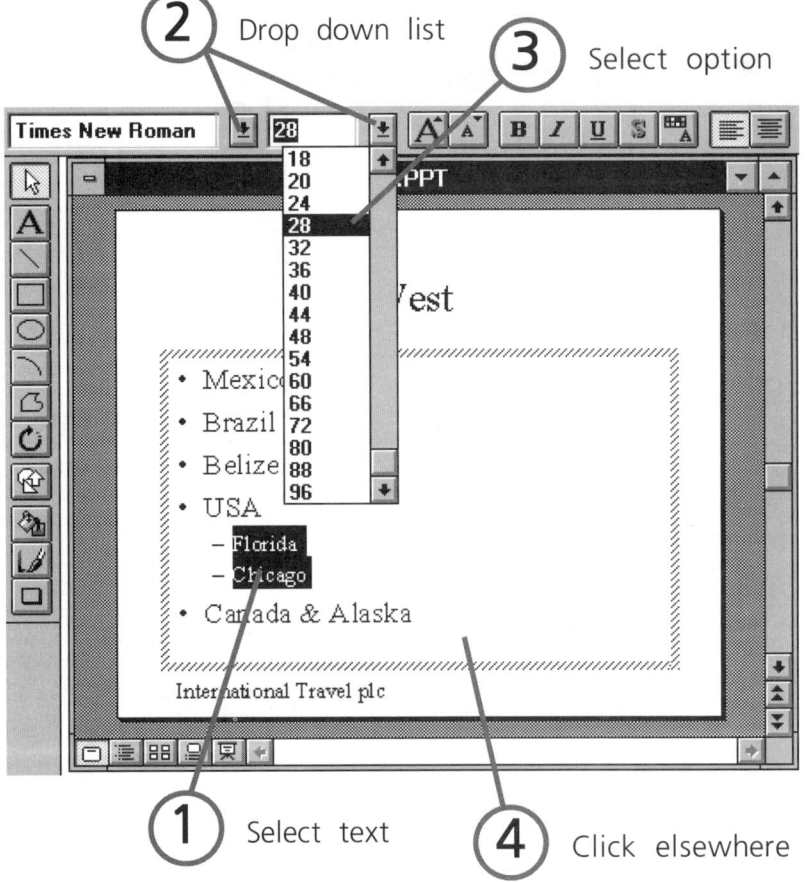

❑ **To change the font**

1 Select the text you want to format

2 Drop down the list of options

3 Choose the font or font size required

4 Deselect the text by clicking on another part of the slide

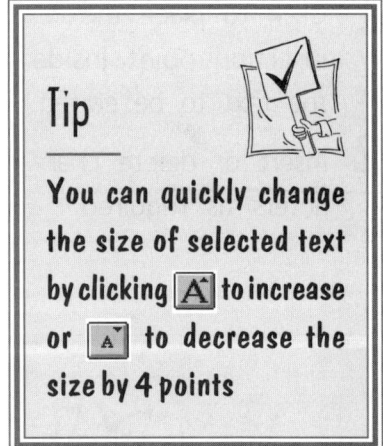

Tip

You can quickly change the size of selected text by clicking 𝐀 to increase or 𝐀 to decrease the size by 4 points

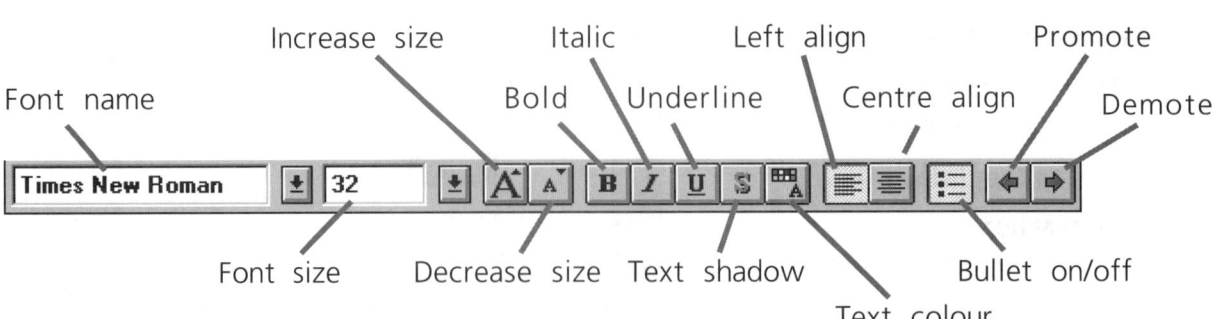

Font name · Increase size · Bold · Italic · Underline · Left align · Centre align · Promote · Demote · Font size · Decrease size · Text shadow · Text colour · Bullet on/off

54

Basic steps

- ❑ **To set styles**

1 Select the text

2 Click the Bold, Italics, Underline or Shadow tools to toggle the style on and off

3 Deselect the text

- ❑ **To change the colour**

1 Select the text

2 Click the Text Color tool to display the range available

3 Click on a colour (or on `Other Color...` if you want a larger choice)

4 Deselect the text

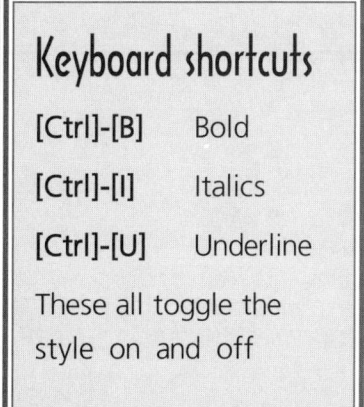

Keyboard shortcuts

[Ctrl]-[B]   Bold

[Ctrl]-[I]   Italics

[Ctrl]-[U]   Underline

These all toggle the style on and off

---

2 Toggle a style

Times New Roman ▼ 28 ▼ A⁺ A⁻ **B** *I* U S ▒A ≡ ≡

TRAVEL.PPT

Go West

- Mexico
- Brazil
- Belize and Jamaica
- USA
  - *Florida*
  - *Chicago*
- Canada & Alaska

International Travel plc

1 Select the text   **2** Click Colour tool

Times New Roman ▼ 44 ▼ A⁺ A⁻ **B** *I* U S ▒A ≡ ≡

TRAVEL.PPT

Go West

3 Pick a colour

Other Color...

- Mexico
- Brazil
- Belize and Jamaica
- USA
  - *Florida*
  - *Chicago*
- Canada & Alaska

International Travel plc

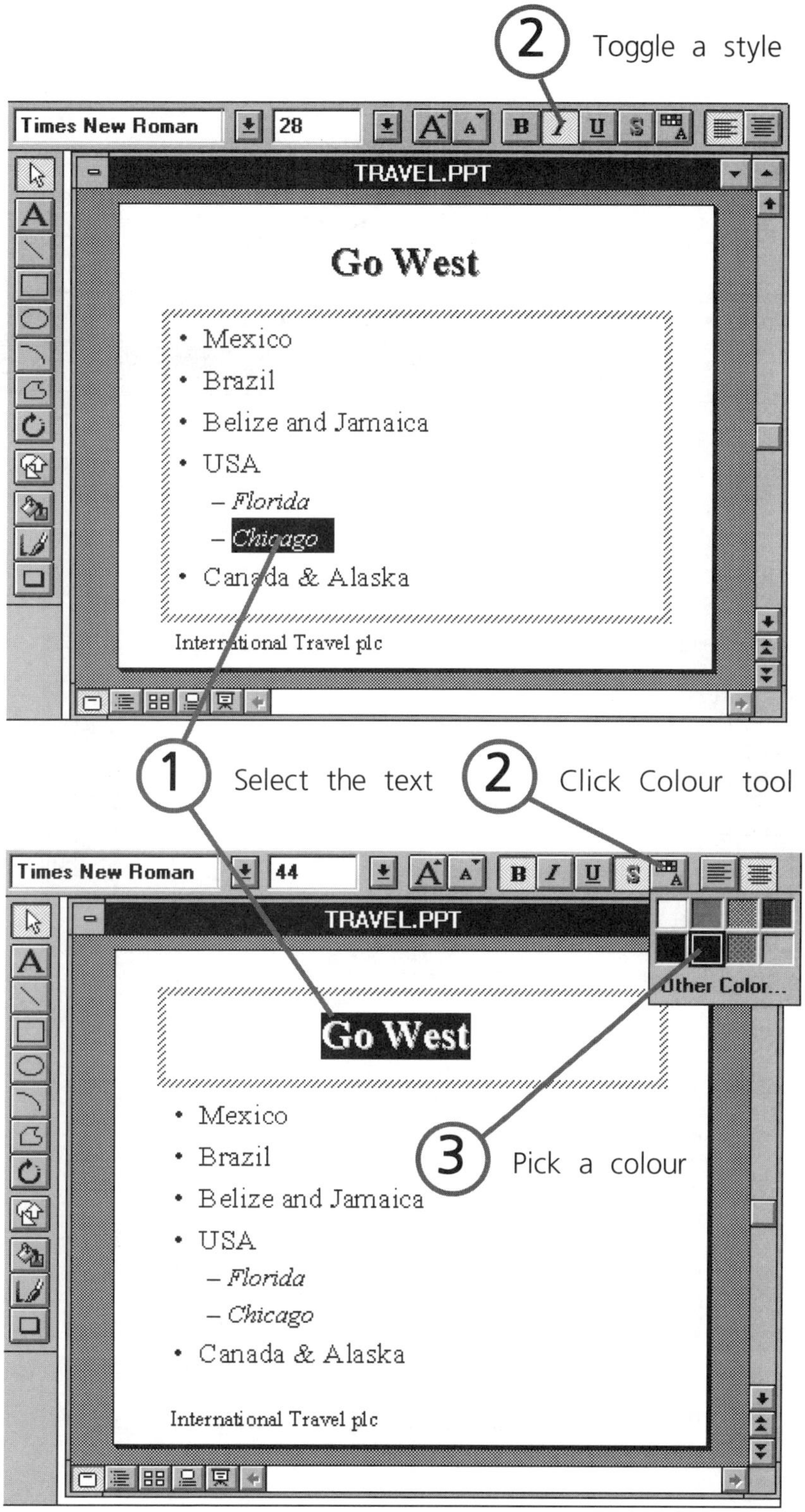

- **To justify text**

1 Select the text you want to format – a paragraph is selected as long as the insertion point is within it

2 Click the **Left Alignment** ▤ or **Center Alignment** ▤ tool

3 If you have selected multiple paragraphs or several characters, deselect the text

① Select paragraph

② Choose alignment

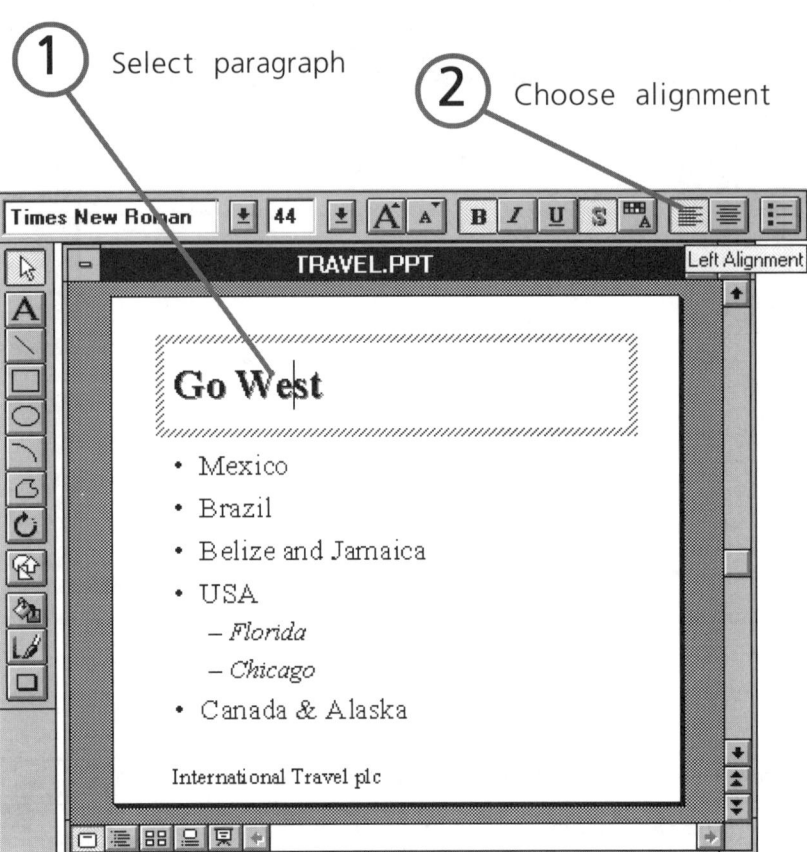

Keyboard shortcuts

[Ctrl]-[L] Left Align,
[Ctrl]-[R] Right Align
[Ctrl]-[J] Justify
[Ctrl]-[E] Centre

Take note

Options for Right Alignment and Justify (make the text meet both left and right margins) are available on the Format – Alignment menu.

❑ **To switch bullets on and off**

1 Select the point(s) where you want to add or remove bullets

2 Click the **Bullet On/Off** icon 📇 to toggle the display

❑ **Choosing a bullet**

1 Select the point(s) whose bullet you wish to change

2 Open the **Format** menu and choose **Bullet**

In most slide layouts the text objects are formatted to display bullets at each point listed. The bullets can be switched off (and on again) as required.

As well as switching them on and off, you can choose your own bullet character to customise your presentation.

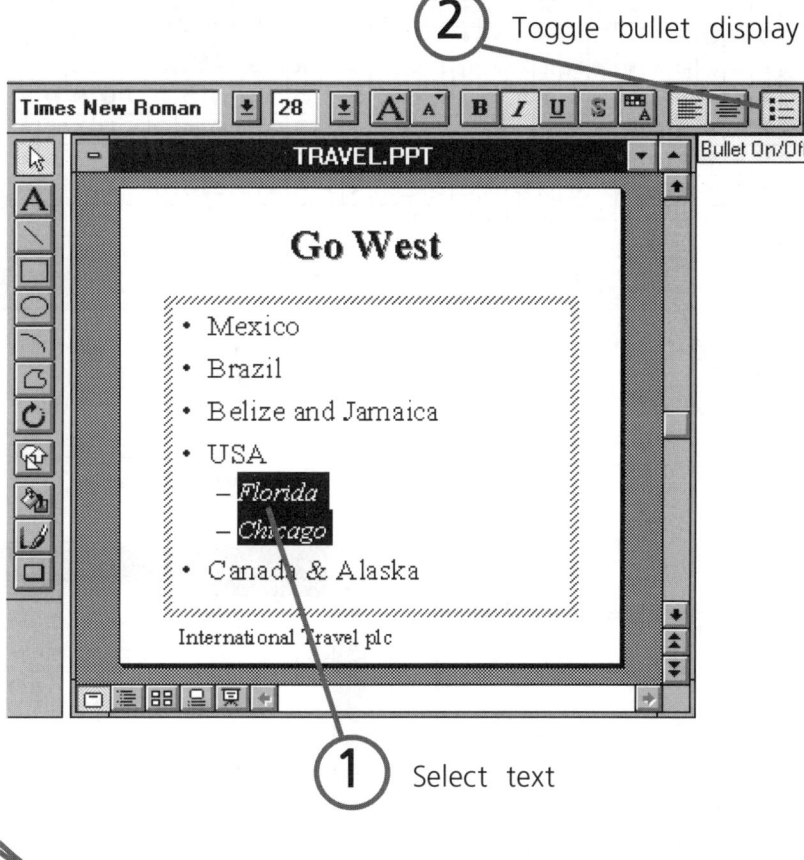

② Toggle bullet display

① Select text

② Chose Bullet from the Format menu

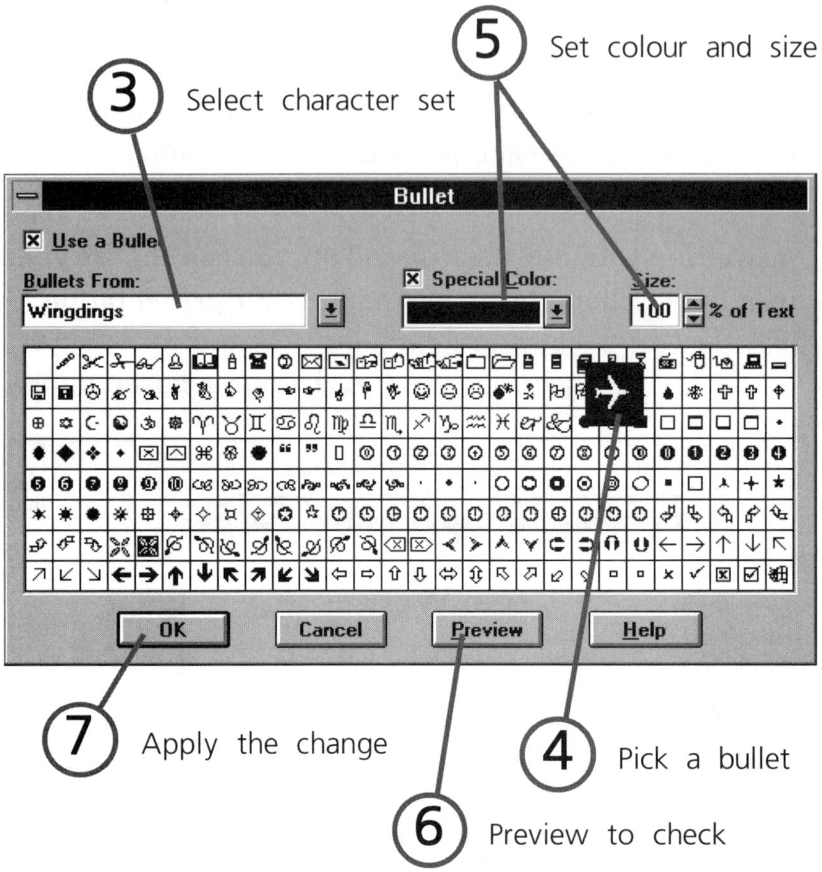

(5) Set colour and size

(3) Select character set

3 Choose the character set that contains the character you wish to use as a bullet

4 Select the character

5 Specify the colour and size if necessary

6 Click the Preview button to see the effect of your changes (you might need to move the Bullet dialog box to see your slide)

7 Click OK to apply your changes to the slide

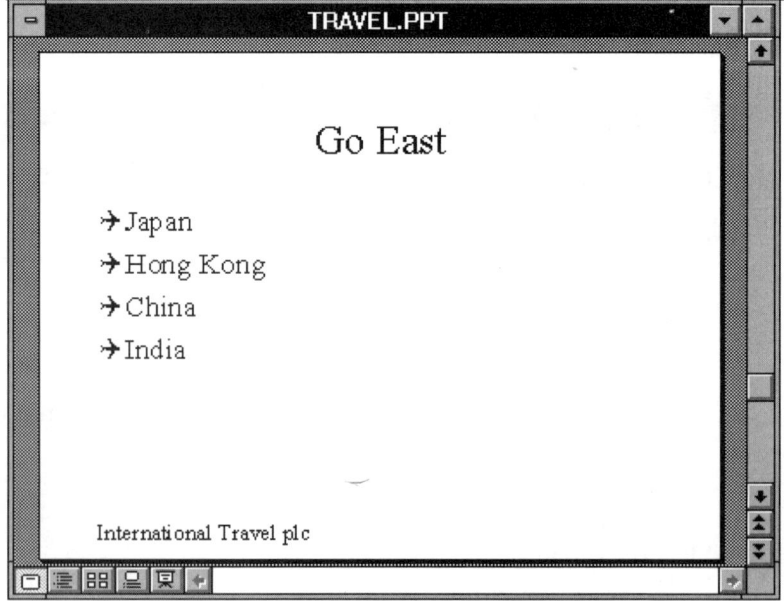

Bullet

☒ Use a Bullet

Bullets From:
Wingdings

☒ Special Color:

Size:
100 % of Text

OK   Cancel   Preview   Help

(7) Apply the change

(4) Pick a bullet

(6) Preview to check

Tip

Don't change the text formatting on every slide. If you overdo things you will give your presentation an inconsistent look.

TRAVEL.PPT

Go East

→ Japan
→ Hong Kong
→ China
→ India

International Travel plc

Basic steps

1 Click 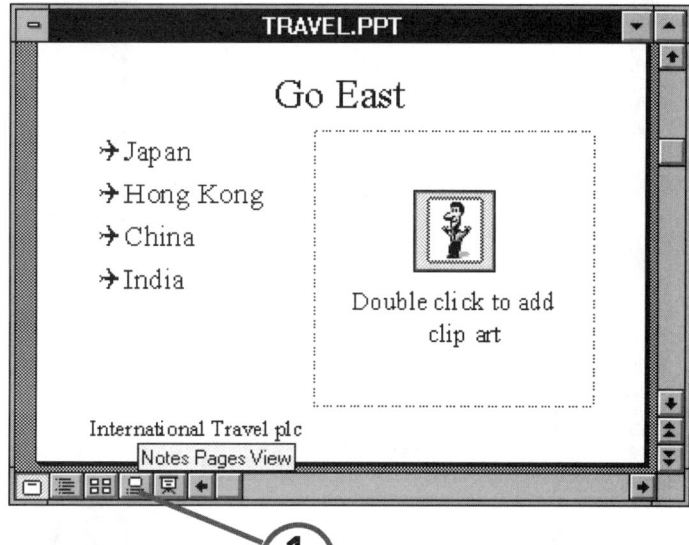 to go into Notes Pages view

2 Locate the slide to make notes for

3 Click in the notes area of the screen

4 Zoom in to 75% to make it easier to read

5 Key in your notes

Take note

Your notes are saved automatically when you save your presentation.

Adding notes to slides

To help you through your presentation, you'll find things easier if you have some notes to accompany your slides. You can add notes in Notes Pages view. The Notes pages consist of a copy of the slide plus the notes you type in yourself. These pages can be printed out so you can refer to them as you do your presentation (see Section 12).

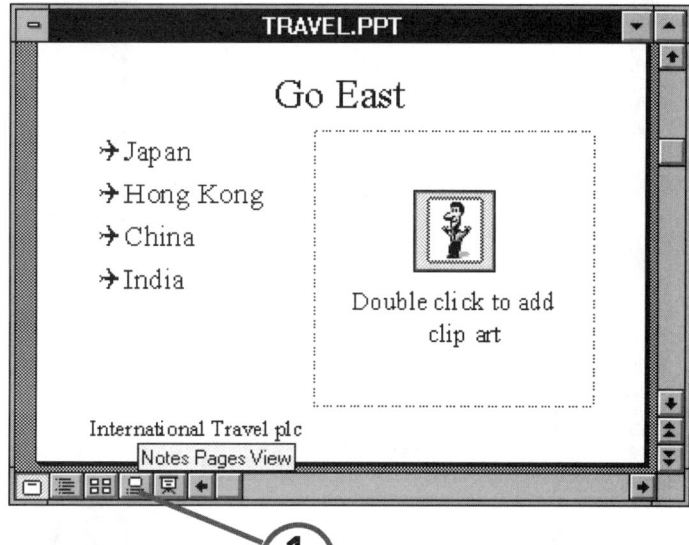

① Click Notes Pages view

② Locate slide

③ Click in Notes area

④ Zoom in

⑤ Key in text

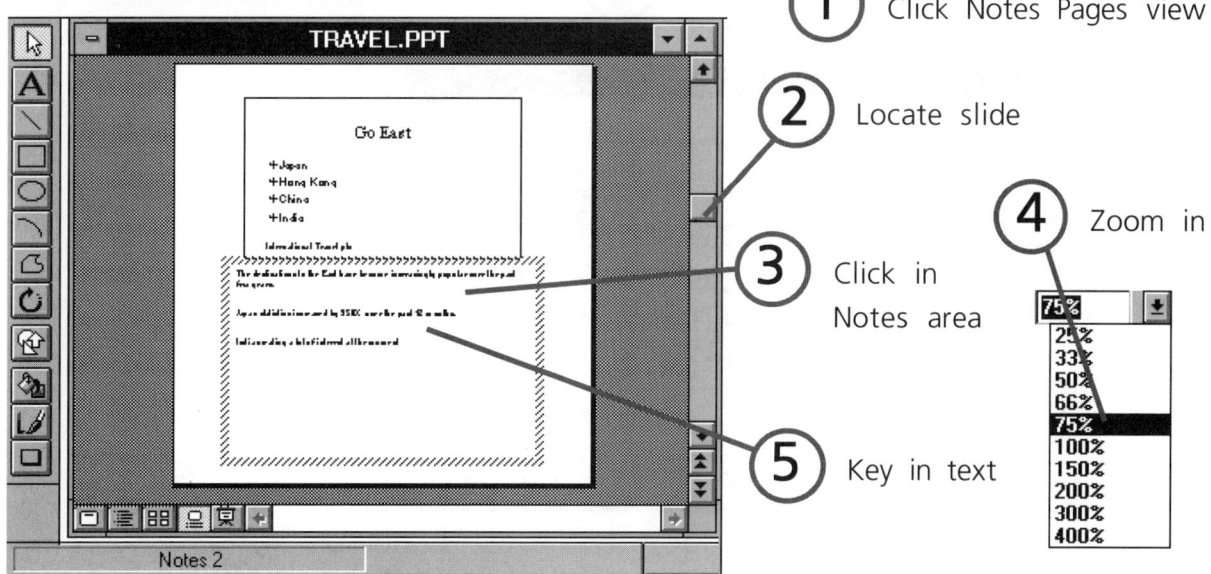

Changing a slide layout

If you decide you have chosen the wrong layout for a slide, this is easily changed from Slide view.

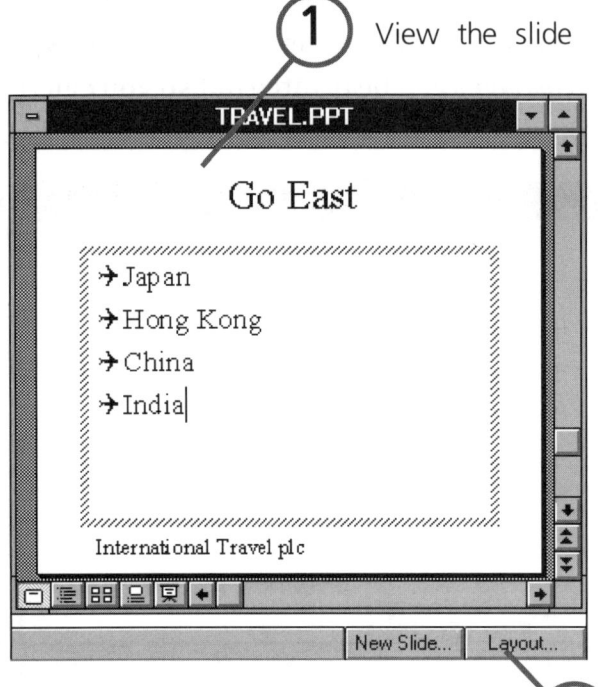

(1) View the slide

(2) Click Layout

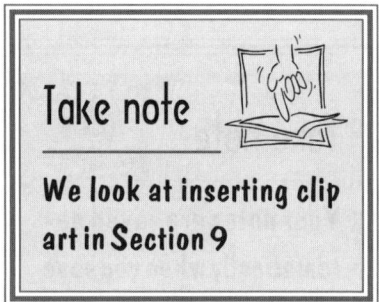

Take note

We look at inserting clip art in Section 9

(3) Choose a layout

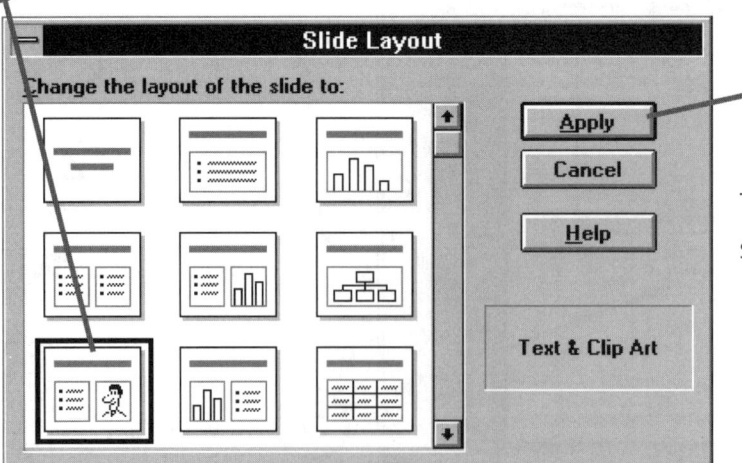

(4) Click Apply

The new layout is shown opposite

Basic steps

1 Click [Template...] on the Status Bar

2 Change the drive and directory if necessary

3 Select the Template you want to use

4 Click [**Apply**]

You can change your presentation template at any time. The template determines the design elements of your presentation - colour, fonts, alignment of text etc.

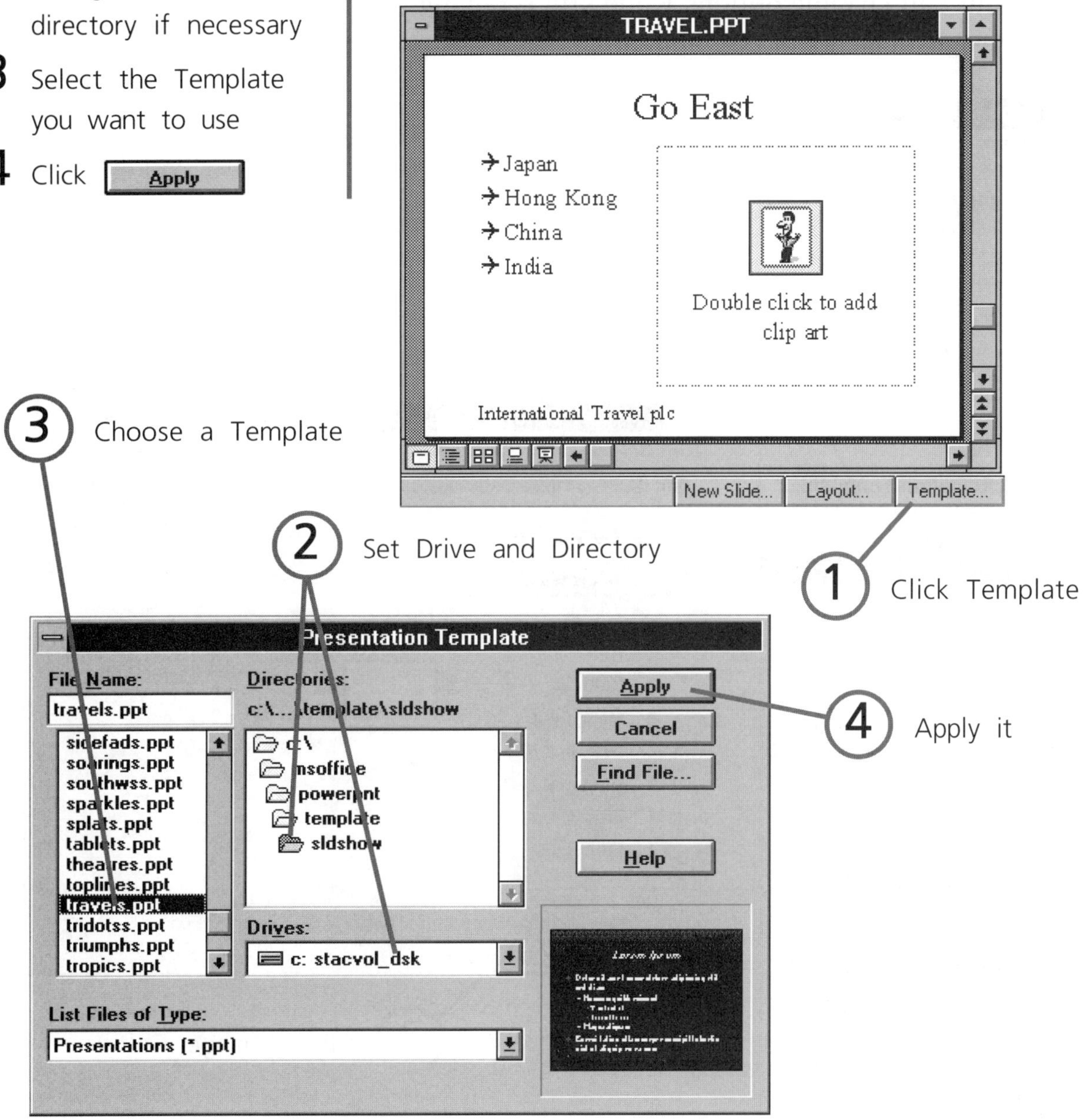

TRAVEL.PPT

Go East

→ Japan
→ Hong Kong
→ China
→ India

Double click to add clip art

International Travel plc

[New Slide...] [Layout...] [Template...]

③ Choose a Template

② Set Drive and Directory

① Click Template

Presentation Template

File **N**ame:
travels.ppt

sidefads.ppt
soorings.ppt
southwss.ppt
sparkles.ppt
splats.ppt
tablets.ppt
theatres.ppt
toplines.ppt
travels.ppt
tridotss.ppt
triumphs.ppt
tropics.ppt

Directories:
c:\...\template\sldshow

c:\
msoffice
powerpnt
template
sldshow

Dri**v**es:
c: stacvol_dsk

[**Apply**]
[**Cancel**]
[**Find File...**]
[**Help**]

④ Apply it

List Files of **T**ype:
Presentations (*.ppt)

Background styles

When you select a template for your presentation, the slide background colour and shading is picked up from the options set in the template. You can easily change the colour and shading options while still retaining the other design elements of the template.

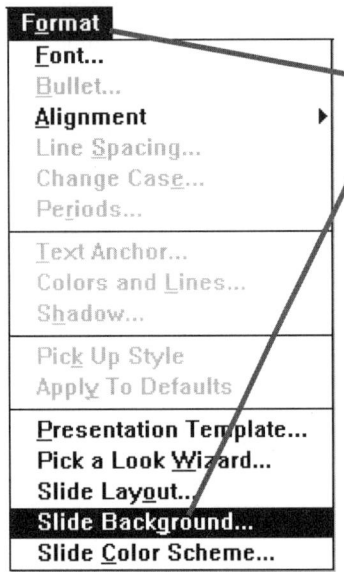

Select Format –
Slide Background..

Basic steps

1 Choose **Slide Background...** from the **Format** menu

2 Click [**Change Color...**]

3 Choose the **Background Colour** you want from the palette

4 Click **OK**

5 Select the shading style you want to use

Tip

This feature could be useful if your presentation were in sections, eg on departments, or regional sales figures. You could set a different colour for each section.

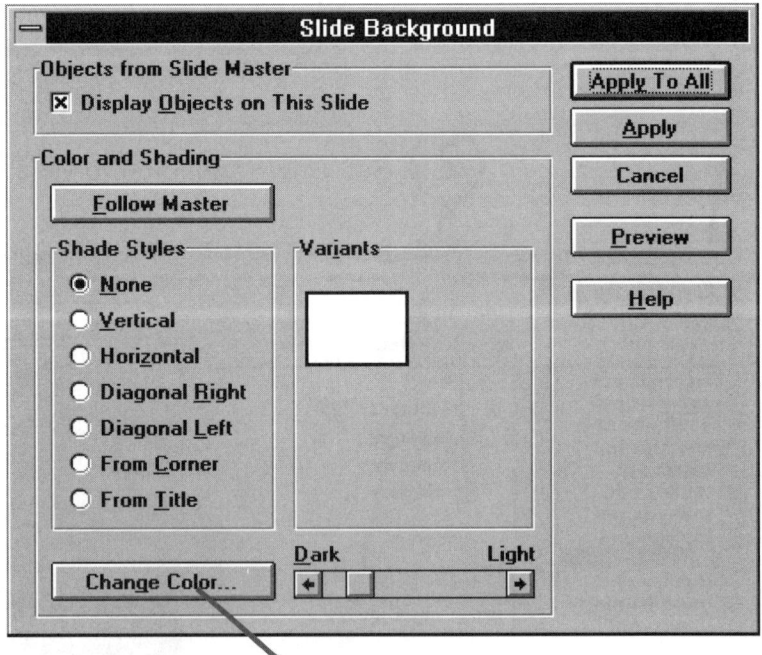

Click Change Colour..

62

6 Experiment with the Dark/Light slidebar until you have the shade you want

7 Click [**Apply**] to apply the colour to the selected slide only, or [**Apply To All**] to apply it all slides in the presentation

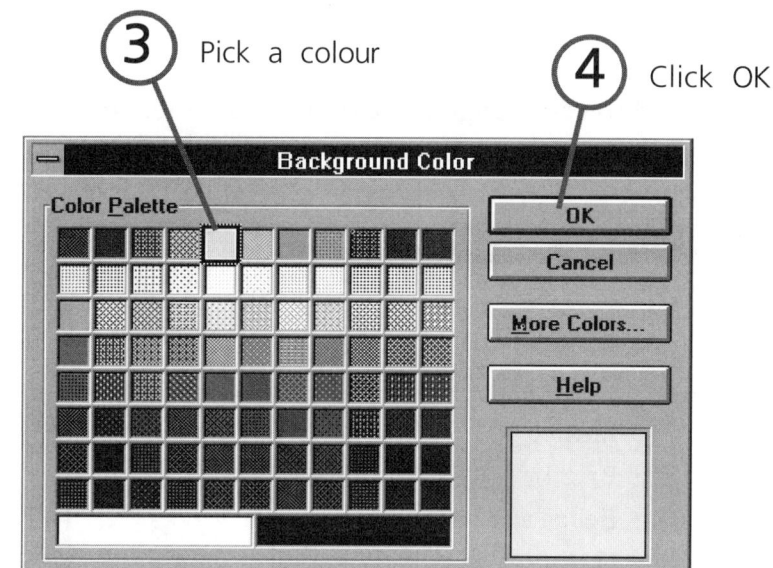

③ Pick a colour

④ Click OK

⑤ Pick a shading style

⑦ Apply it

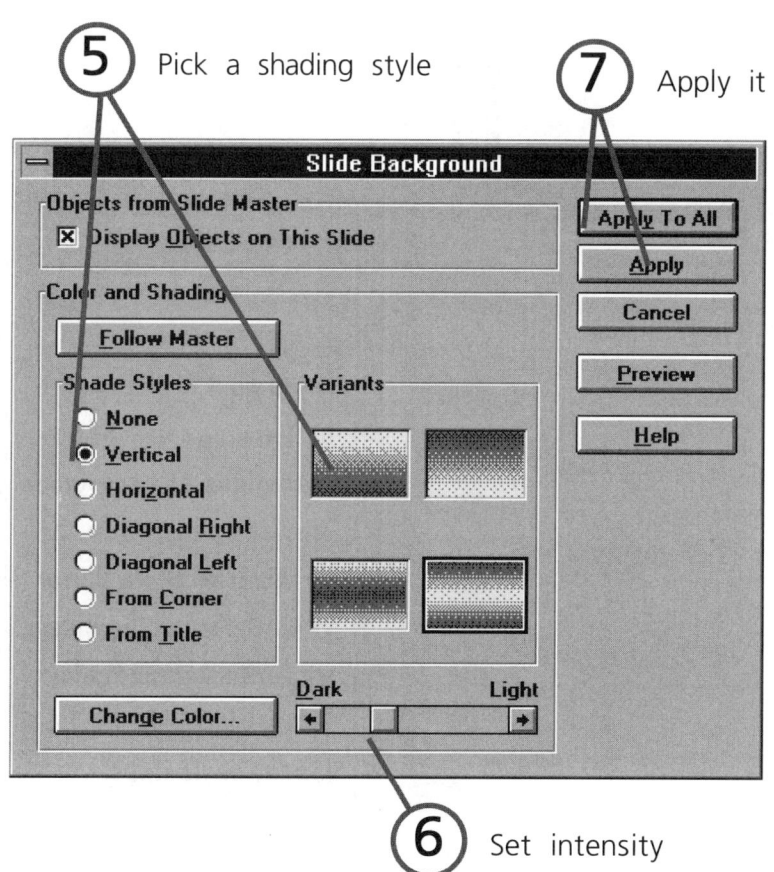

⑥ Set intensity

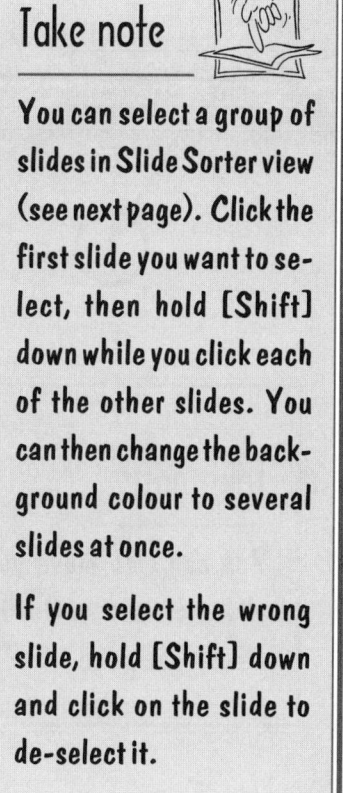

Take note

You can select a group of slides in Slide Sorter view (see next page). Click the first slide you want to select, then hold [Shift] down while you click each of the other slides. You can then change the background colour to several slides at once.

If you select the wrong slide, hold [Shift] down and click on the slide to de-select it.

Re-arranging your slides

If you need to re-arrange the order your slides are in, go into Slide Sorter view.

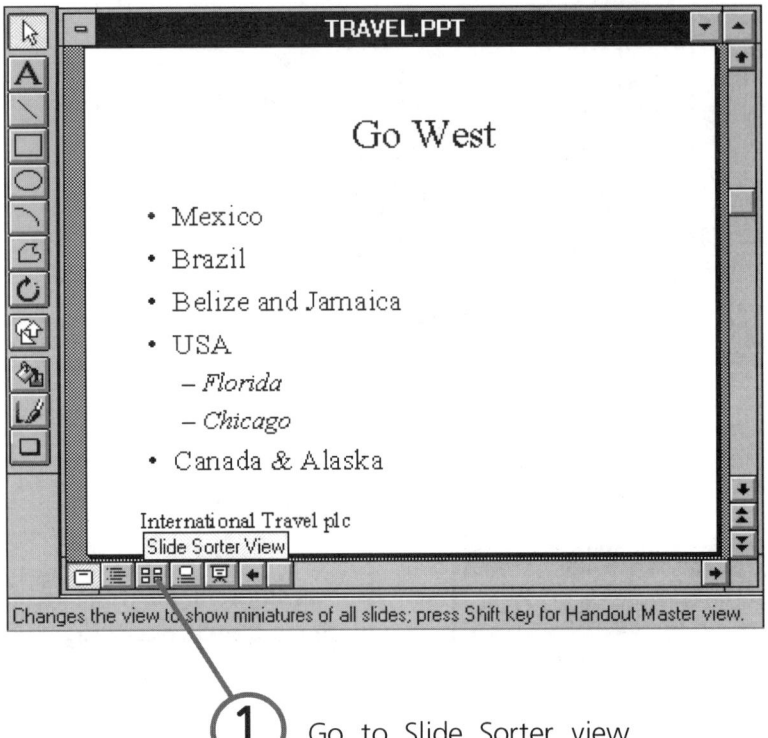

(1) Go to Slide Sorter view

Take note

You can also move your slides around in Outline view – see page 46.

1 Click the Slide Sorter view tool 🔡 to go into Slide Sorter view

2 Click on the slide you want to move, to select it

3 Drag the selected slide to its new position – the dimmed dotted vertical line indicates where the slide will go

Tip

If you want to change the background colour of several slides at once (see previous page), you can do this from Slide Sorter view. Select all the slides whose background colour is to be changed, then follow the basic steps!

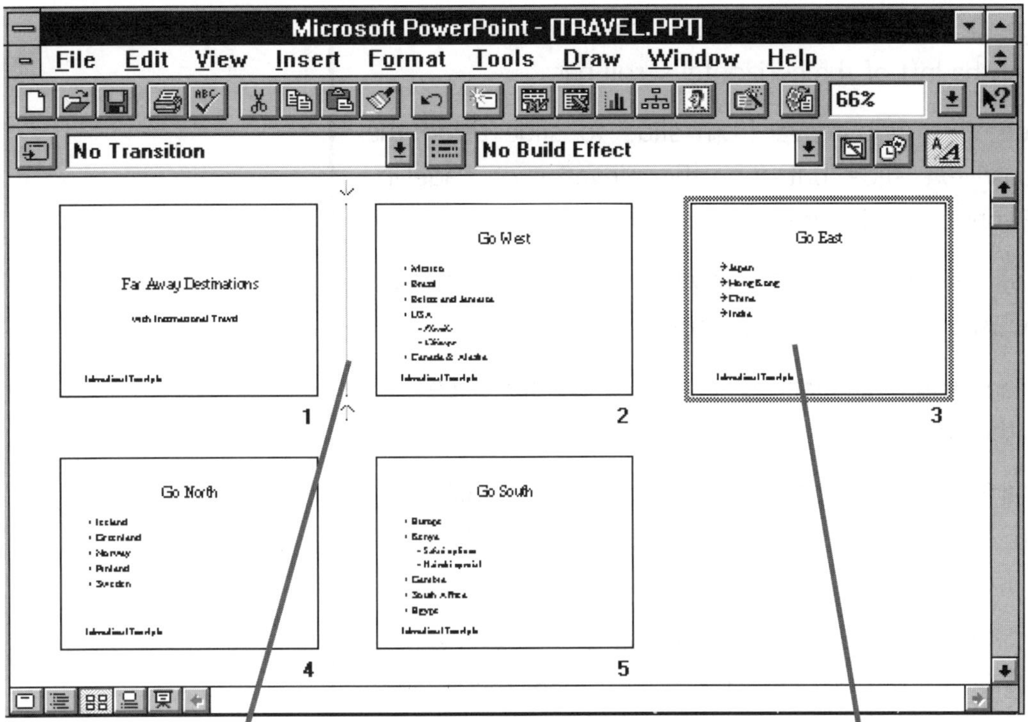

The screenshot shows a Microsoft PowerPoint window with slide sorter view.

Menu bar and toolbars with "Microsoft PowerPoint - [TRAVEL.PPT]", File Edit View Insert Format Tools Draw Window Help, "No Transition", "No Build Effect", "66%".

Slides shown:
1. Far Away Destinations
2. Go West
3. Go East (selected)
4. Go North
5. Go South

(3) Drag into its new position

(2) Select a slide

Deleting slides

If you want to delete a slide, you can delete it in this view as well. Just select the slide and press **[Delete]** or use the menu option **Edit – Delete Slide**

Tip

If you delete a slide by mistake, click the Undo tool on the standard toolbar, or use the keyboard shortcut - [Ctrl]-[Z].

65

Summary

- **Change views** in your presentation using the view icons at the left of the horizontal scroll bar

- In **Slide** View you move from slide to slide using the Previous/Next slide buttons, the elevator or PageUp and PageDown on your keyboard

- New slides can be added anywhere in your presentation using the `New Slide...` button

- You can delete a slide by choosing **Delete Slide** from the **Edit** menu

- To change the **layout** of a slide, click the `Layout...` button on the status bar then choose the layout you want from the dialog box

- To change the presentation **Template**, click the `Template...` button on the status bar, then select an alternative Template from the list

- Go into Slide Sorter view to **re-arrange** your slides. Then simply click and drag your slides to their new positions

- You can **add notes** to accompany your slides in Notes Pages view

6 Drawing

Selecting objects

So far, we have dealt with Text objects – slide headings and points listed for discussion on the slides.

In this section we are going to consider how the tools on the Drawing toolbar can be used to customise and add interest to your slides. You must be in Slide view for this.

We'll work from the top down!!

Selection Tool

The Selection tool is used to select objects on your slide. Once an object has been selected, you can move it, resize it, delete it (and lots of other things as we'll soon see). The Selection tool on the Drawing toolbar is always selected unless you are using another tool.

Basic steps

❑ **To select a text object**

1 Click within the text placeholder area – this places the insertion point within it and shows the grey border

2 Point and click on the border

❑ Note the handles that appear at the corners and along the edges of the selected object.

❑ **To select any other objects**

1 Click anywhere inside the object placeholder

❑ **To Deselect an object**

1 Click anywhere outside the selected object (click inside or outside a text object)

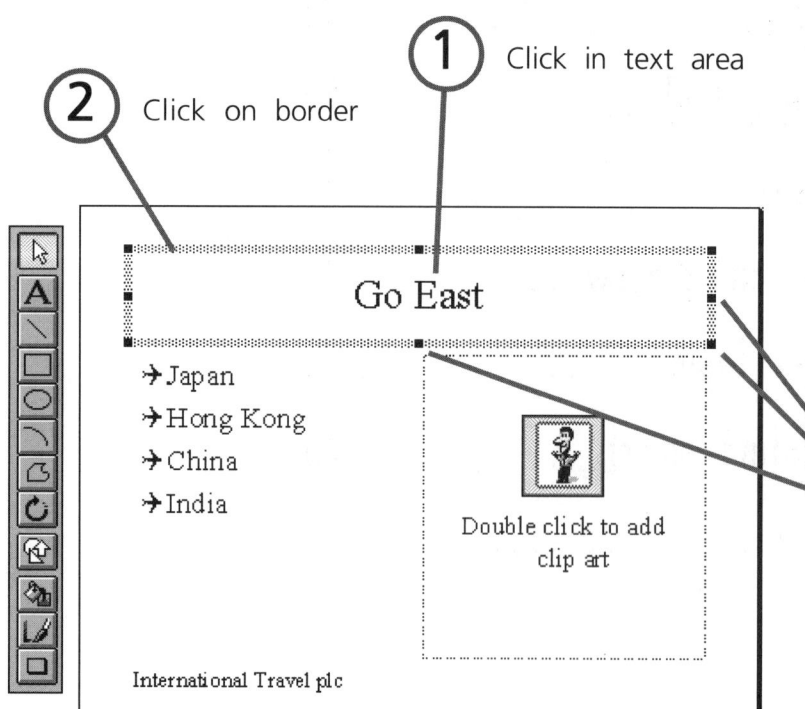

① Click in text area

② Click on border

Go East

→ Japan
→ Hong Kong
→ China
→ India

Double click to add clip art

International Travel plc

Handles

Selected objects can be

❏ **Moved**

Point to the **border** of a text object, or anywhere *within* any other type of object (not a handle) and drag the object to its new position

❏ **Resized**

Point to one of the **handles** (note the mouse pointer) and drag the handle until the object is the required size

❏ **Deleted**

Press **[Delete]** on your keyboard

Take note

If you delete an object by mistake, click the Undo tool on the Standard toolbar.

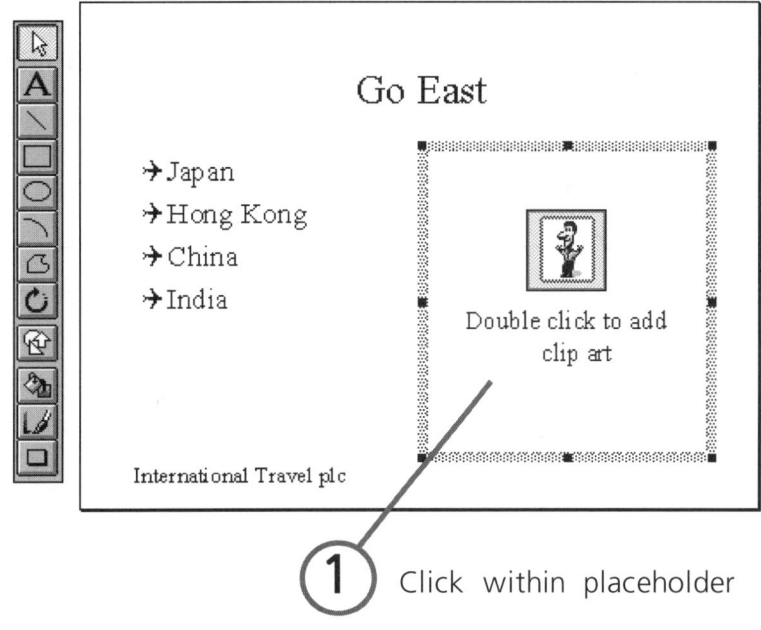

Go East

→ Japan
→ Hong Kong
→ China
→ India

Double click to add clip art

International Travel plc

① Click within placeholder

The Drawing toolbar

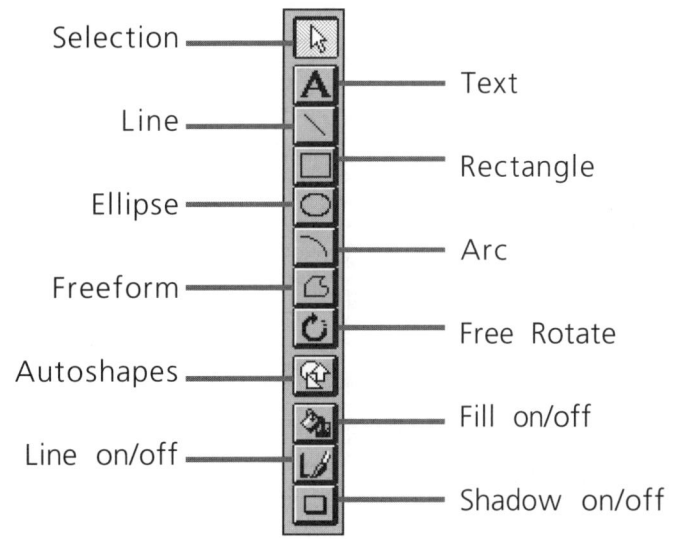

Selection

Line

Ellipse

Freeform

Autoshapes

Line on/off

Text

Rectangle

Arc

Free Rotate

Fill on/off

Shadow on/off

Text tool

You can use the text tool to enter text **anywhere** on your slide (not necessarily within an existing text placeholder).

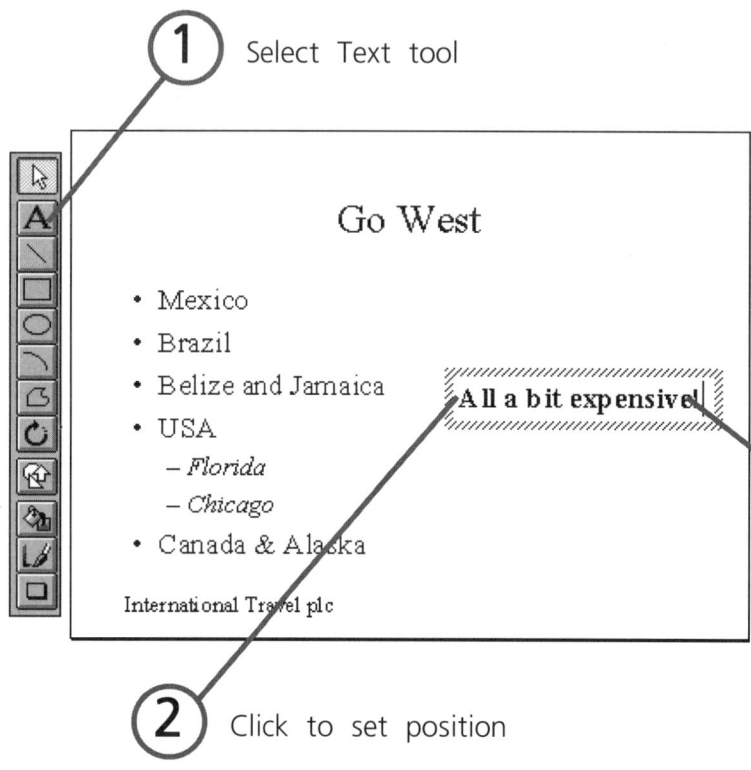

(1) Select Text tool

Go West

- Mexico
- Brazil
- Belize and Jamaica
- USA
  - *Florida*
  - *Chicago*
- Canada & Alaska

International Travel plc

All a bit expensive

(3) Key in text

(2) Click to set position

Basic steps

1 Select A the Text tool

2 Click anywhere on your slide to position the insertion point

3 Key in the text

❑ The text object you have created can be selected, moved, resized and deleted (see page 70).

Take note

You can format the text using any of the text formatting options available - bold, size, font style, italics, underline etc.

Tip

The line drawing and Freeform tools can all be locked on. Double click the tool to lock it. Select any other tool (or press [ESC]) to unlock it.

Drawing tools

❑ **Line-based tools**

1 Select a tool

2 Click to set the start

3 Drag to draw the shape on your slide

☞ Hold **[Shift]** down as you click and drag if you want a straight line (line tool), a square (rectangle tool) or circle (ellipse tool).

❑ **Freeform tool**

1 Select the Freeform tool 🖸

2 Click and drag (note the pencil shaped mouse pointer) to draw a line freehand

☞ Click at each corner of your shape to get straight lines

3 Press **[Esc]** when you are finished

The line, rectangle, ellipse and arc tool all work in a similar way. The more adventurous/artistic among you will have fun with the Freeform tool. Experiment with them on your slides.

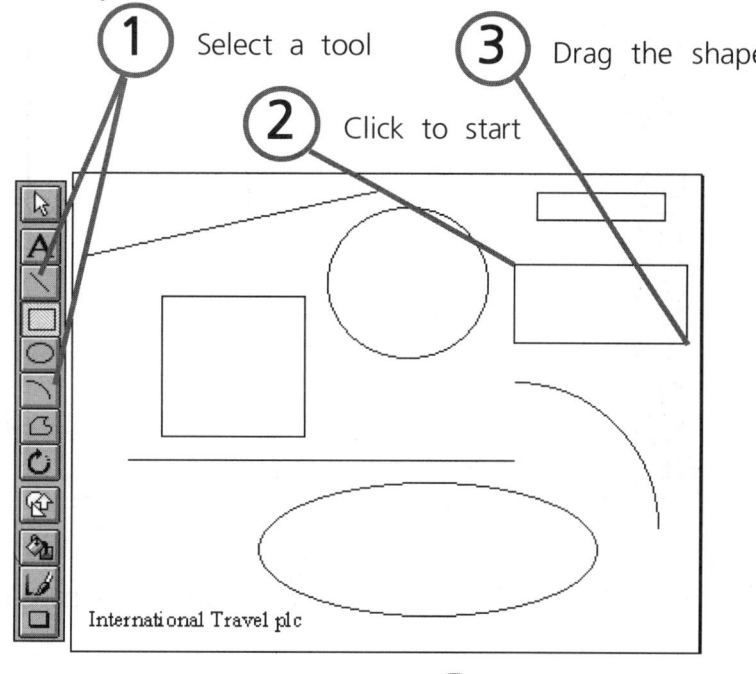

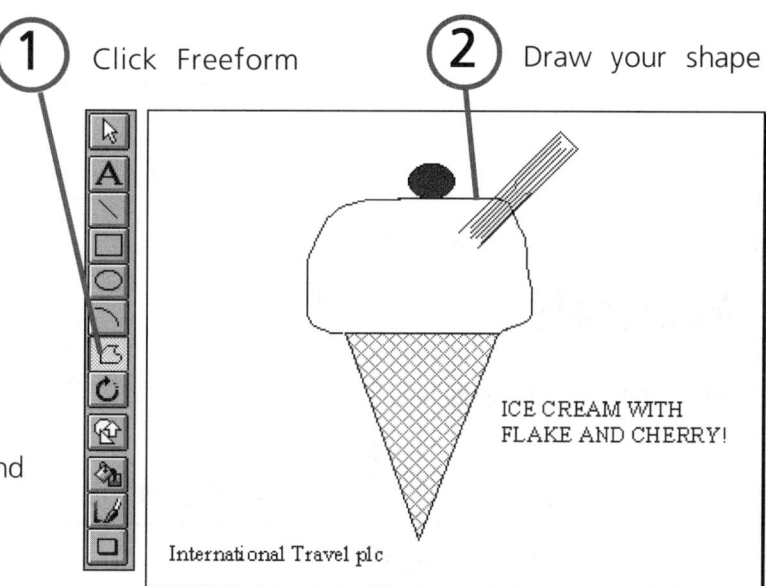

Free rotate tool

The Free Rotate Tool is used to rotate an object.

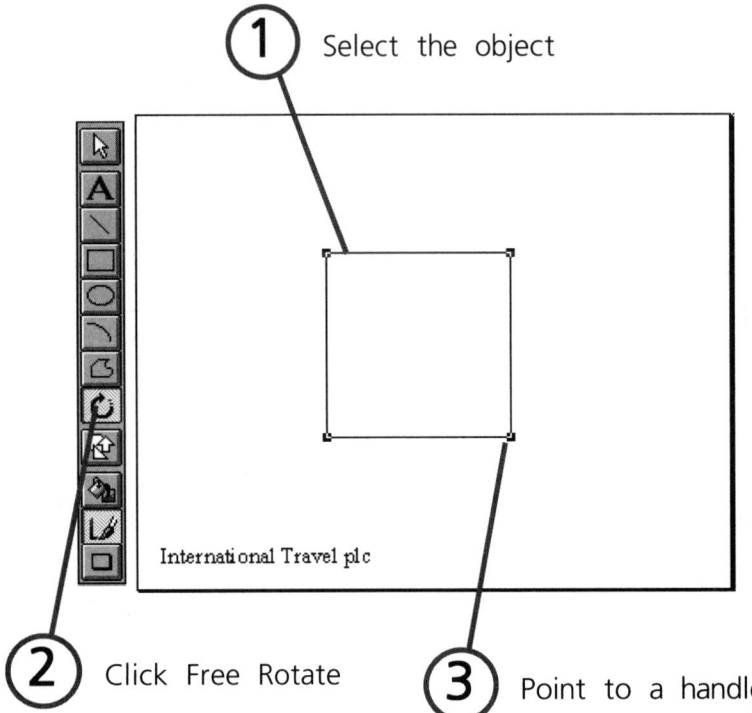

① Select the object

② Click Free Rotate

③ Point to a handle

1 Select the object you want to rotate

2 Click the **Free Rotate** tool

3 Position the mouse pointer (note its appearance) over one of the handles of the selected object

4 Drag the handle until the object is rotated to its new position

5 Press **[Esc]** to switch off Free Rotate (or select another tool)

④ Drag to rotate

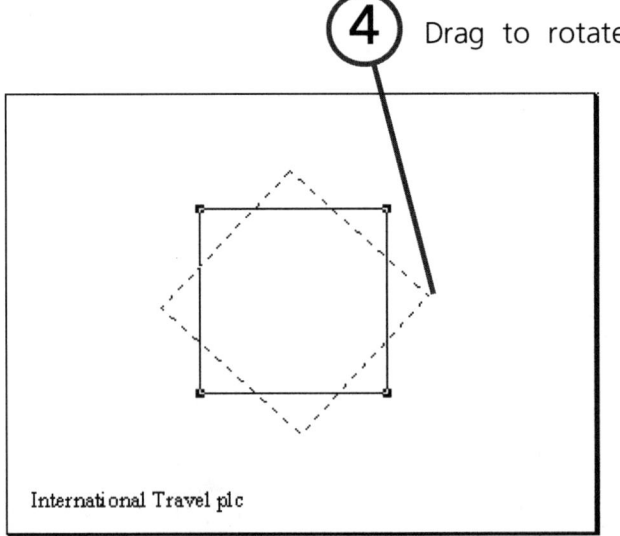

Mouse pointers

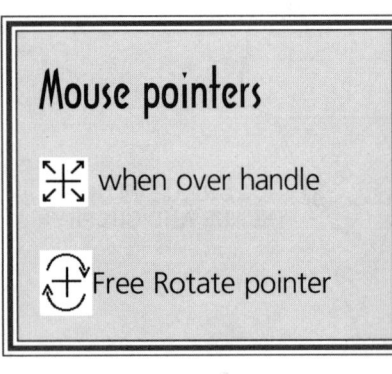

when over handle

Free Rotate pointer

72

Basic steps

1 Click the **AutoShapes** tool to display the AutoShapes toolbar

2 Select the shape you want

3 Click and drag on your slide to draw your shape

4 Click to hide the toolbar again

AutoShapes

If you want stars, triangles, arrows etc on your slide it's worth looking at the AutoShapes provided. If the shape you want is here, it's a lot easier to use an AutoShape than to draw the design from scratch!

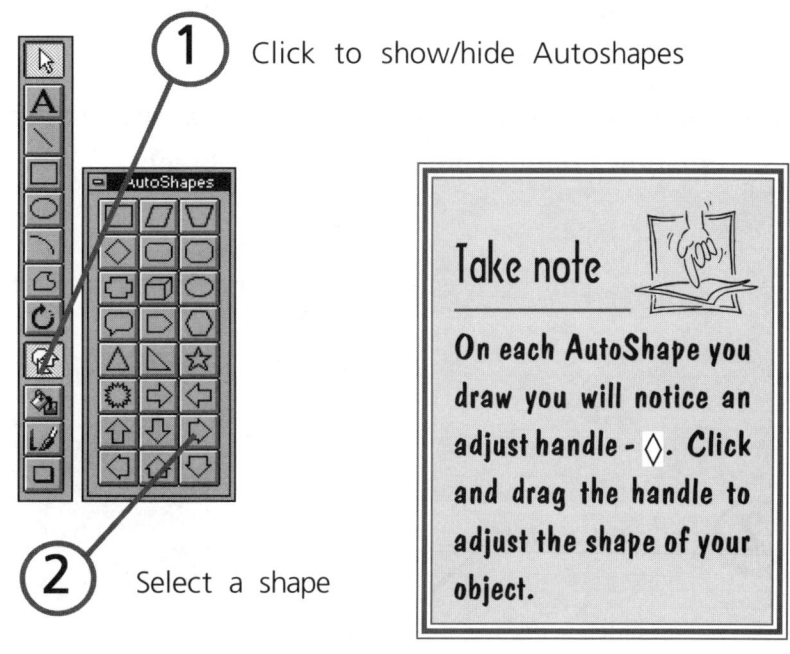

① Click to show/hide Autoshapes

② Select a shape

Take note

On each AutoShape you draw you will notice an adjust handle - ◊. Click and drag the handle to adjust the shape of your object.

Tip

If you use the AutoShapes a lot, leave the toolbar showing. You can drag it to one of the docking areas - top, bottom, right or left of your screen - so it doesn't obscure your slides. To move the toolbar, drag its title bar.

Adjust handle ③ Drag to draw shape

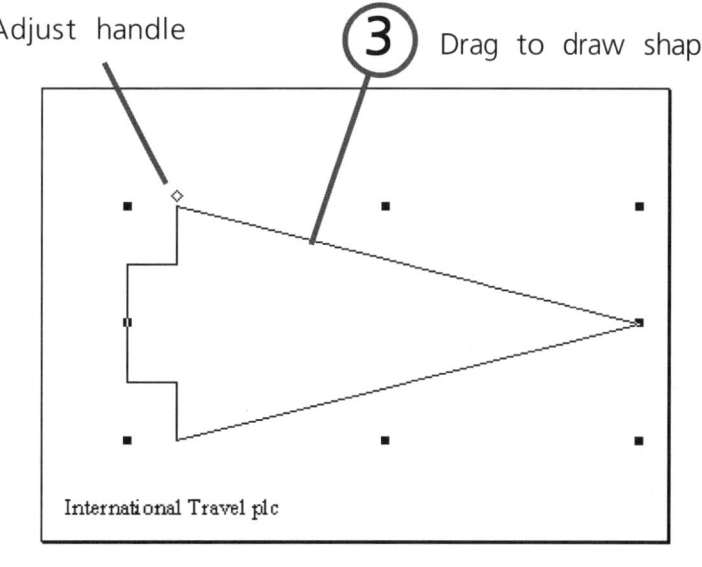

International Travel plc

Fill, line and shadow

These tools are all toggles.

Fill On/Off adds and removes the default fill colour from the selected object

Line On/Off adds and removes the default line colour from the selected object

Shadow On/Off adds and removes the default shadow colour from the selected object.

Basic steps

1 Select the object

2 Click the tool – Fill On/Off, Line On/Off or Shadow On/Off

3 Deselect the object (click anywhere off it)

(1) Select the object

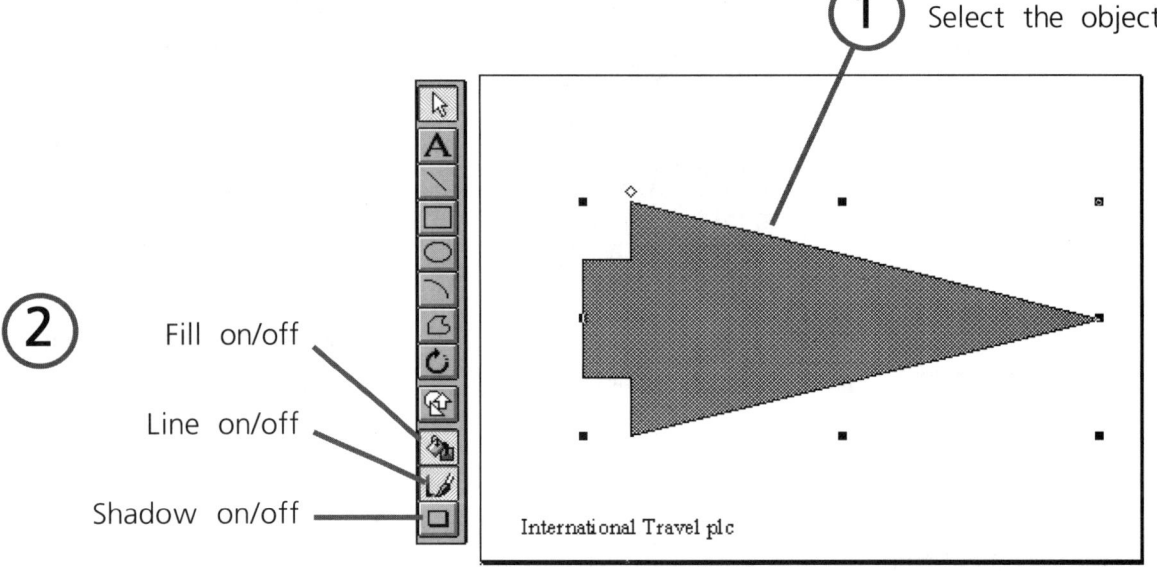

(2)

Fill on/off

Line on/off

Shadow on/off

International Travel plc

(3) Deselect

Take note

If you switch all three off - the Fill, Line and Shadow - you can't see your object!

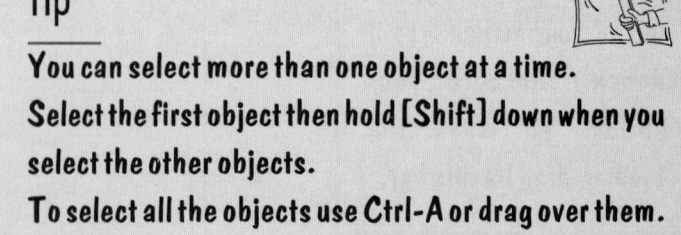

Tip

You can select more than one object at a time. Select the first object then hold [Shift] down when you select the other objects.
To select all the objects use Ctrl-A or drag over them.

Basic steps

1 Position the mouse pointer over any toolbar on screen and click the **right** mouse button to display the toolbar shortcut menu

2 Select the **Drawing+** toolbar from the list

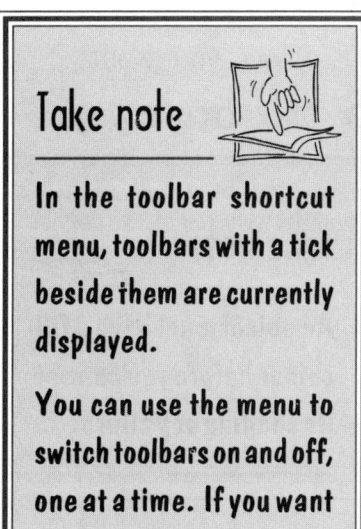

Take note

In the toolbar shortcut menu, toolbars with a tick beside them are currently displayed.

You can use the menu to switch toolbars on and off, one at a time. If you want to switch several toolbars on or off at the same time, open the View menu and choose Toolbars.

Drawing+ toolbar

Now that you have used the tools on the Drawing Toolbar, you might like to experiment with the Drawing+ Toolbar!

The Drawing+ Toolbar allows you to edit the Fill colour, Line colour, Line style and Shadow. You can also use it to pile objects one on top of the other to get special effects, group objects and flip them over! What more could you want!

Display the Drawing+ Toolbar and try out some of the tools.

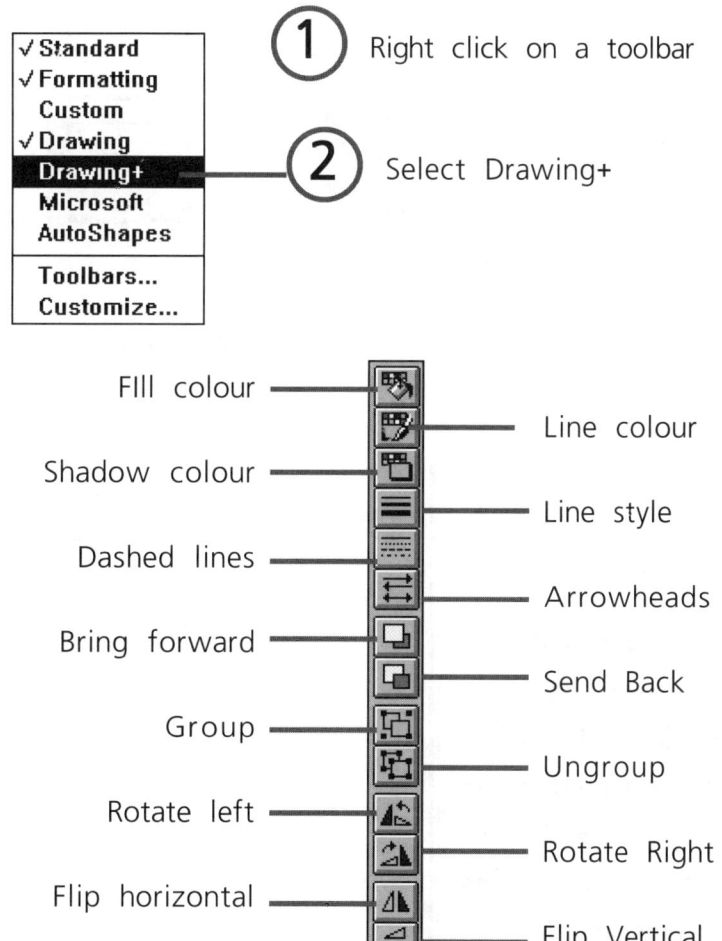

75

Changing the fill colour

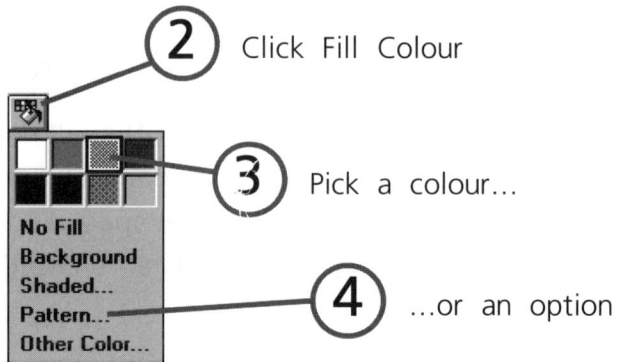

② Click Fill Colour

③ Pick a colour...

④ ...or an option

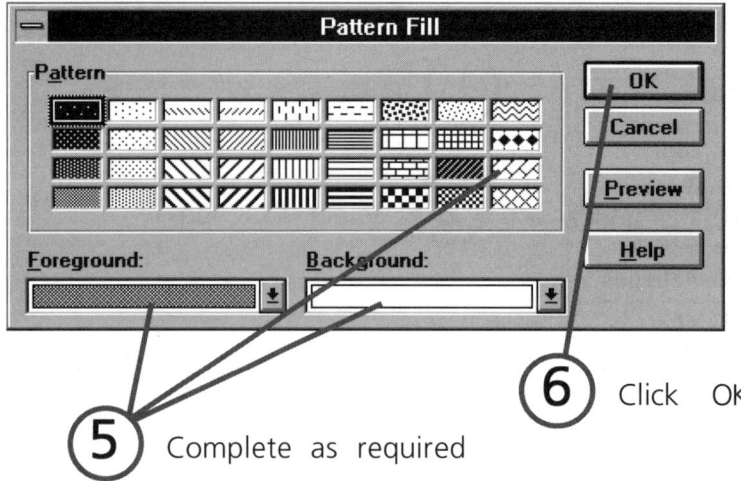

⑤ Complete as required

⑥ Click OK

1 Select the object

2 Click the **Fill Colour**
   tool

3 Select a colour

OR

4 Choose **Shaded...**,
   Pattern... or **Other**
   Colour.. for more
   options

5 Select the effect or
   colour you want

6 Click **OK**

Take note

An object must have a fill
colour before you can set
its shading or pattern.

Tip

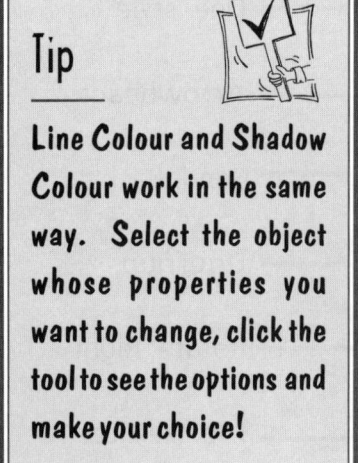

Line Colour and Shadow
Colour work in the same
way. Select the object
whose properties you
want to change, click the
tool to see the options and
make your choice!

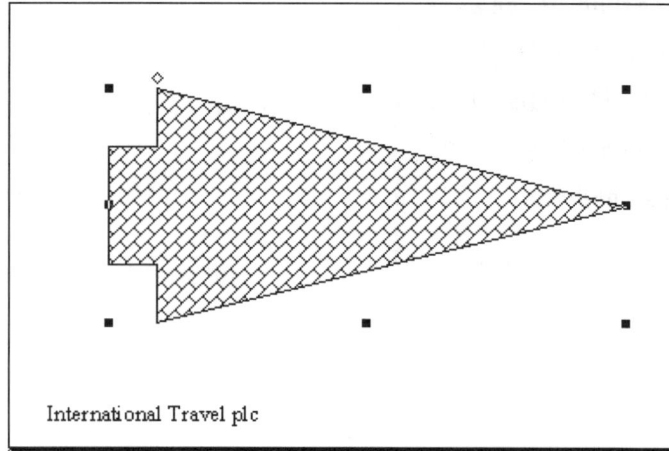

Lines and arrowheads

❑ **Line styles**

1 Select your object

2 Click the **Line Style**
   ▤ or **Dashed Lines**
   ▦ tool

3 Make your choice

❑ **Arrowheads**

1 Draw your line

2 Select it

3 Click the **Arrowheads**
   ⇄ tool

4 Select the arrowhead
   style you want

You can select an alternative line style for your object, or if you want to point to something on your slide you can add arrowheads to a line.

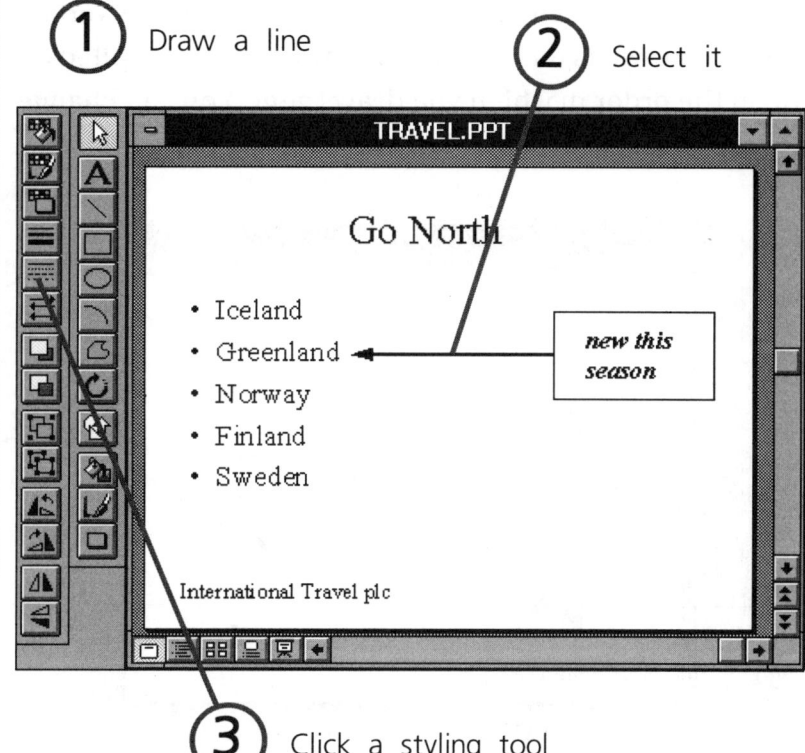

① Draw a line   ② Select it

③ Click a styling tool

④ Choose your style

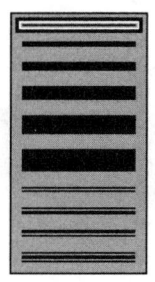

Line styles

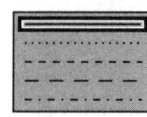

Dashed lines

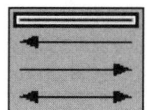

Arrowheads

Manipulating objects

Bring forward, send back

These are useful if you have overlapping objects and need to change their relative level. When objects overlap, the first drawn is underneath, and the others are piled on top in the order in which you draw them. You can change the order with the Bring Forward or Send Back tools.

Basic steps

1 Select the object you wish to Bring Forward or Send Backward

2 Click the **Bring Forward** or **Send Back** tool until the object is at the required level

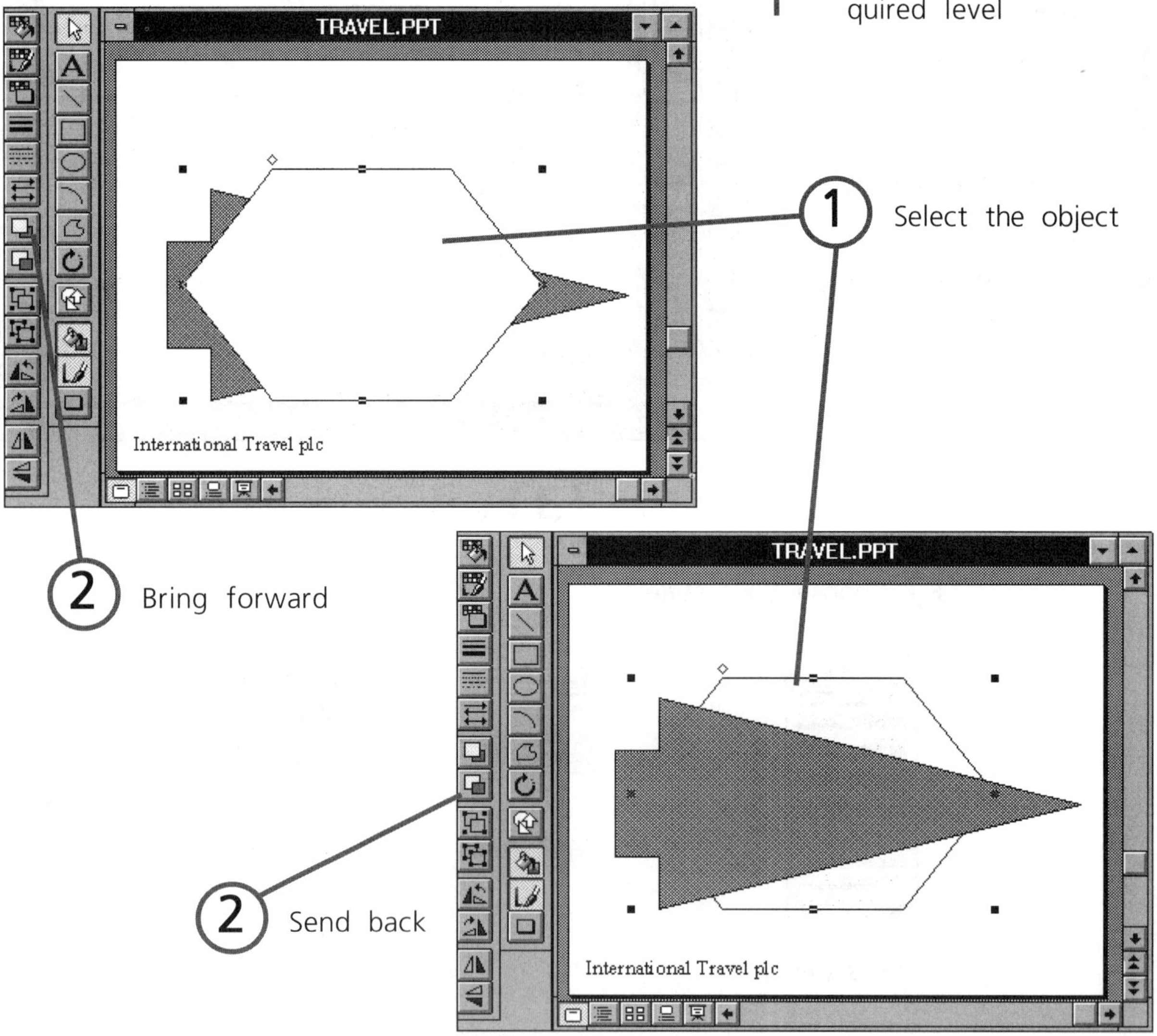

TRAVEL.PPT

International Travel plc

① Select the object

② Bring forward

TRAVEL.PPT

International Travel plc

② Send back

78

Basic steps

- ❏ **To group objects**
- **1** Select the objects
- **2** Click **Group** 🔲

- ❏ **To Ungroup objects**
- **1** Select the grouped object
- **2** Click **Ungroup** 🔲

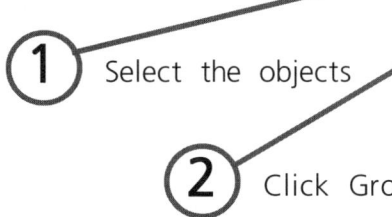

① Select the objects

② Click Group

- ❏ **To Rotate or Flip**
- **1** Select the object
- **2** Click the appropriate Rotate or Flip tool

② Rotate or Flip

Grouping objects

If you have drawn several objects to generate an image, you can group the objects together into one to make it easier to move, copy or resize the whole image.

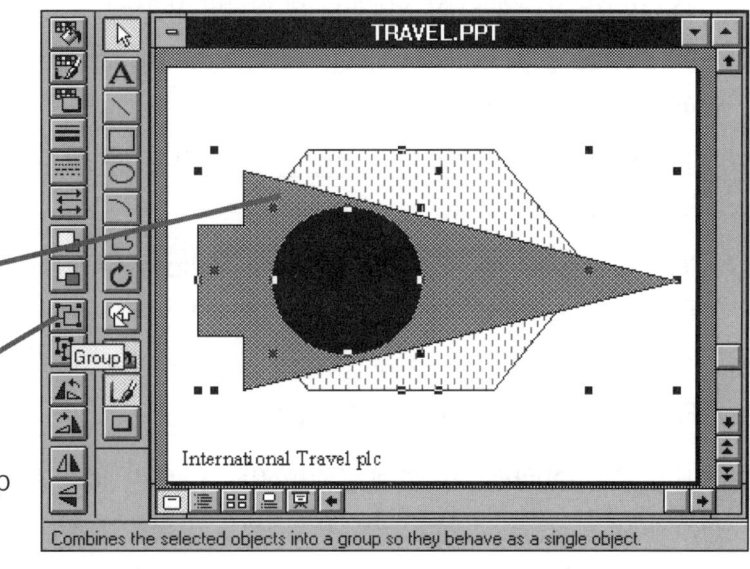

Combines the selected objects into a group so they behave as a single object.

Rotate and flip

The orientation of an object can be changed with the Rotate and the Flip tools.

① Select the object

> **Tip**
>
> The Rotate tools rotate by 90° left or right. Use the Free Rotate Tool to rotate by other amounts.

Summary

- To move, resize or delete an object, you must **select it first**

- To **move** a selected object, drag its border

- To **resize** a selected object, drag one of the handles along its border

- To **delete** a selected object, press **[Delete]** on your keyboard

- You can use the **Line**, **Rectangle**, **Ellipse**, **Arc** or **Freeform** tool to create drawings on your slides

- The orientation of objects can be changed using the **Free Rotate**, **Rotate** or **Flip** tools

- The **AutoShapes** toolbar contains several useful shapes to add impact to your presentations

- **Fill colours**, **lines** and **shadows** are easily toggled on and off

- The **Drawing+ Toolbar** provides many additional features to help you perfect your drawing

7 Graphs

Starting a graph

There will be times when pictures talk louder than words - and when this is the case you can use graphs, organisation charts, clipart, tables etc to help you make your point. In this section we'll look at ways you can add a graph to your slide.

There are three main ways to set up your chart using Microsoft Graph:-

● Choose a slide from the New Slide dialog box that has a Graph placeholder already on it

 or

● Choose a slide from the New Slide dialog box that has an Object placeholder already on it

 or

● Click the Insert Graph tool ▥

Basic steps

❏ Using a Graph placeholder

1 Double click within the Graph placeholder to move into the graphing environment

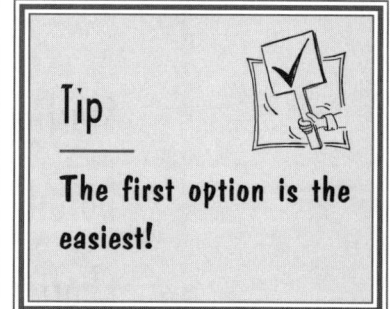

Tip

___

The first option is the easiest!

1 Double click

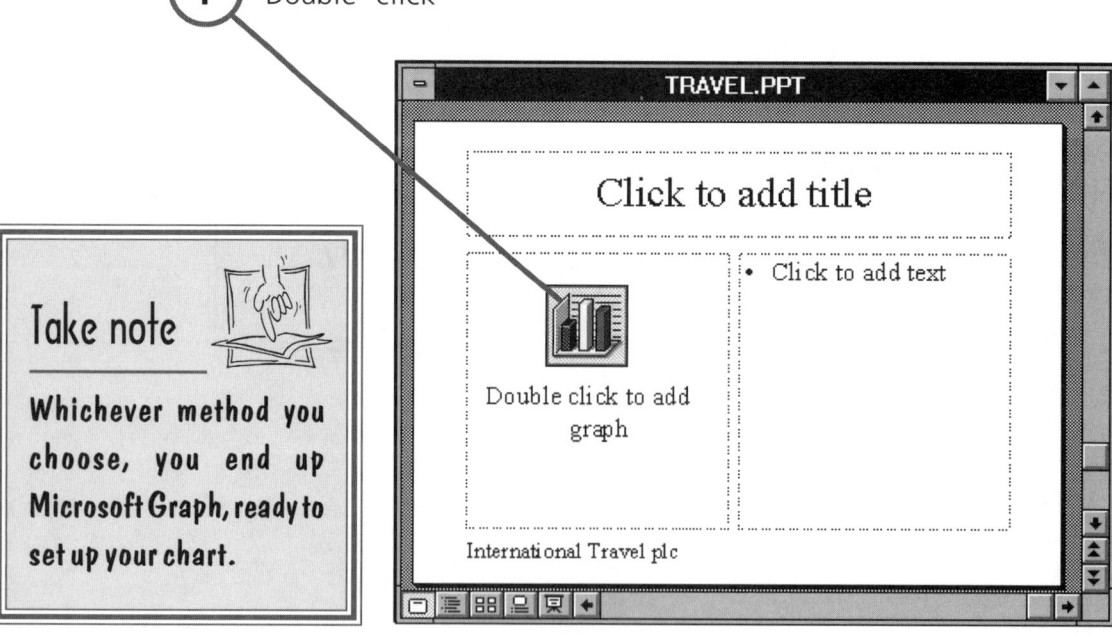

Take note

___

Whichever method you choose, you end up Microsoft Graph, ready to set up your chart.

Basic steps

❑ **Using an Object placeholder**

1 Double click within the Object placeholder on your slide to open the **Insert Object** dialog box

2 Choose **Microsoft Graph 5**

3 Click **OK**

❑ **From a slide with no placeholder set**

1 Click the Insert Graph tool ⬚ on the standard toolbar

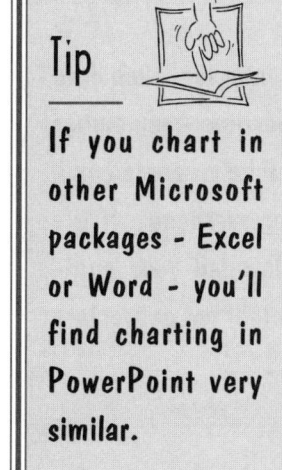

Tip

If you chart in other Microsoft packages - Excel or Word - you'll find charting in PowerPoint very similar.

① Double click

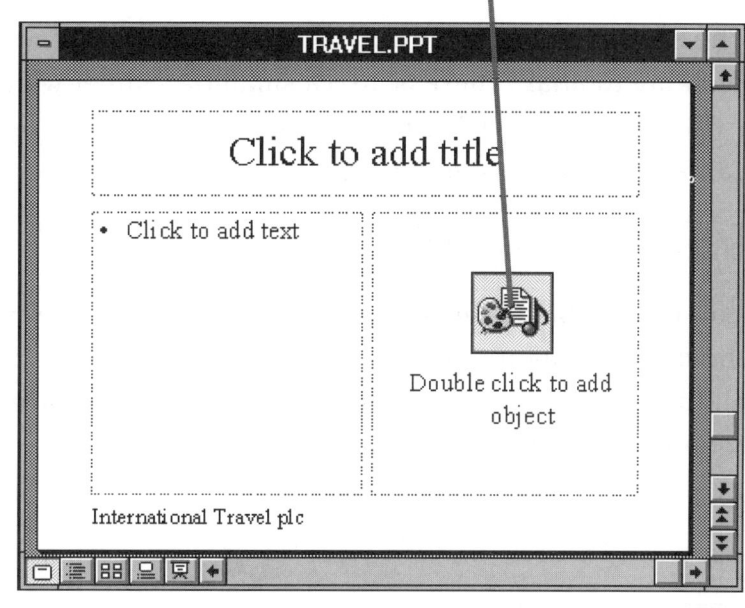

② Choose Graph

③ Click OK

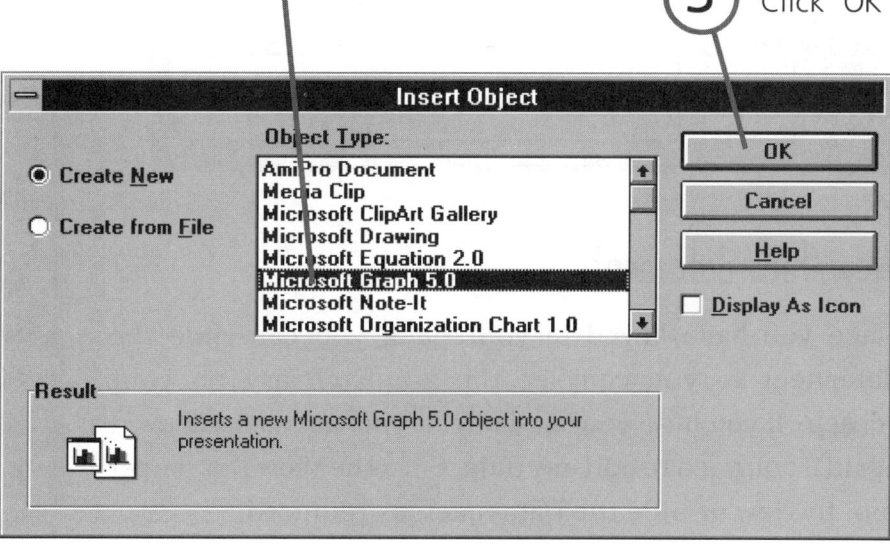

83

Datasheet and toolbars

The Graph environment has its own Standard toolbar and Drawing toolbar. There is also a small Datasheet window (which can be moved or resized as necessary), where you can key in the data you want to chart.

Entering your own data

You must replace the sample data in the datasheet with the data you want to chart. If you do not need to replace all the sample data, delete the cell contents that are not required - go to the cell and press [Delete].

1 Move to the cell   **2** Enter data

Scroll up or down, right or left to access additional rows or columns if you are entering a lot of data.

		A	B	C	D	
		1st Qtr	2nd Qtr	3rd Qtr	4th Qtr	
1	East	20.4	27.4	90	20.4	
2	West	30.6	38.6	34.6	31.6	
3	North	45.9	46.9	45	43.9	
4						
5						
6						

TRAVEL.PPT - Datasheet

View/hide datasheet

Once you have keyed in your data, you can Hide the datasheet so you can see the graph clearly on your screen. If you hide your datasheet, you can easily view it again if you need to edit any data. Click the View Datasheet tool to view or hide the Datasheet, as required.

Tip

Don't enter too much data for charting - remember this will be presented on a slide or overhead. If it's too detailed your audience might not appreciate it fully!

Moving around your datasheet

Tip

Once your data is entered, hide your datasheet. It's easier to work on your chart without the datasheet obstructing your view. You can display it again if you need to edit it.

There are a number of ways to move from cell to cell within the Datasheet. You can use the:-

Arrow keys   one cell in direction of arrow

[Tab]   forward to the next cell

[Shift]-[Tab]   back to the previous cell

[Enter]   down to the next cell in a column

or

Point to the cell and click.

The cell you are in (your *current* cell) has a dark border.

Standard toolbar

Import chart — Cut — Paste — By Row — Chart type — Horizontal gridlines — Textbox — Colour — Help

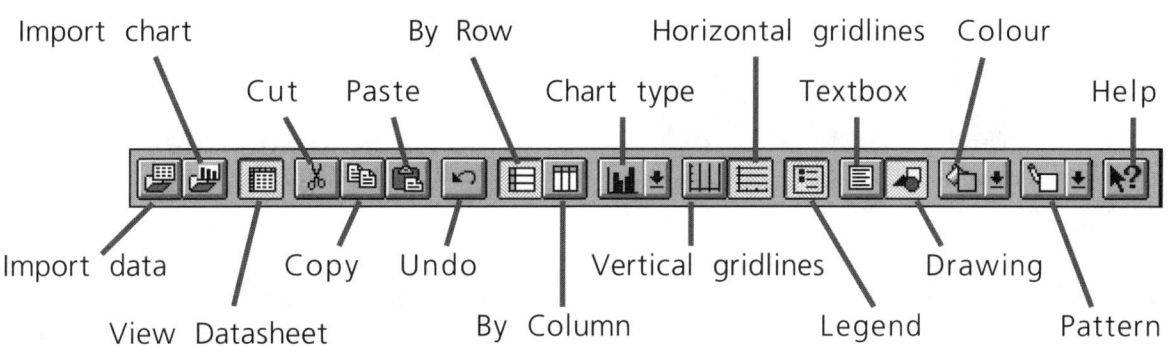

Import data — View Datasheet — Copy — Undo — By Column — Vertical gridlines — Legend — Drawing — Pattern

Drawing toolbar

Line — Freehand — Ellipse — Freeform — Filled Ellipse — Filled Freeform — Selection — Group — Bring to front — Drop Shadow

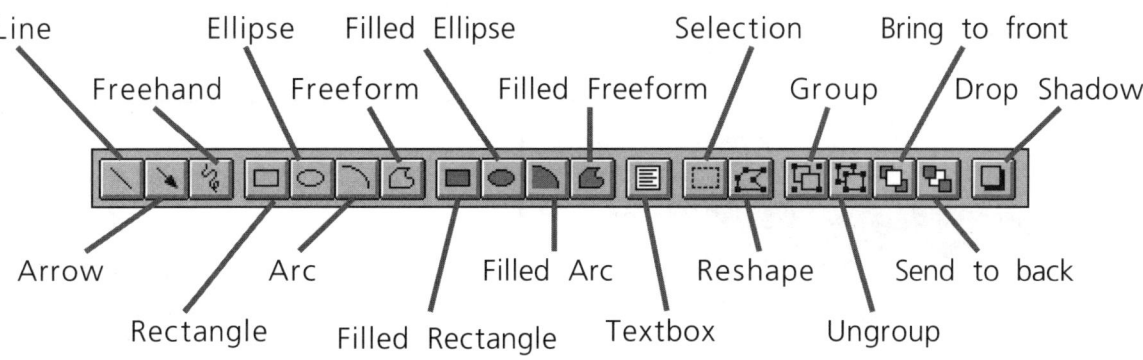

Arrow — Rectangle — Arc — Filled Rectangle — Filled Arc — Textbox — Reshape — Ungroup — Send to back

Chart type

The default chart type is a column chart. You can try out a variety of other chart types using the Chart Type tool on the Standard toolbar.

Basic steps

1 Click the drop down arrow to display the chart types available

2 Choose one

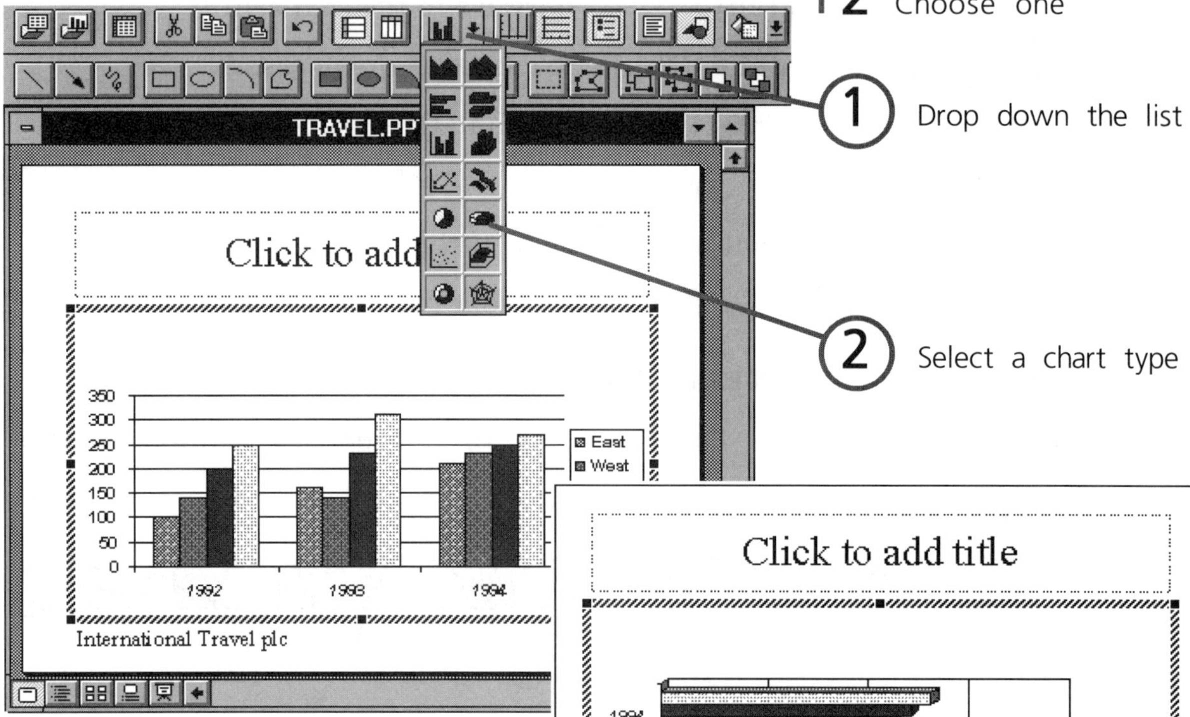

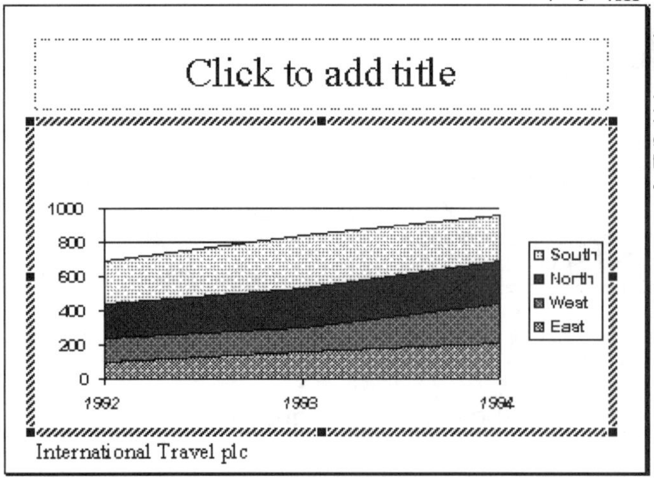

① Drop down the list

② Select a chart type

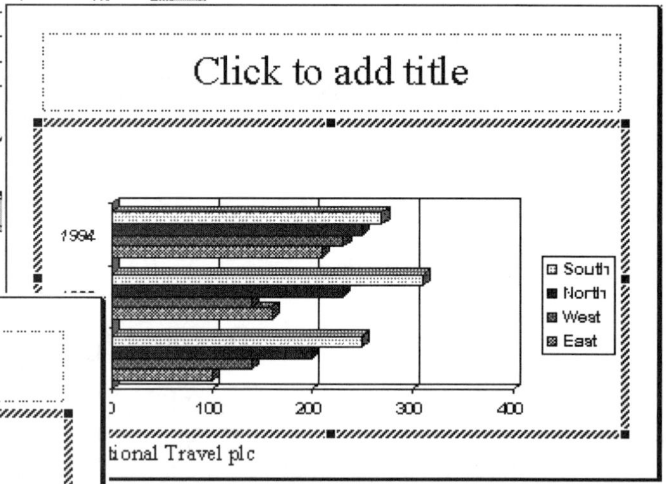

TRAVEL.PP'

Click to add

350
300
250
200
150
100
50
0
1992   1993   1994

☒ East
■ West

International Travel plc

Click to add title

1994

☐ South
■ North
☒ West
☒ East

0   100   200   300   400

...ional Travel plc

Click to add title

1000
800
600
400
200
0
1992   1993   1994

☐ South
■ North
☒ West
☒ East

International Travel plc

If you don't like your first choice of chart type, drop down the list and try another

86

Customising graphs

You can customise the basic chart in a number of different ways, to add your own personal touch.

Gridlines and legends

You can toggle the display of gridlines and legends on your charts with the tools on the standard toolbar.

● Toggle Vertical Gridlines on and off using

● Toggle Horizontal Gridlines on and off using

● Toggle the Legend on and off using

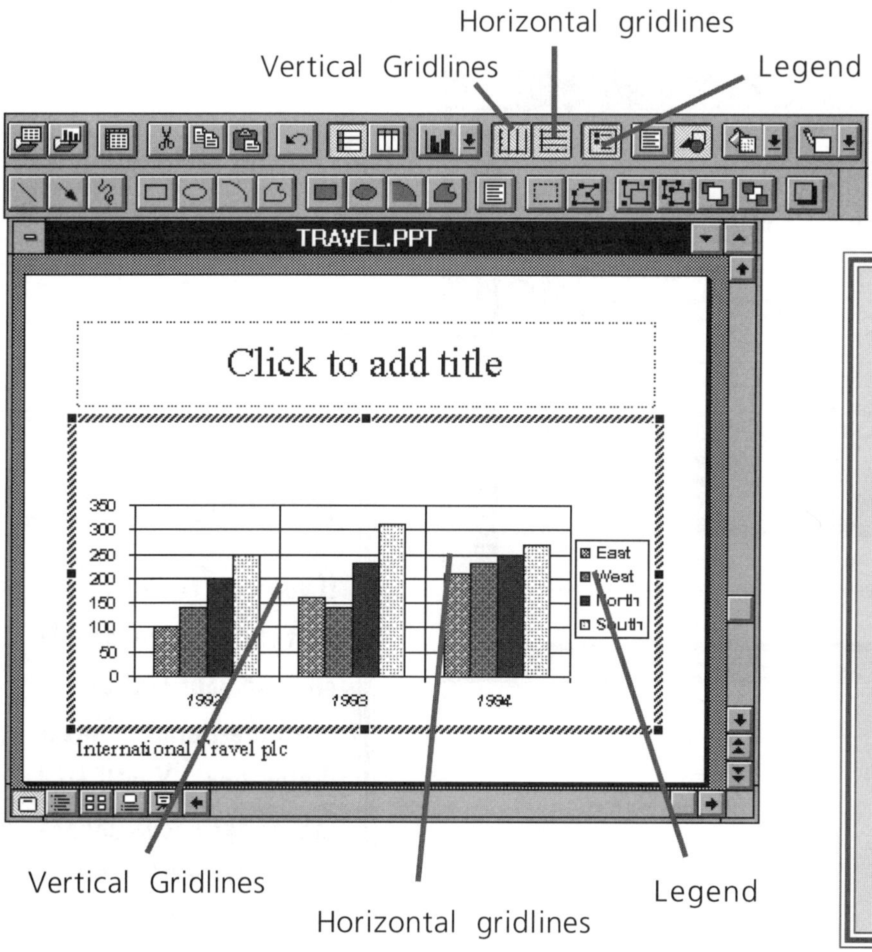

Horizontal gridlines

Vertical Gridlines

Legend

TRAVEL.PPT

Click to add title

350
300
250
200
150
100
50
0

1992   1993   1994

☒ East
☒ West
■ North
□ South

International Travel plc

Vertical Gridlines

Horizontal gridlines

Legend

Text Box

If you want to add text within the chart area, you can use a Text Box for this. The Text Box is a separate object which can be moved, resized or deleted as required.

● If you make your Text Box too large or too small, select it then drag the handles to resize it.

● If you put it in the wrong place, select it then click and drag from within the selected area to move it.

Basic steps

1 Click the Text Box tool 📧 on either toolbar

1 Click and drag to position the Text Box within the chart area

3 Key in your text

4 Click outside the Text Box

(1) Click Text Box

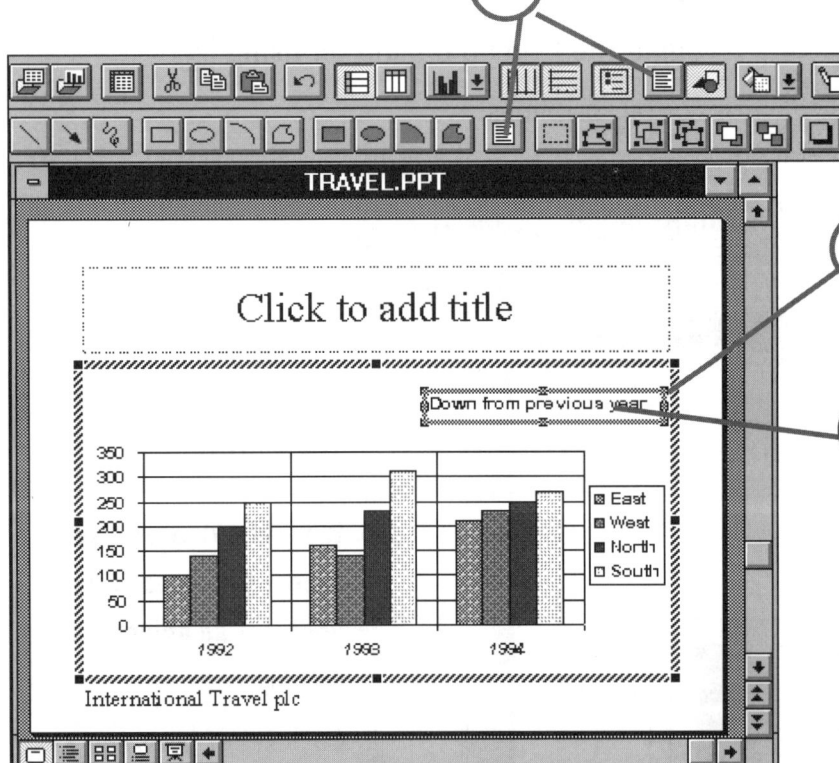

(2) Drag to draw box

(3) Enter text

(4) Click outside box

Take note

If you want to change the font style or size, double click on your text box to open the Format Object dialog box. You'll find lots of options to choose from in there!

Basic steps

Colours and patterns

1 Select the object

2 Click the drop down arrow beside the Colour tool to display the list of colours you can choose from

3 Pick a colour

If you don't like the colour of the bars (or other objects) on your chart, or if you want to experiment with patterns as well as colour, try out the options.

① Select the object

② Drop down the list

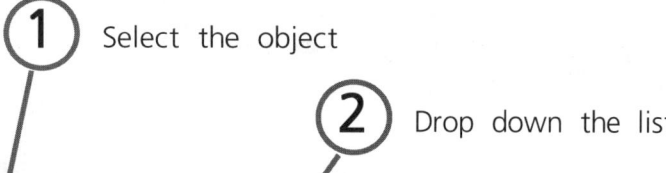

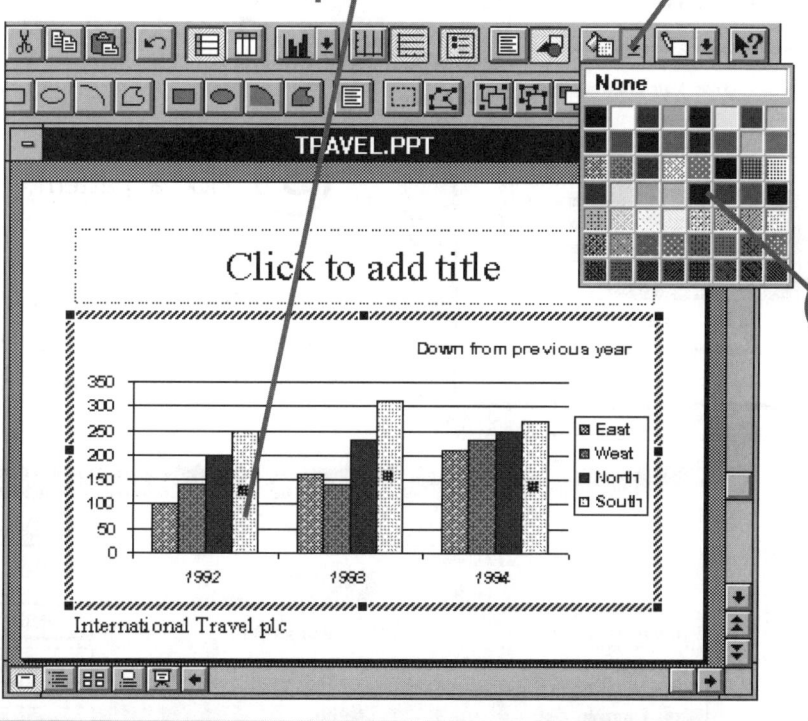

③ Choose a colour

Tip

Selecting one bar in a data series, selects them all

Take note

You can further enhance your charts using the tools on the Drawing toolbar. Toggle its display by clicking the Drawing tool on the standard toolbar. Many of the tools are very similar to the ones on the Drawing toolbars in Slide view.

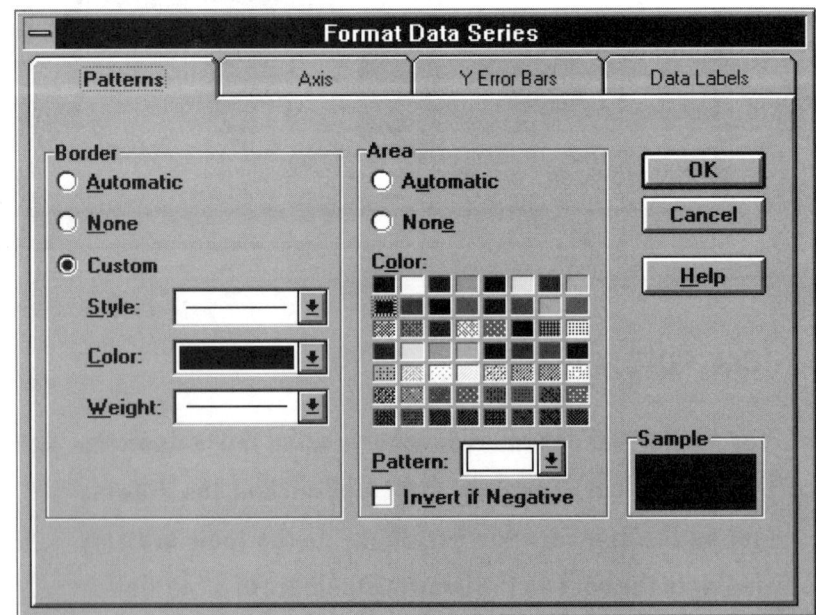

① Select an object

② Open the palette

③ Pick a pattern

TRAVEL.PPT

Click to add title

Down from previous year

East
West
North
South

1992   1993   1994

International Travel plc

Automatic

To change patterns

1 Select the object

2 Click the drop down arrow beside the Pattern tool to display the palette of patterns

3 Choose a pattern

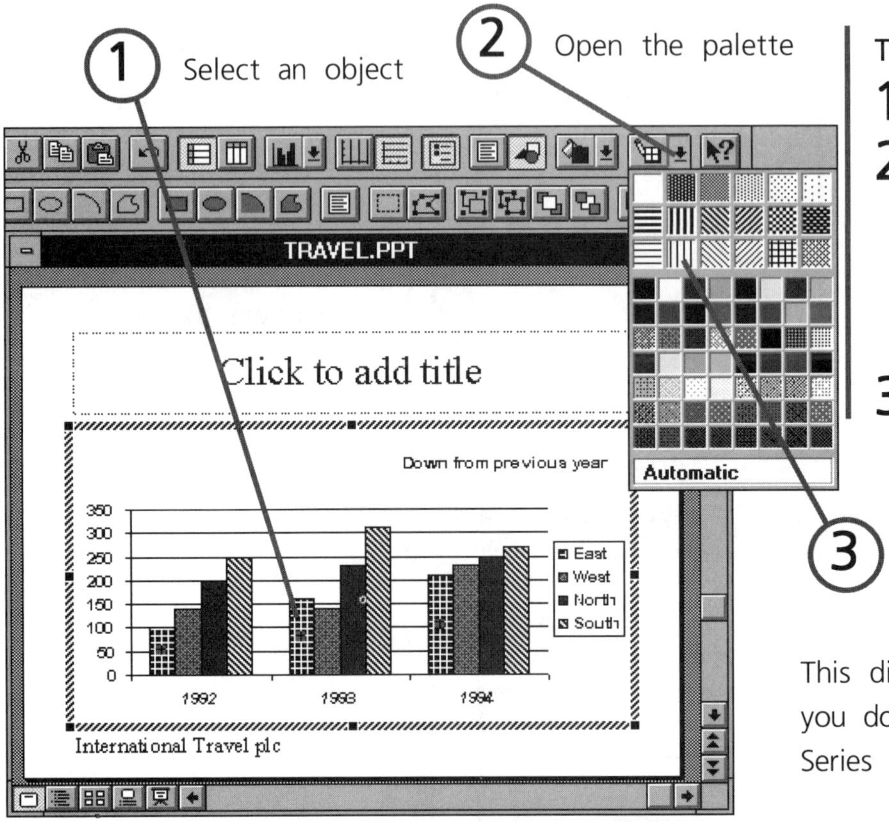

This dialog box opens when you double click on a Data Series (bar or line on chart)

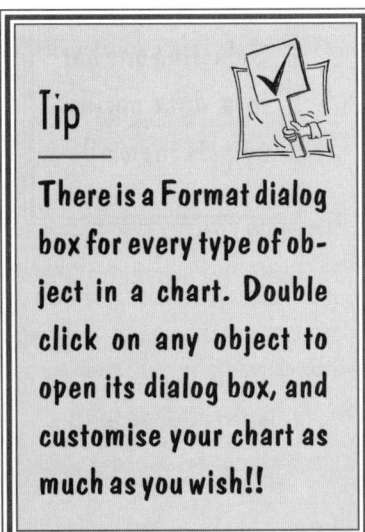

Tip

There is a Format dialog box for every type of object in a chart. Double click on any object to open its dialog box, and customise your chart as much as you wish!!

Format Data Series

| Patterns | Axis | Y Error Bars | Data Labels |

Border
- ○ Automatic
- ○ None
- ● Custom

Style: _____ ±

Color: _____ ±

Weight: _____ ±

Area
- ○ Automatic
- ○ None

Color:

Pattern: _____ ±

☐ Invert if Negative

OK

Cancel

Help

Sample

Leaving the graph

When your chart is complete, click anywhere on the slide outside its placeholder to return to your presentation.

If you wish to take your chart back into the graphic environment, simply double click on it.

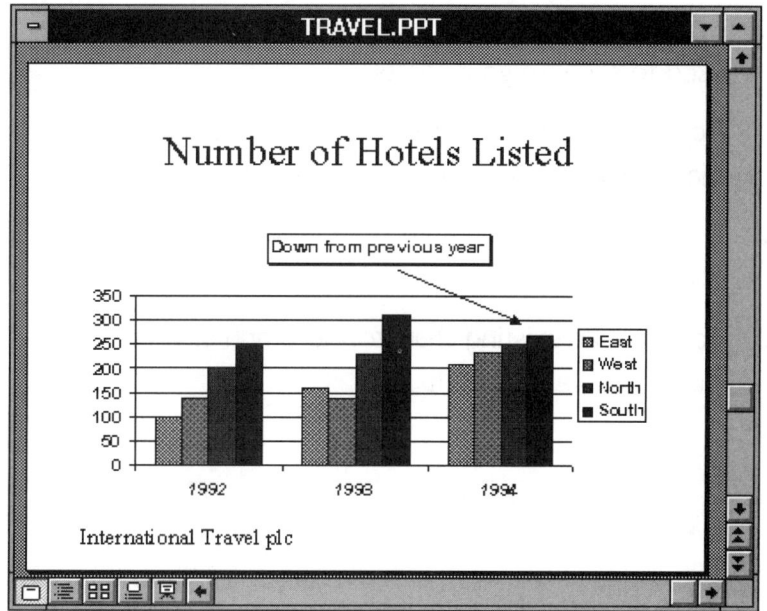

TRAVEL.PPT

Number of Hotels Listed

Down from previous year

East
West
North
South

International Travel plc

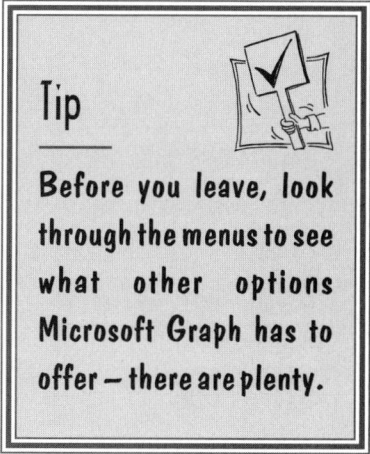

Summary

❏ **Charts** can be used on any of your slides

❏ Working in the Graph environment is similar to working and charting in **Excel**

❏ There are several **chart types** to choose from – bar, line, area etc

❏ **Colours, patterns, text** and **drawings** can all be used to enhance your charts

❏ Double click on any object to open its **Format dialog box** where you can customise its appearance

❏ To **leave Graph**, and return to your presentation, click anywhere outside the chart placeholder

❏ To **return an existing chart** to the Graph environment, double click on it

8 Organisation Charts

Starting up

Organisation charts give you another opportunity to make your point using a diagram rather than words.

Microsoft Organisation Chart is shipped with Microsoft Office, and if you've installed all the shared applications, you will have access to it.

This section introduces Organisation Chart and some of its features. If you use a lot of organisation charts, tour through its menus and the On-line help to appreciate its full potential.

As with graphs, there are a number of ways to start:

●   Choose a slide from the New Slide dialog box with an
    Organisation Chart placeholder on it
    or

●   Choose a slide with an Object placeholder on it
    or

●   Click the Insert Organisation Chart tool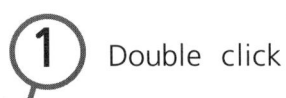

❑   **With an Organisation Chart placeholder**

1 Double click within the Organisation Chart placeholder on your slide

① Double click

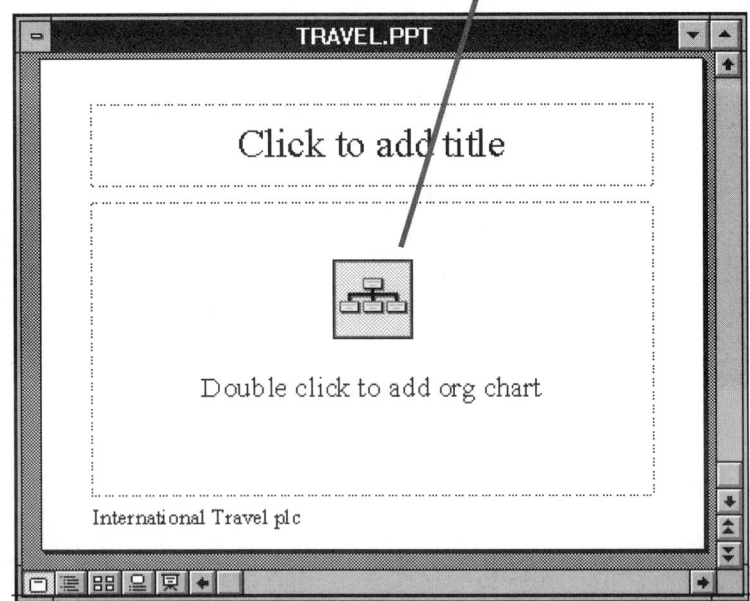

94

Basic steps

❑ **With another Object placeholder**

1 Double click within the Object placeholder on your slide to open the **Insert Object** dialog box

2 Choose **Microsoft Organisation Chart**

3 Click **OK**

❑ **From a slide with no placeholder set**

3 Click the **Insert Org Chart** tool 🔲 on the standard toolbar

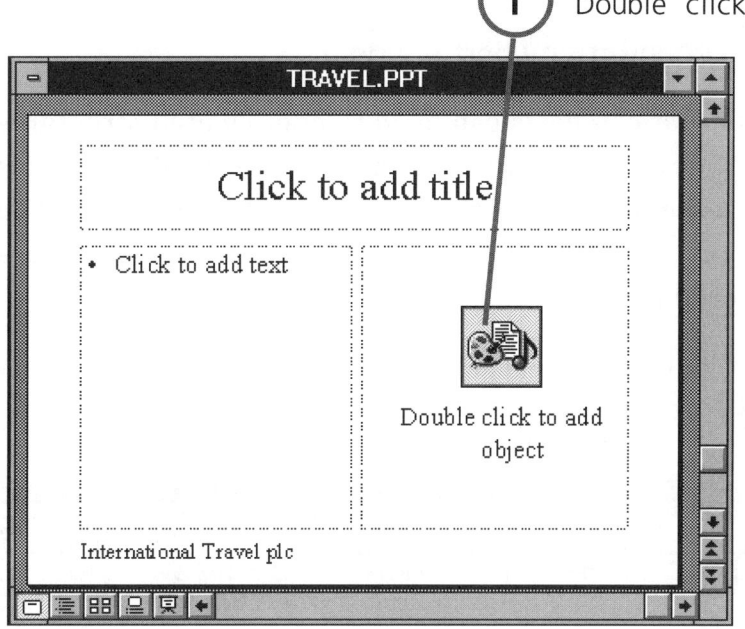

(1) Double click

(2) Select Organization Chart

(3) Click OK

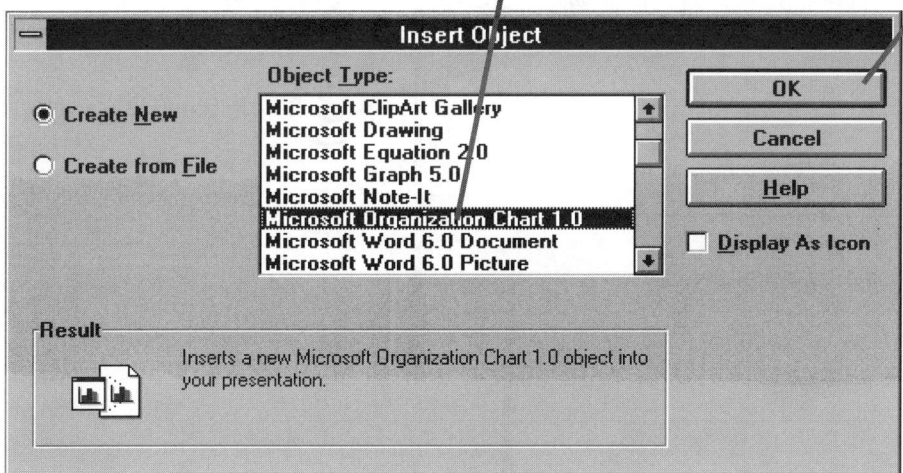

Text and boxes

The Organisation Chart window

Organisation charts can be very complicated structures but they have only simple elements. The small set of tools in this window are all that you need. Most are for adding boxes, and all the normal range of relationships are covered here.

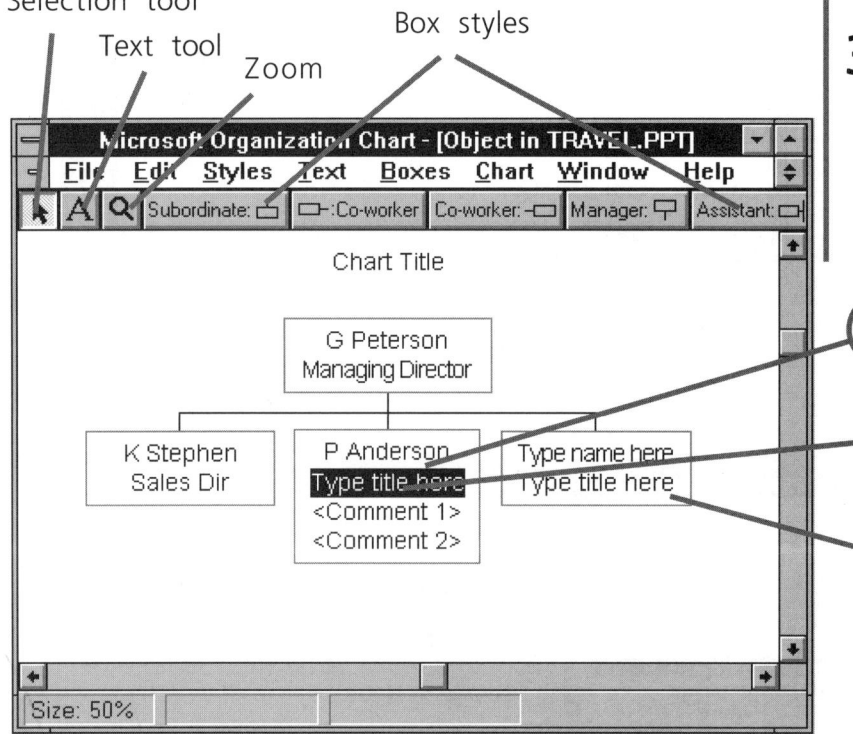

Entering text

Entering text into the boxes in the organisation chart is like entering data into a text object in PowerPoint itself.

Basic steps

1 Click on the box you wish to write in. The box drops down to take 4 lines of data

2 Key in your data and press **[Enter]** or the arrow keys to move to the next row

3 Click on the next box to be completed, or anywhere outside the box, when you are finished

Basic steps

Adding and deleting boxes

□ **To Add a box**

1 Select the box type from the Toolbar

2 Click on the box to which the new box is related

□ **To Delete a box**

1 Click to select the box you wish to delete

2 Press [Delete]

You can easily build your chart up by adding boxes where needed. Deleting boxes is even easier !

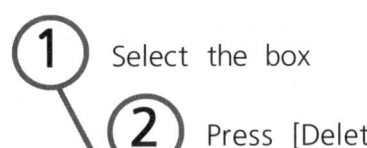

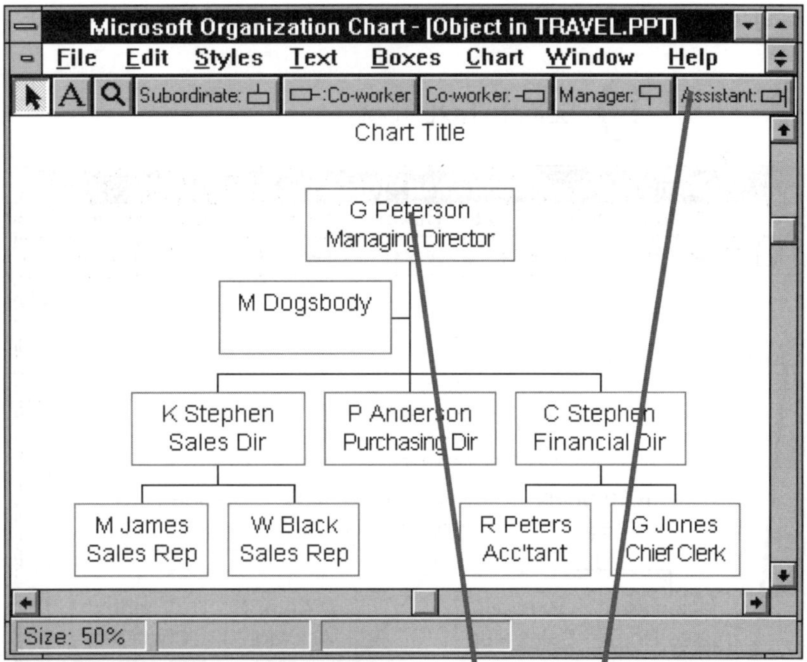

Select the box

Press [Delete]

Select a box type

Click on the related box

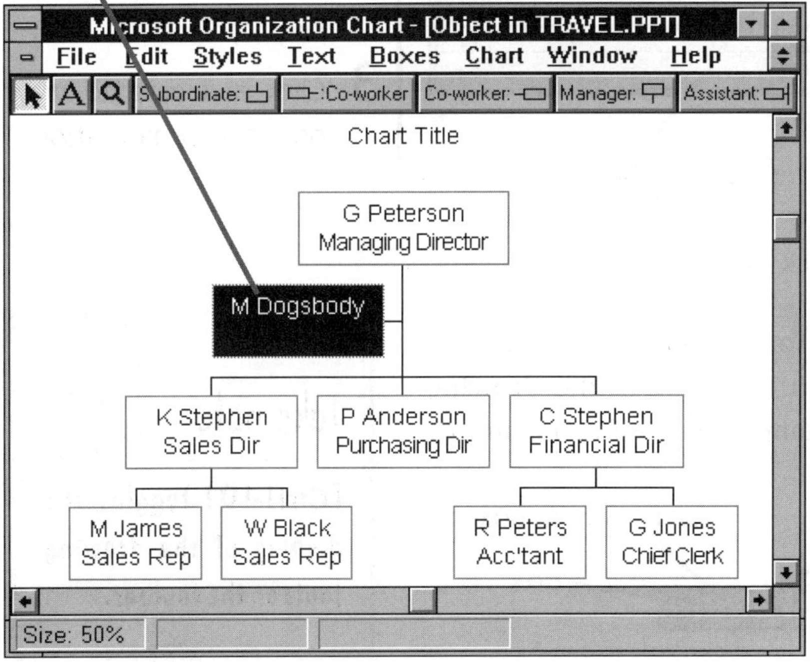

Text and drawing tools

The text and drawing tools can be used to add the finishing touches to your organisation chart. If you need text outwith the boxes on your chart, use the Text tool.

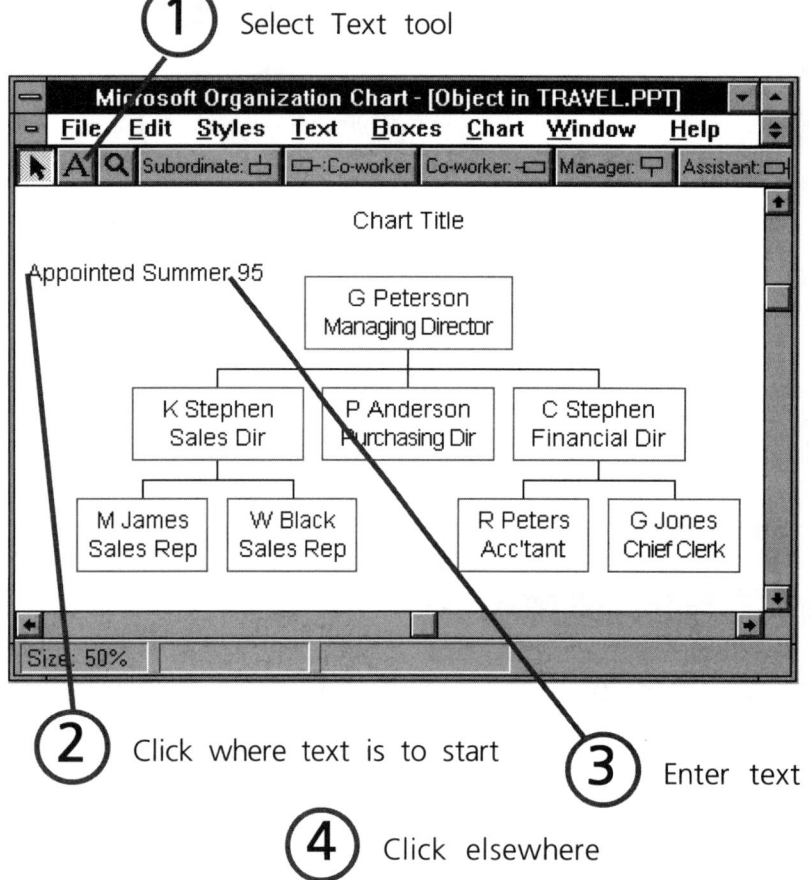

① Select Text tool

② Click where text is to start

③ Enter text

④ Click elsewhere

There are also a few drawing tools to help you complete your organisation chart. You can display the drawing tools all the time or toggle them on and off as required.

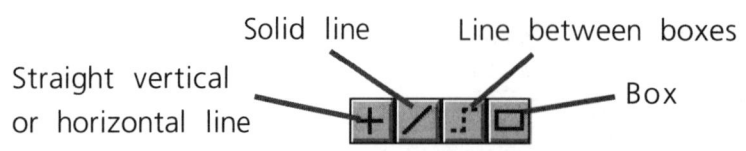

Straight vertical or horizontal line

Solid line

Line between boxes

Box

❑ **Text**

1 Click the Text tool on the toolbar

2 Click to position the insertion point where you want the text

3 Key in the text

4 Click anywhere outside the text area

❑ **Drawing**

1 Press **[Ctrl]-[D]** to display the drawing tools

2 Select the one you want to use (there are only 4)

3 Click and drag to draw on your organisation chart

Take note

[Ctrl]-[D] toggles the display of the drawing tools on the toolbar.

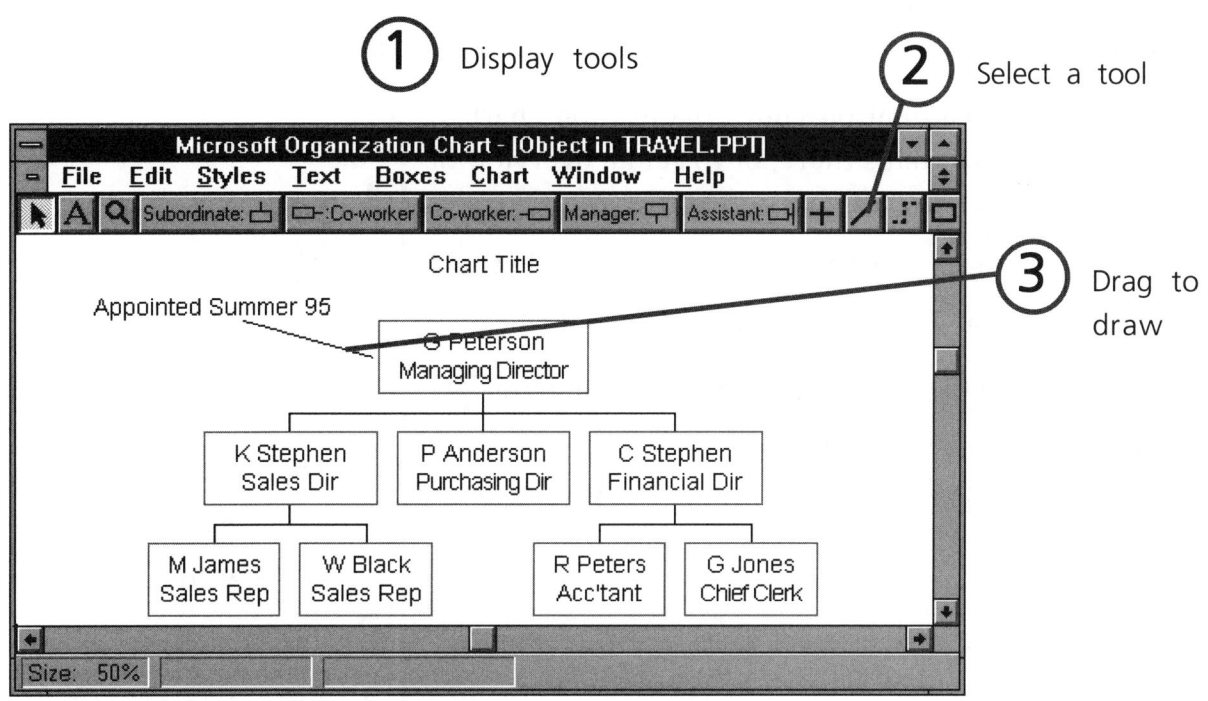

3 Drag to draw

Chart title

1 Select the Chart Title prompt

2 Either key in the title

or

2 Press [Delete] to remove the title prompt

You can give your chart a title here or using the Slide Title or a text box in your presentation. If you opt to key in the title in the presentation, delete the *Chart Title* prompt.

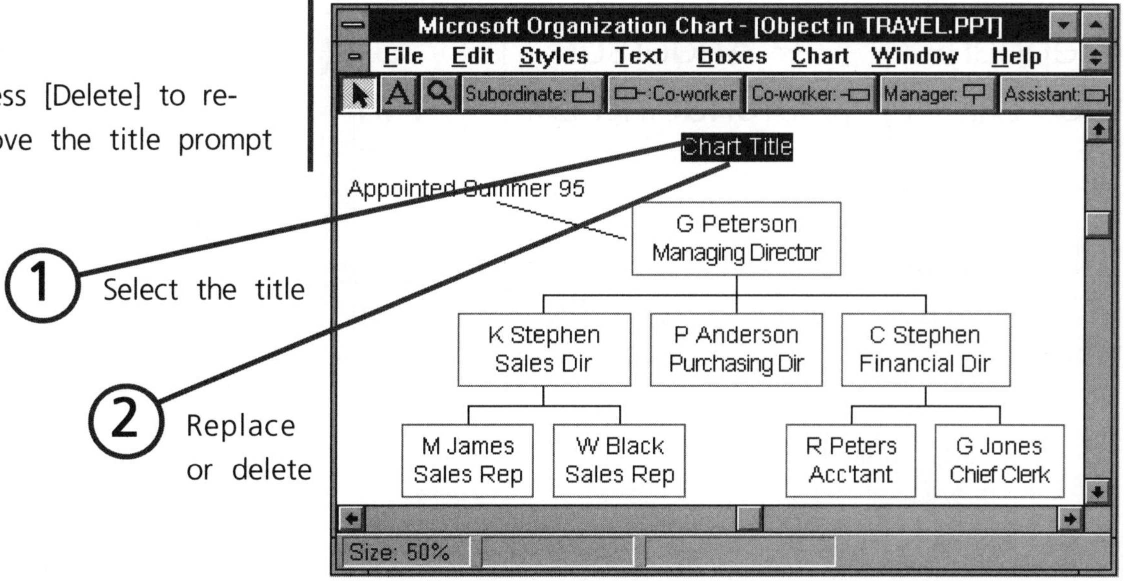

1 Select the title

2 Replace or delete

Zoom options

You can zoom in and out on your organisation chart to get a closer look at what's there, or to get an overview of the whole thing. There are four options:

● Size to Window – for an overview of the whole chart

● 50% of Actual – the best mode for normal work

● Actual Size (100%) – in this mode the Zoom tool toggles to Size to Window 🔲

● 200% of Actual – if you want to get really close

❏ **Zoom to Actual size**

1 Select the Zoom tool 🔍

2 Click on the place on chart that you want to zoom in on

❏ **Zoom out**

1 Select the Size to Window tool 🔲

2 Click on the chart

❏ The whole thing reduces so you can see the entire chart in your window.

① Select Size to Window tool

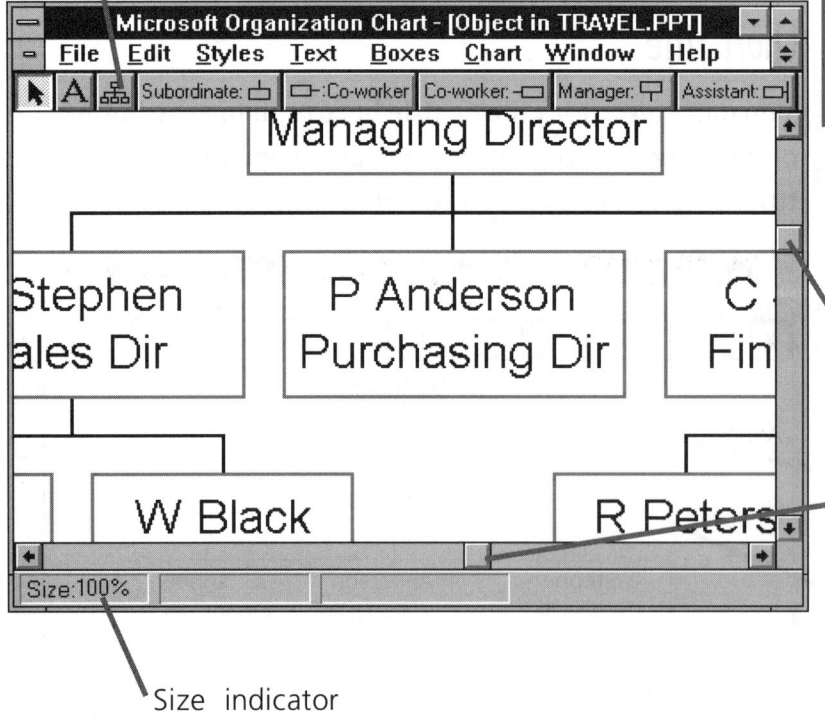

Scroll to examine other parts of your chart

Size indicator

Basic steps

- ❏ **Return to Normal**
- **1** Open the **Chart** Menu
- **2** Select **50% of Actual**
- ❏ Note the other sizes can be selected here

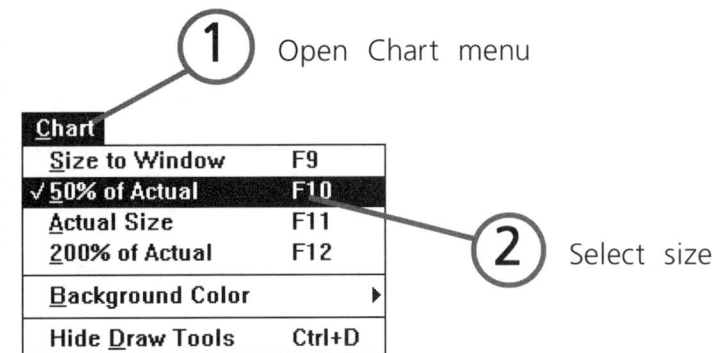

① Open Chart menu

② Select size

Zoom to Actual size if wanted

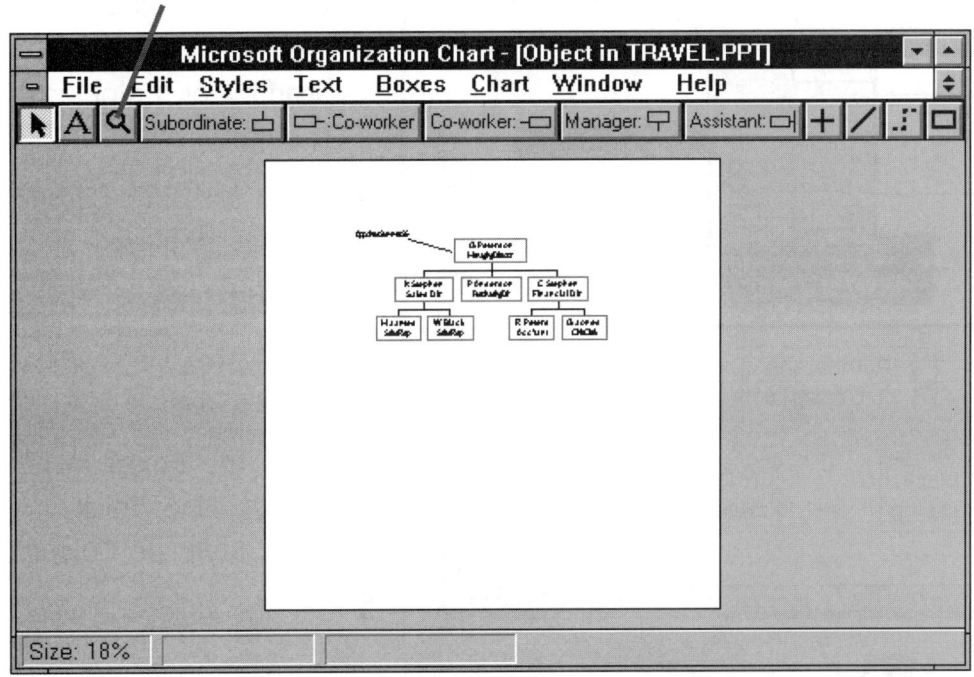

Keyboard shortcuts

[F9]	Size to Window
[F10]	50% of Actual
[F11]	Actual Size
[F12]	200% of Actual Size

Finishing touches

Using the Boxes and Text menus, you can add the finishing touches to your organistion chart – edit the line styles, add shadows to the boxes, change the colour, size and font of text etc.

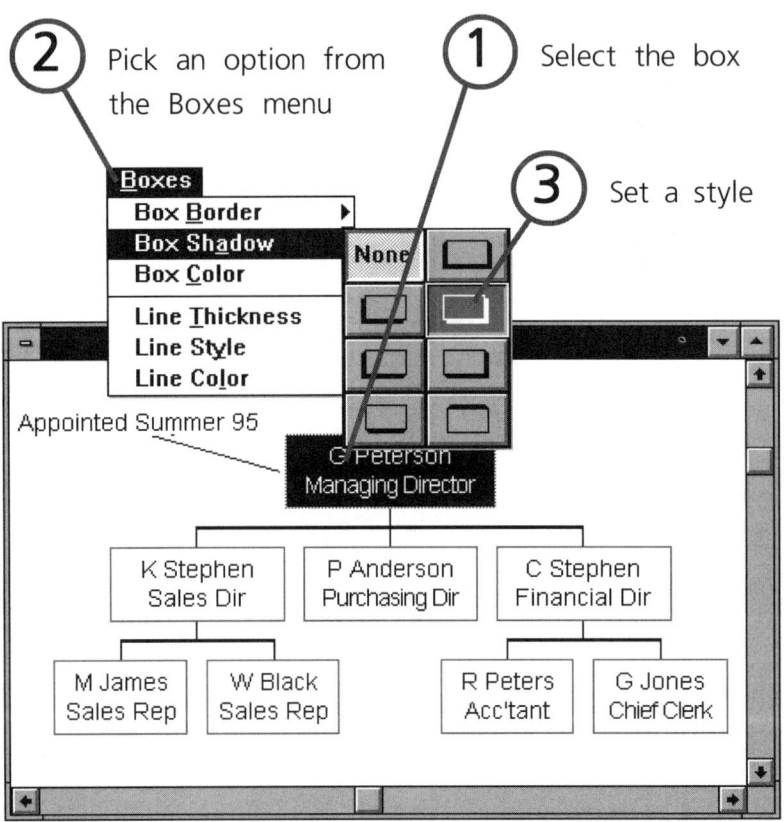

② Pick an option from the Boxes menu

① Select the box

③ Set a style

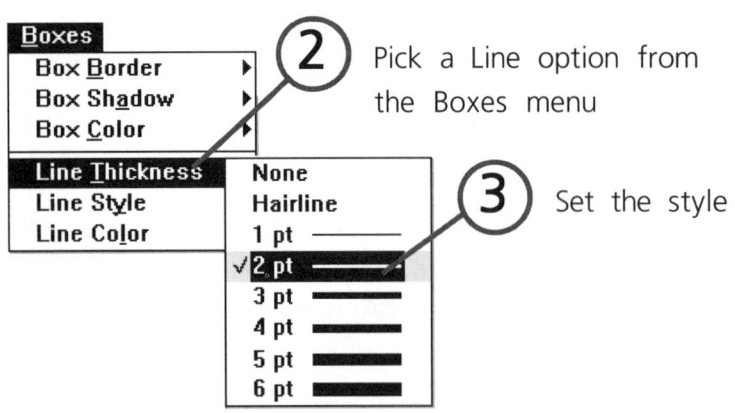

② Pick a Line option from the Boxes menu

③ Set the style

❑ **To restyle a box**

1 Select the box you want to edit

❑ To select multiple boxes, select one then hold **[Shift]**, and click on the others

2 Open the **Boxes** menu and choose **Border**, **Shadow** or **Color** as required

3 Select an option from the set displayed

❑ **To edit lines**

1 Select the line(s) you want to edit

2 From the **Boxes** menu choose **Line Thickness**, **Style** or **Colour**

3 Set the style or colour

Take note

Using the Text menu you can set the colour, font style and size, and the alignment of text.

Update and exit

□ **Update the presenta-tion**

1 Open the **File** menu

2 Choose **Update** *PRES-ENTATION NAME*

3 Your slide will be updated to display your organisation chart.

□ **Exit Organisation Chart**

1 Double click the Con-trol Menu button on the application Title Bar

or

1 Open the **File** menu

2 Choose **Exit and Return to** *PRESENTA-TION NAME*

Tip

If you want to take your chart back into Organisa-tion Chart for editing, simply double click on it.

Once you've completed your organisation chart, you will need to update the slide in your presentation and return to the presentation proper to continue working on it.

You exit Organisation Chart just as you would any other Windows application

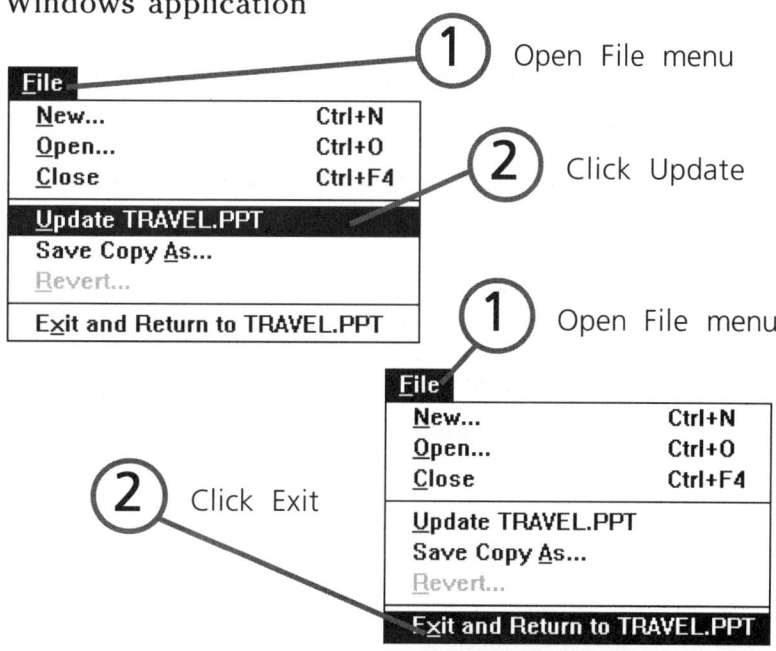

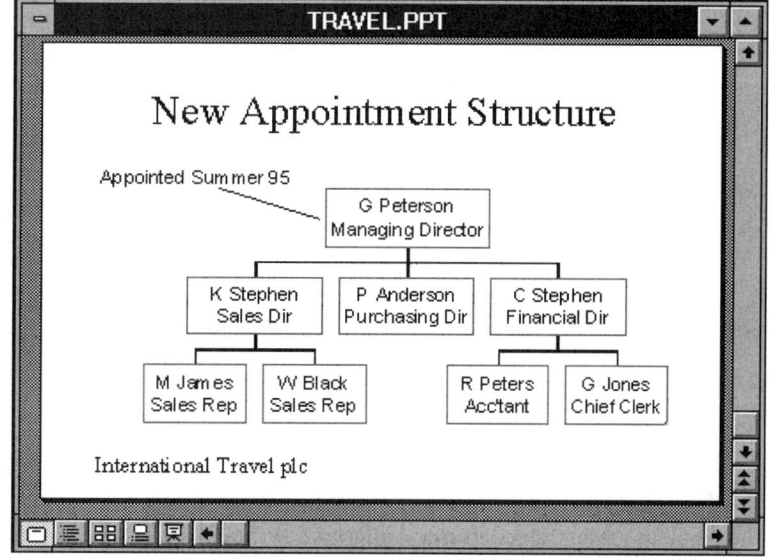

Summary

❑ **Organisation Chart** is a separate application shipped with Microsoft Office

❑ Charts can **easily be added** to your slides

❑ **Boxes** are added to and deleted from organisation charts as required

❑ **Text** and **drawing tools** are available to further enhance your chart

❑ There are several **Zoom** options so you can get a close up look or an overview of your chart

❑ The **colour** and **format** of items on your chart can be controlled from the Boxes and Text menus

❑ Remember to **Update your presentation** before exiting the Organisation Chart

9 ClipArt

The ClipArt gallery

PowerPoint comes with over 1000 ClipArt pictures that can be added to your slides. As with Graph and Organisation Chart, there are 3 main ways of getting your hands (or mouse) on the ClipArt.

● Choose a slide from the New Slide dialog box that has an ClipArt placeholder already on it

or

● Choose a slide from the New Slide dialog box that has an Object placeholder already on it

or

● Click the Insert ClipArt tool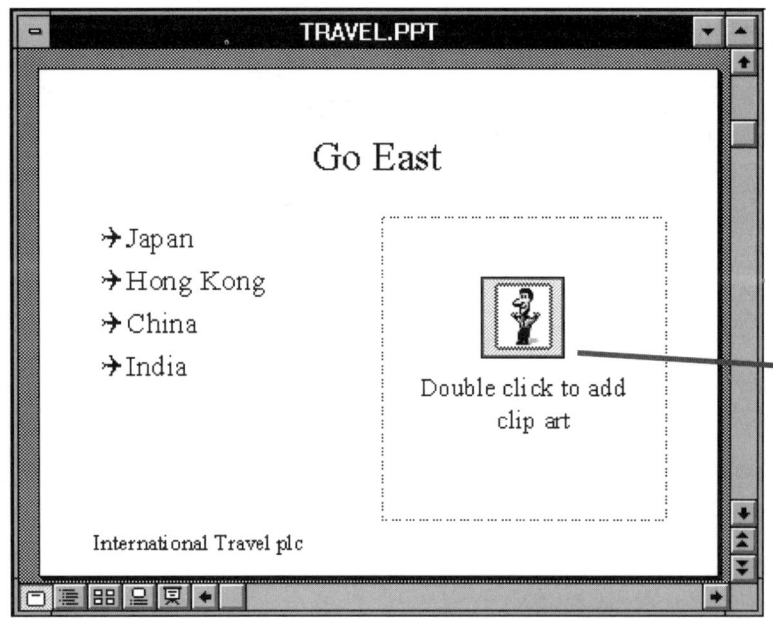

❑ **From a slide with a ClipArt placeholder**

1 Double click in the ClipArt placeholder

❑ **From a slide with an Object placeholder**

1 Double click within the Object placeholder to open the **Insert Object** dialog box

2 Choose **Microsoft ClipArt Gallery**

3 Click **OK**

❑ **From a slide with no placeholder set**

1 Click the Insert ClipArt tool on the standard toolbar

(1) Double click

Tip

It's simplest to start with a slide with a ClipArt placeholder.

106

The ClipArt gallery window

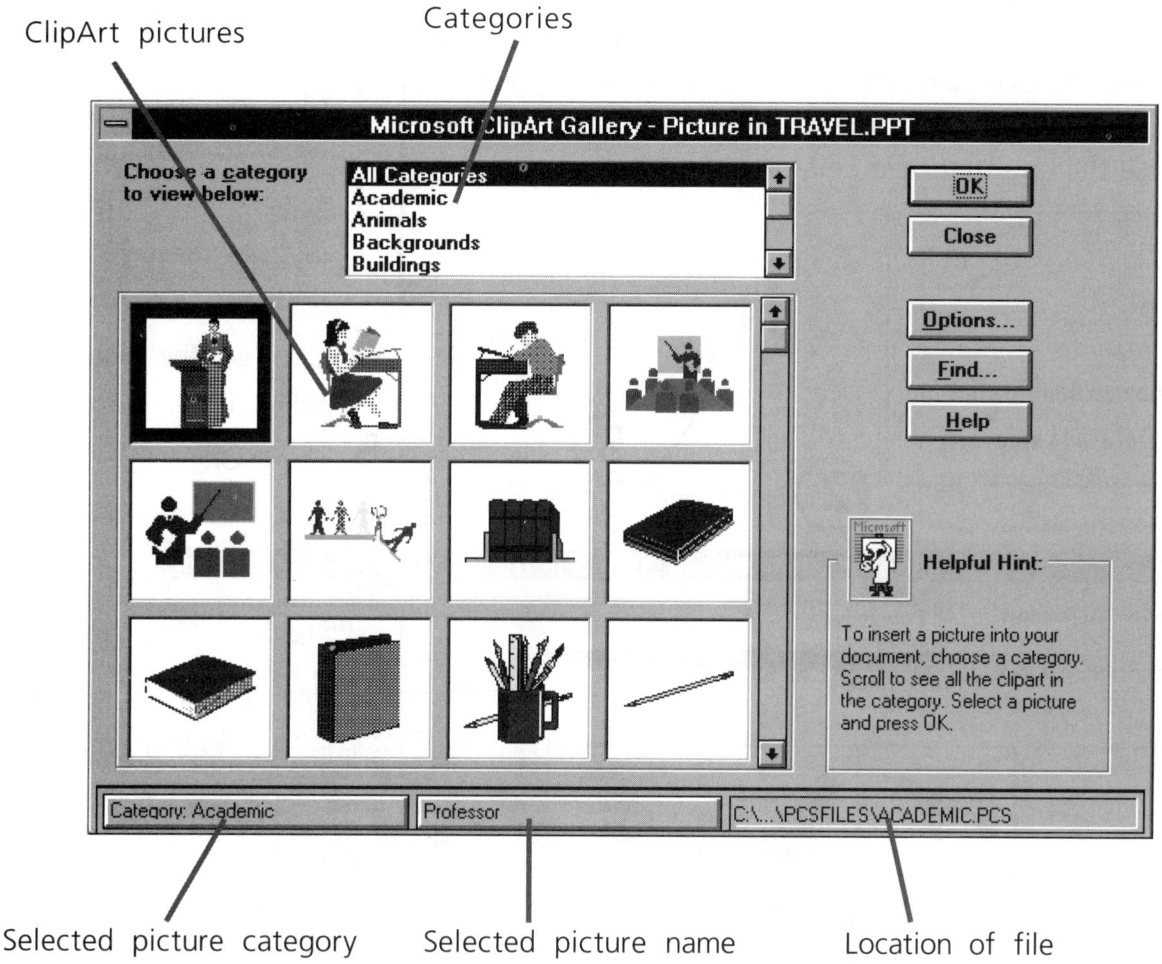

ClipArt pictures

Categories

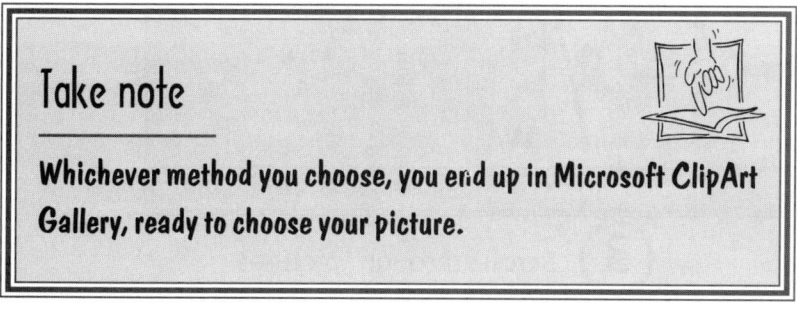

Selected picture category

Selected picture name

Location of file

Take note

Whichever method you choose, you end up in Microsoft ClipArt Gallery, ready to choose your picture.

Choosing a picture

The ClipArt is organised into categories to make it easier for you to locate the picture you want. You can browse through them to see what is available. Once you have selected the category, thumbnail images of its pictures are displayed in the ClipArt Gallery window. Simply choose the one that best suits your purpose.

Basic steps

1 Scroll through the **Choose a category** list to find a set

2 Click on the Category name to select it

3 Scroll through the pictures until you see one you want

4 Click on the picture to select it

5 Click **OK**

> **Tip**
>
> **You can double click on a picture to select it.**

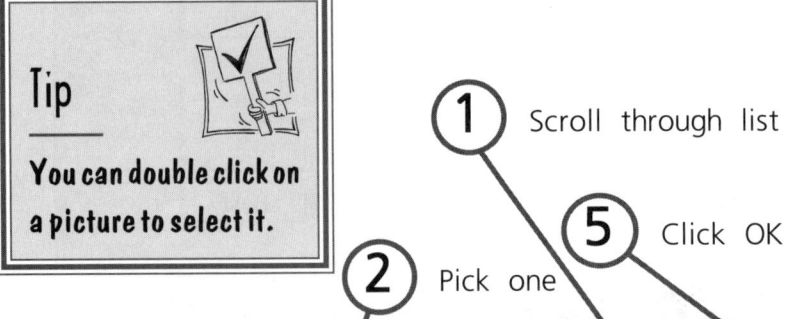

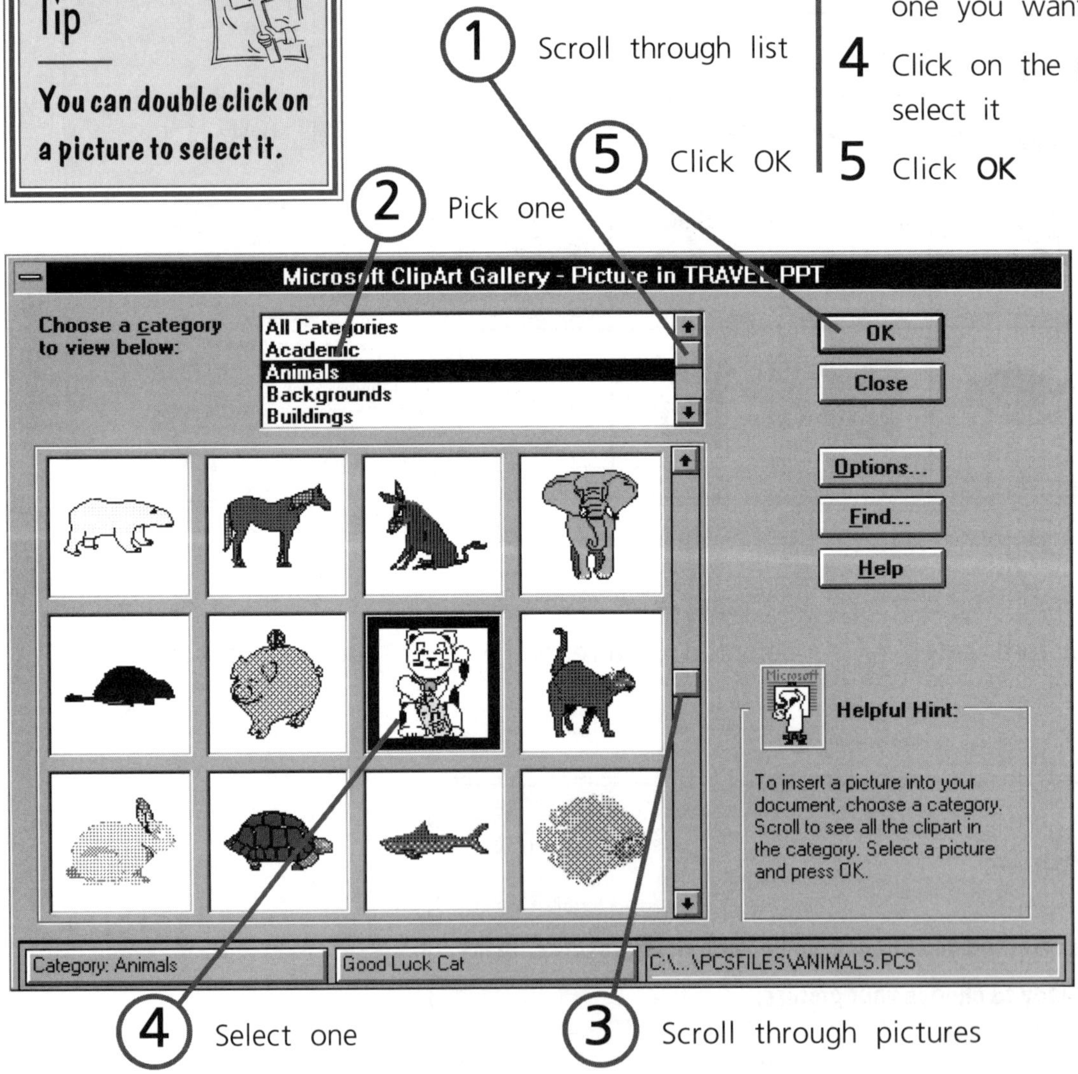

① Scroll through list

⑤ Click OK

② Pick one

④ Select one

③ Scroll through pictures

Fine tuning the picture

With a selected picture you can..

❑ Press **[Delete]** to **delete** the picture

❑ Click and drag any of the **handles** around the edges of the picture to **resize** it

❑ Click and drag the **edge** (not a handle) of the picture to **move** it

Deselect it by clicking anywhere off it.

The picture can be edited in the same way as any other object on your slide.

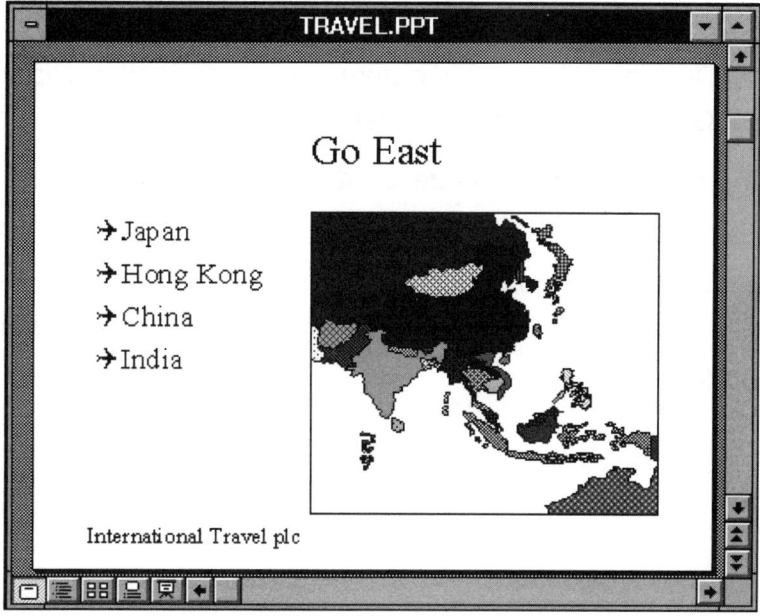

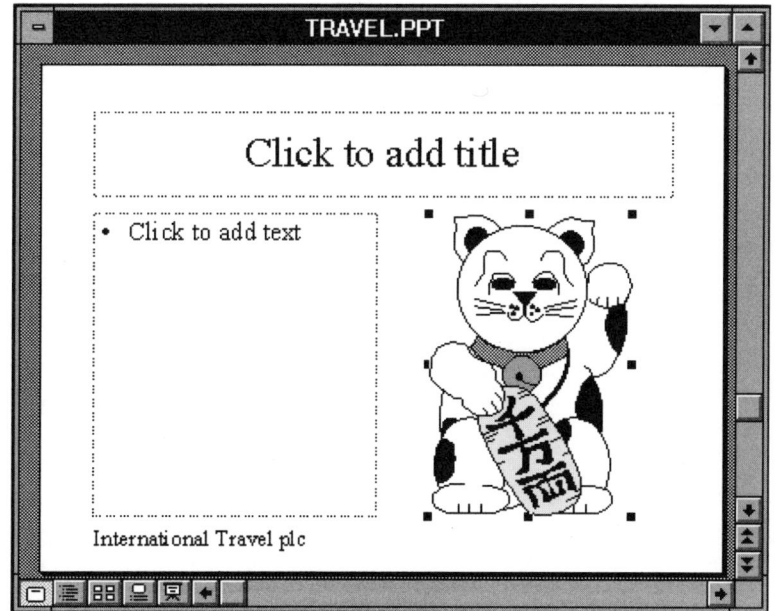

Tip

Use the ClipArt, Drawing and Text tools to create less formal slides!

Summary

❑ The simplest way to **add ClipArt** is to start with a slide that has a ClipArt placeholder.

❑ The ClipArt gallery contains over **1000 pictures**, arranged in several **categories**

❑ Double click on the picture you want in the **ClipArt Gallery** dialog box to insert it onto your slide

❑ You can **move**, **resize** or **delete** the ClipArt object once it is on your slide

❑ Double click on your ClipArt object to return to the Gallery dialog box if you wish to **choose a different picture**

10 Masters

Slide master

The Slide Master holds the formatted placeholders for the slide title and text. Changes to the Slide Master will be reflected in every slide that follows the slide master format. Any slides where you have made changes to the text formatting at slide level will be treated as exceptions and will retain the custom formatting you applied to them (unless you go back and change it).

Any background objects you want to appear on every slide (like your company name or logo) should be added to the Slide Master.

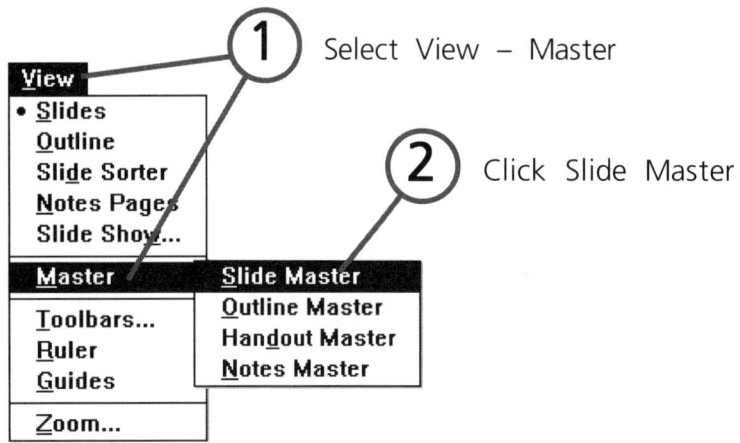

Select View – Master

Click Slide Master

Basic steps

1 Choose **Master** from the **View** menu

2 Select **Slide Master**

3 Amend the Slide Master as required (using the same tools and techniques you use on a slide in your presentation)

4 Choose **Slide view** to return to your presentation and see the slides with the changes applied

Tip

You can view the Slide Master if you hold down [Shift] when you click the Slide View icon.

Take note

Deleted title and content placeholders can easily be added again. Choose Master Layout... from the Format menu and select Add Title or Add Text at the Master layout dialog box.

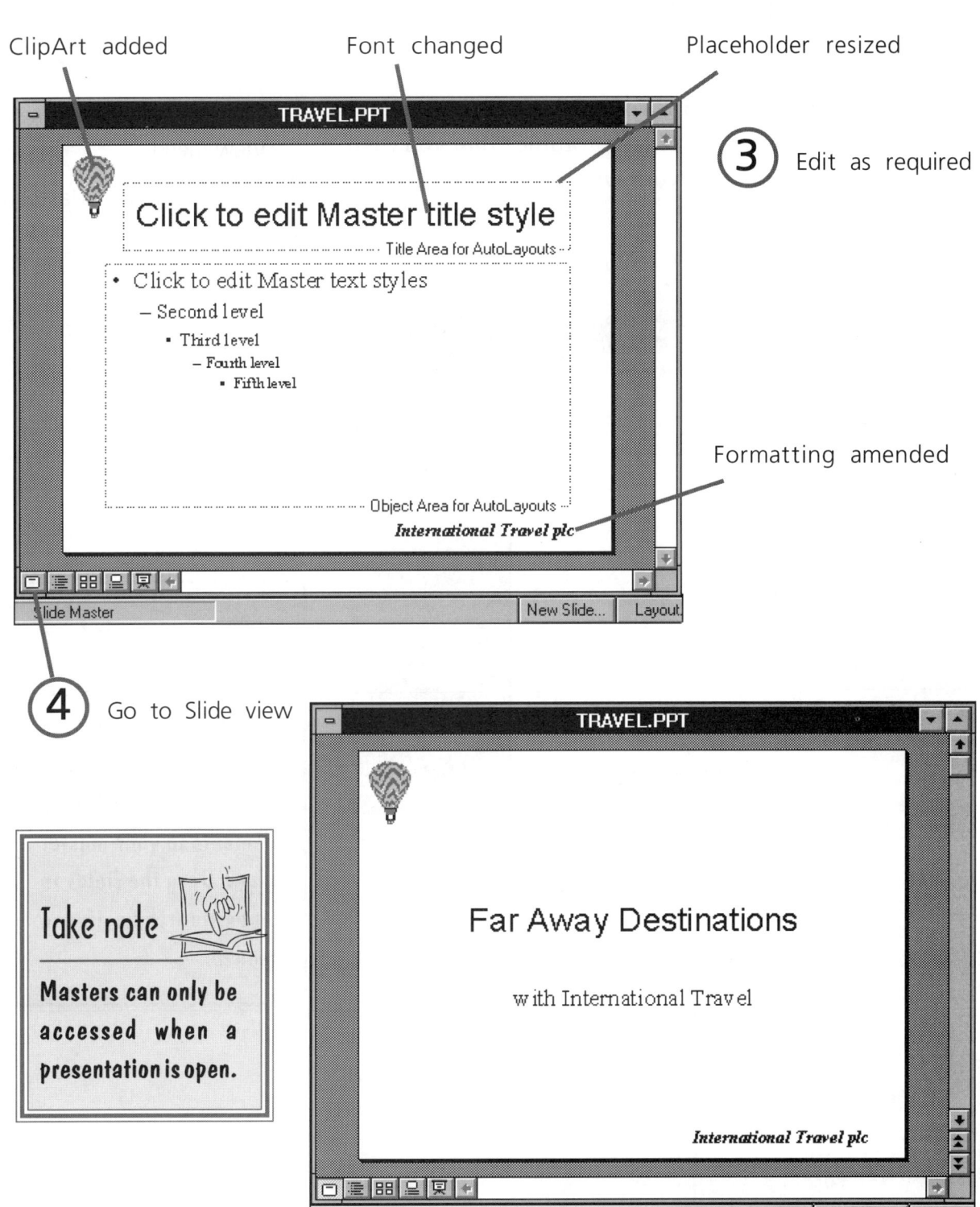

ClipArt added

Font changed

Placeholder resized

③ Edit as required

TRAVEL.PPT

Click to edit Master title style

Title Area for AutoLayouts

- Click to edit Master text styles
  - Second level
    - Third level
      - Fourth level
        - Fifth level

Object Area for AutoLayouts

International Travel plc

Formatting amended

Slide Master

New Slide... Layout

④ Go to Slide view

Take note

Masters can only be accessed when a presentation is open.

TRAVEL.PPT

Far Away Destinations

with International Travel

International Travel plc

Slide 1

New Slide... Layout

Outline master

The Outline Master holds the format for the page layout of your Outline. If you have text or graphics that you wish to display on every page of your Outline, add them to the Outline master.

1 Choose **Master** from the **View** menu

2 Select **Outline Master**

3 Amend the master page as required

4 Choose an alternative view to leave your Outline Master

Company name added

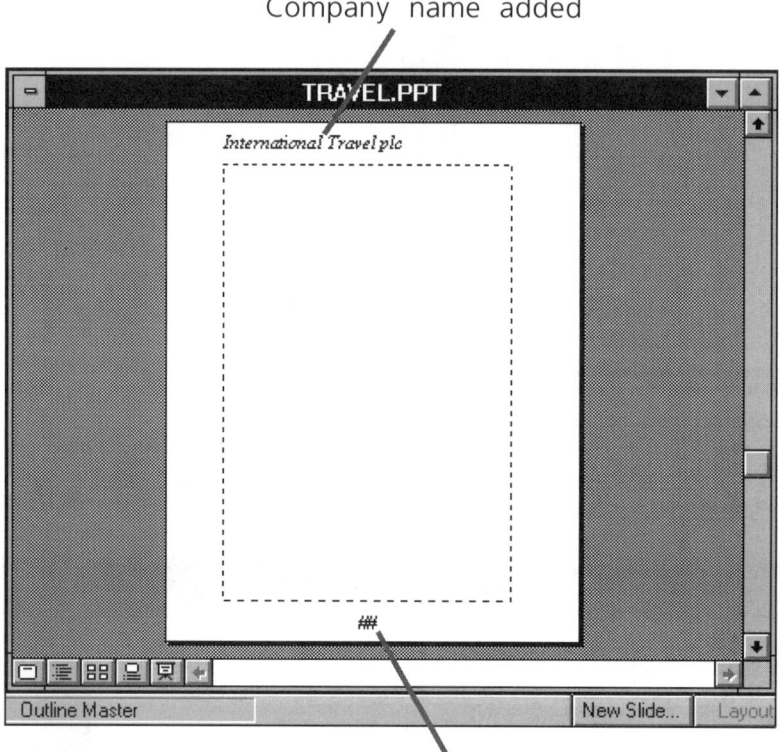

TRAVEL.PPT

International Travel plc

###

Outline Master

New Slide... Layout

Page number field inserted

Tip

From the Insert Menu, you can choose Page Number, Date or Time to add these elements to your master page. Drag the fields to reposition them if you need to.

Take note

You can view the Outline Master if you hold [Shift] down when you click the Outline View icon.

Handout master

1 Choose **Master** from the **View** menu

2 Select **Handout Master**

3 Amend the Handout Master as required

4 Choose an alternative view to leave your Handout Master

You can support your presentation with audience handouts if you wish. Handouts consist of smaller, printed versions of your slides, either 2, 3 or 6 to the page (see section 12 for details on printing).

If you want additional information on the handout pages - your company name or logo, the presentation title, page numbers, date, or lines for your audience to write on - you add the detail to the Handout Master.

Company name keyed in   ClipArt added

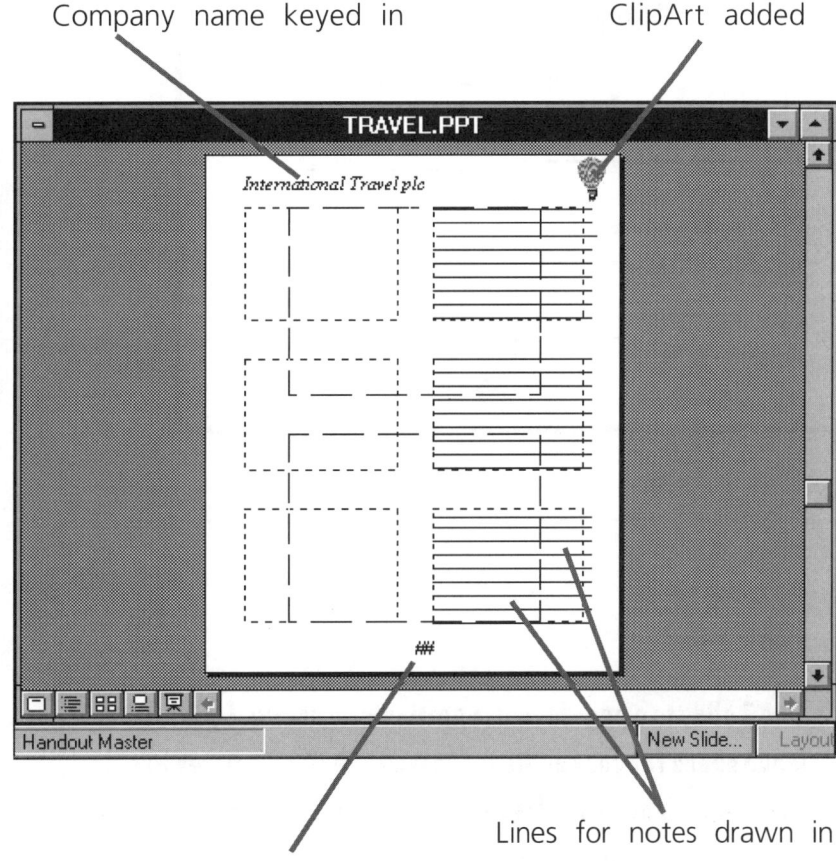

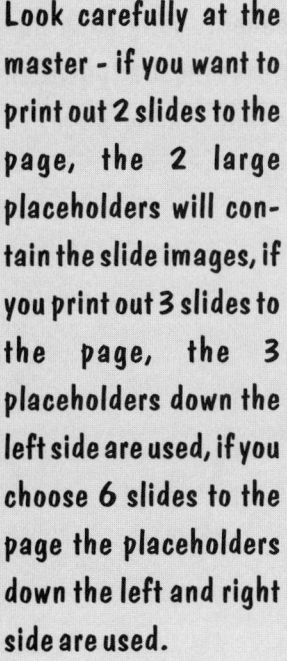

Take note

Look carefully at the master - if you want to print out 2 slides to the page, the 2 large placeholders will contain the slide images, if you print out 3 slides to the page, the 3 placeholders down the left side are used, if you choose 6 slides to the page the placeholders down the left and right side are used.

Lines for notes drawn in

Page number field inserted

115

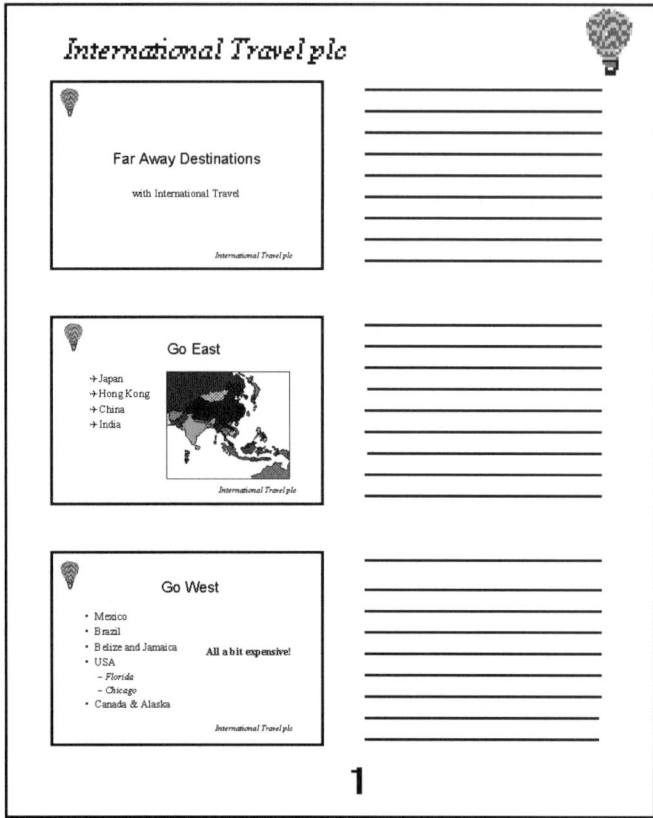

An example of a printed handout. This has had lines added for notes.

Tip

If you are adding lines for your audience to make notes on, draw the first line, select it, then use [Ctrl]-[D] to duplicate it to get the number of lines needed. Drag each line into the required postition on your handout page.

Take note

The 3 slide to a page layout is particularly useful if you want to leave space for your audience to make their own notes beside each slide. You could draw in dotted lines for them to write on down the right hand side of the sheet if you wish.

Basic steps

1 Choose **Master** from the **View** menu

2 Select **Notes Master**

3 Amend the Notes Master as required

4 Choose an alternative view to leave your Notes Master

Notes master

Each slide in your presentation has an accompanying notes page which consists of a smaller version of the slide along with room for any notes you want to make.

If you want to add information to your notes pages (company name or page number perhaps), or change the size of the placeholders (to allow more space for notes and less for the slide image) do so on the Notes Master.

Placeholder resized

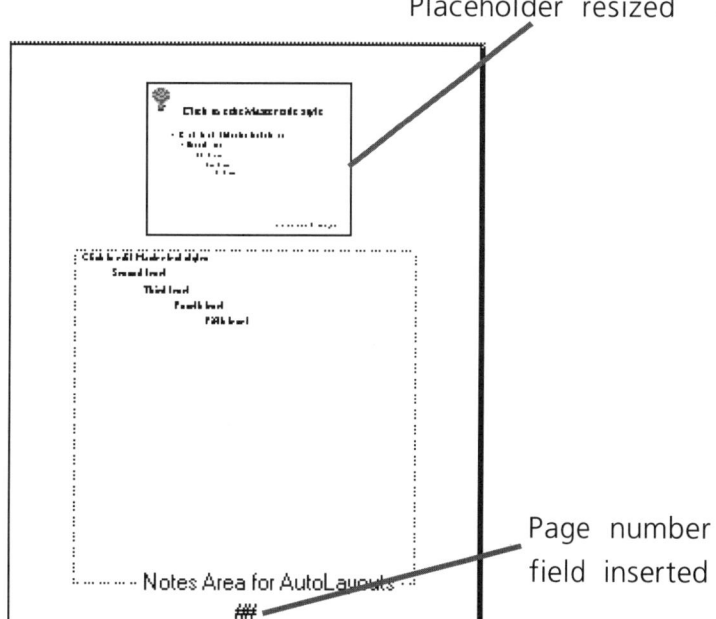

Page number field inserted

Tip

You can view the Notes Master if you hold [Shift] down when you click the Notes Pages View icon.

Take note

Deleted image and text placeholders can easily be added again. Choose Master Layout... from the Format menu and select Add Slide Image or Add Notes Text at the dialog box.

Summary

❏   If you want to add or amend an element on **every slide** in your presentation, change the Slide Master, not the individual slides

❏   **Text, graphics, page numbers, time** and **date fields** added to the Slide, Outline, Handouts and Notes Masters appear on every slide or page

❏   Hold **[Shift]** down when you click the View icons to get the Masters

11 Slide Shows

Slide sorter view

Slide Sorter view was introduced in Section 5 where we considered how you could rearrange the order of your slides. There are several other useful features worth exploring in Slide Sorter view, including:-

● Hiding slides

● Setting up transitions

● Building slides

● Rehearsing timings

We'll look at these features in this section, and see how they can help enhance your presentations.

You should be in Slide Sorter view for this section.

Take note

The topics introduced in this section are useful if you will be giving on-screen presentations (a slide show). They do not apply to overheads and 35mm slides.

Slide Sorter toolbar

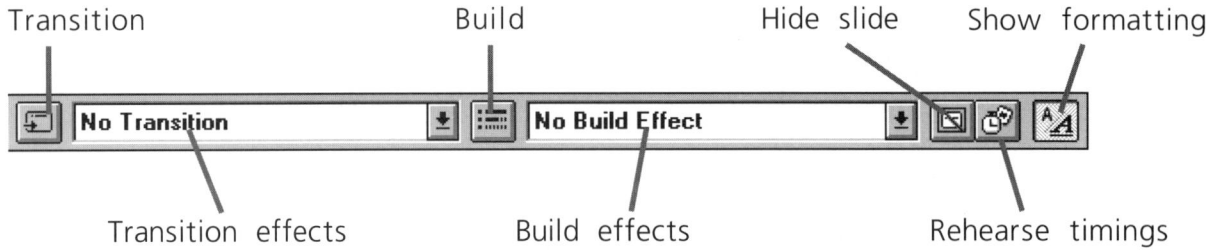

Transition   Build   Hide slide Show formatting

Transition effects   Build effects   Rehearse timings

Take note

Transitions, Builds and Hiding Slides can be specified in any view using the Tools menu, but I find it easiest to do them from Slide Sorter view using the Slide Sorter toolbar.

Basic steps

Hide slide

1. Select the slide
2. Click the Hide Slide tool
- ❑ The slide number is crossed out

This option can prove useful if you're not sure whether or not you will really need a particular slide for your presentation. You can include the slide in your presentation, but hide it. The hidden slide will be by-passed during your slide show, unless you decide you need to use it.

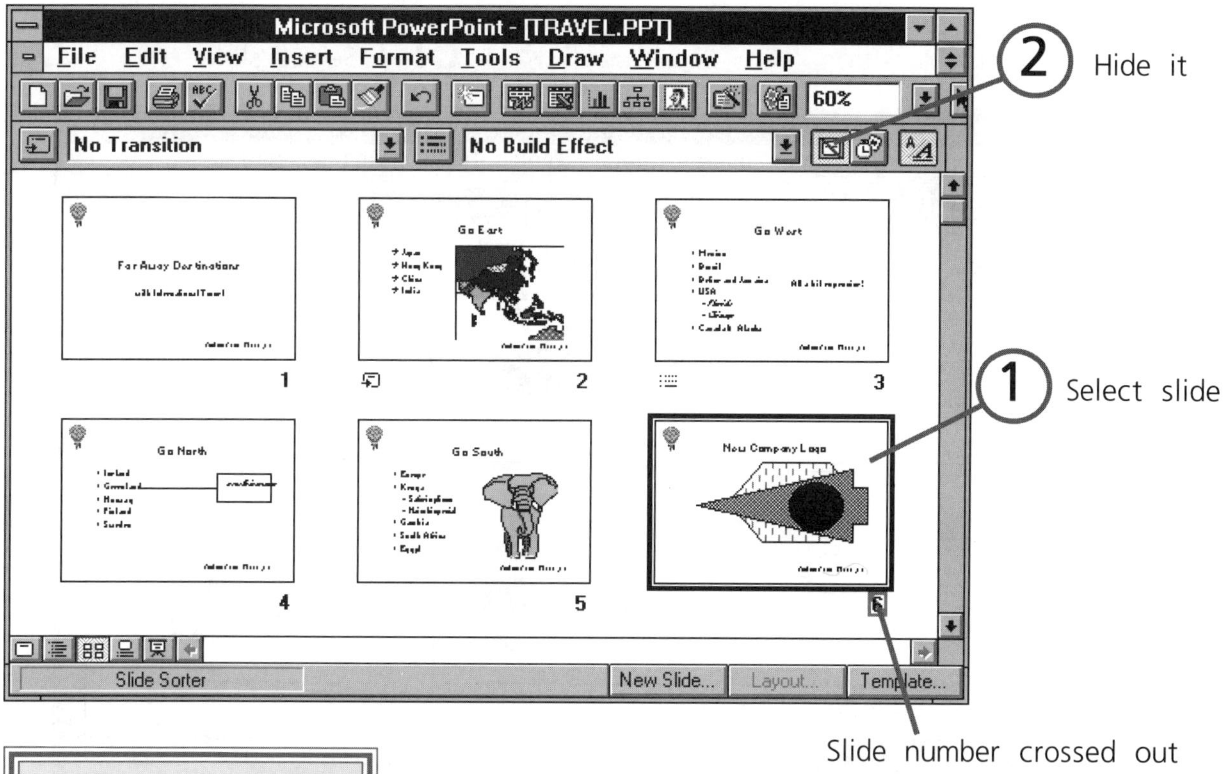

Tip

To remove the hidden status from a slide, select it and click the Hide Slide tool again.

Take note

During your slide show, if you move the pointer, a hide icon appears in the lower right corner of the slide before the hidden one. If you decide to show the hidden slide, click the icon.

Transitions

A transition is an effect used between slides in a slide show. The default option is that No Transition is set, but there are several interesting alternatives you might find effective for your presentation. Experiment with the Transition options until you discover those best suited to your presentation.

Basic steps

1 Select the slide to which you want to specify a transition

2 Click the Transition tool

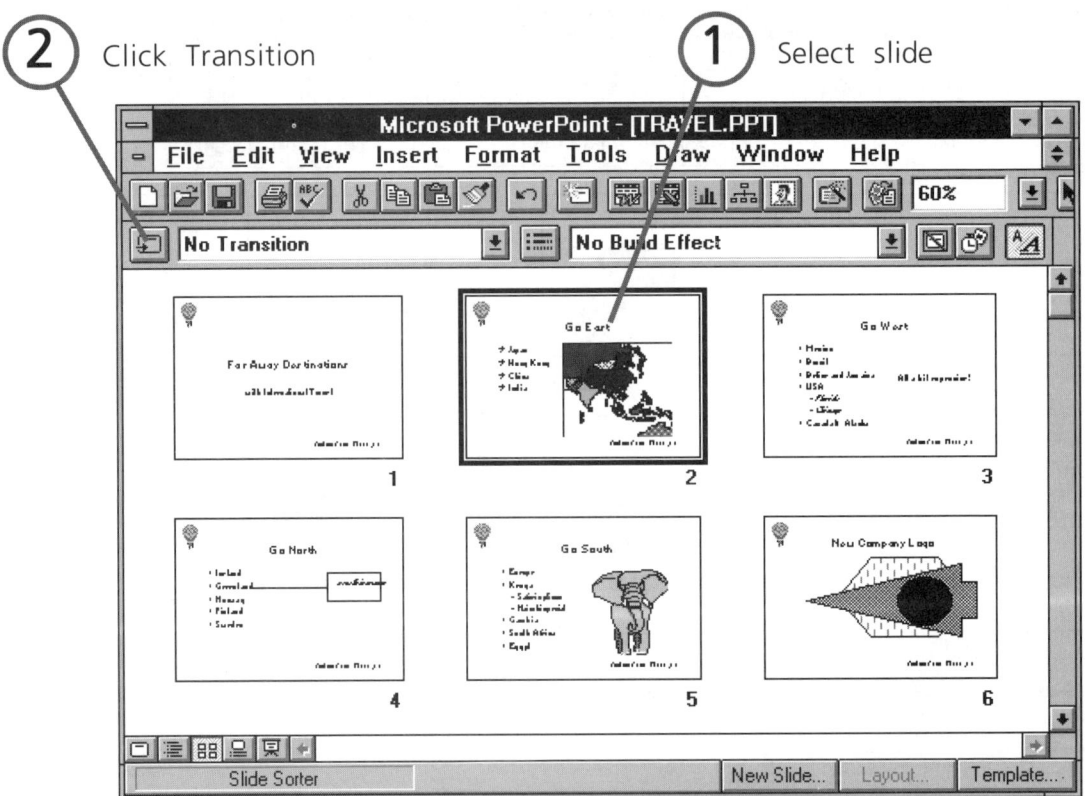

② Click Transition

① Select slide

Tip

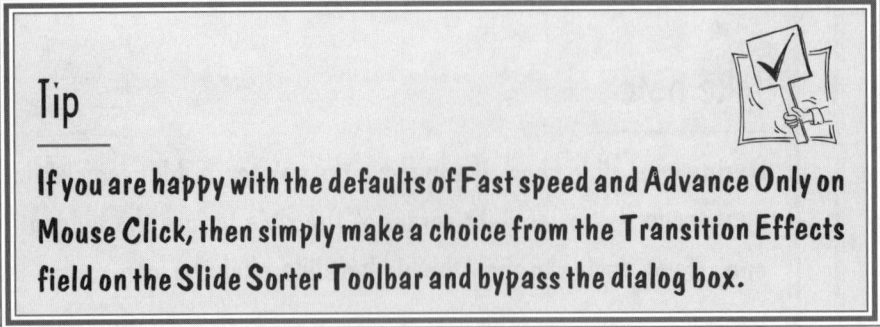

If you are happy with the defaults of Fast speed and Advance Only on Mouse Click, then simply make a choice from the Transition Effects field on the Slide Sorter Toolbar and bypass the dialog box.

3 Select the Effect from the drop down list

The Preview window demonstrates the transition – click on it to see the effect again

4 Set the Speed to Fast. Focus your audiences on your slides, not the transition method!

5 Choose an Advance option

6 Click OK

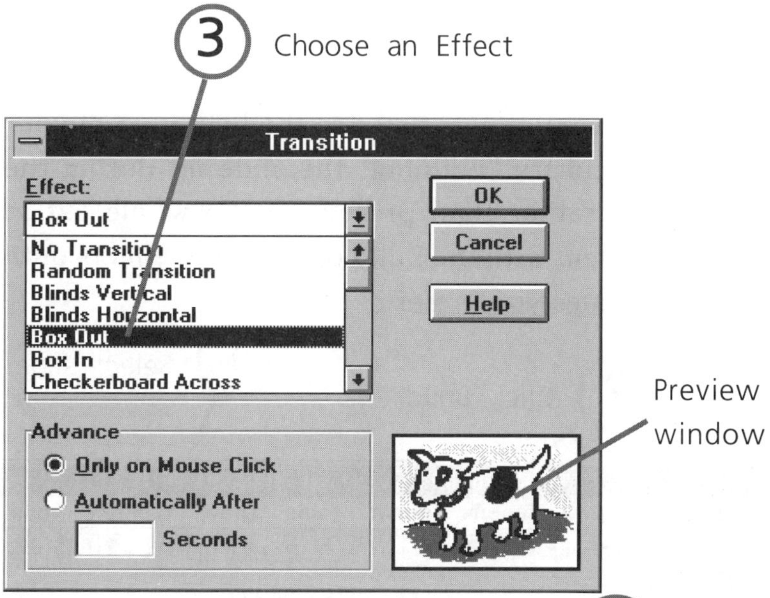

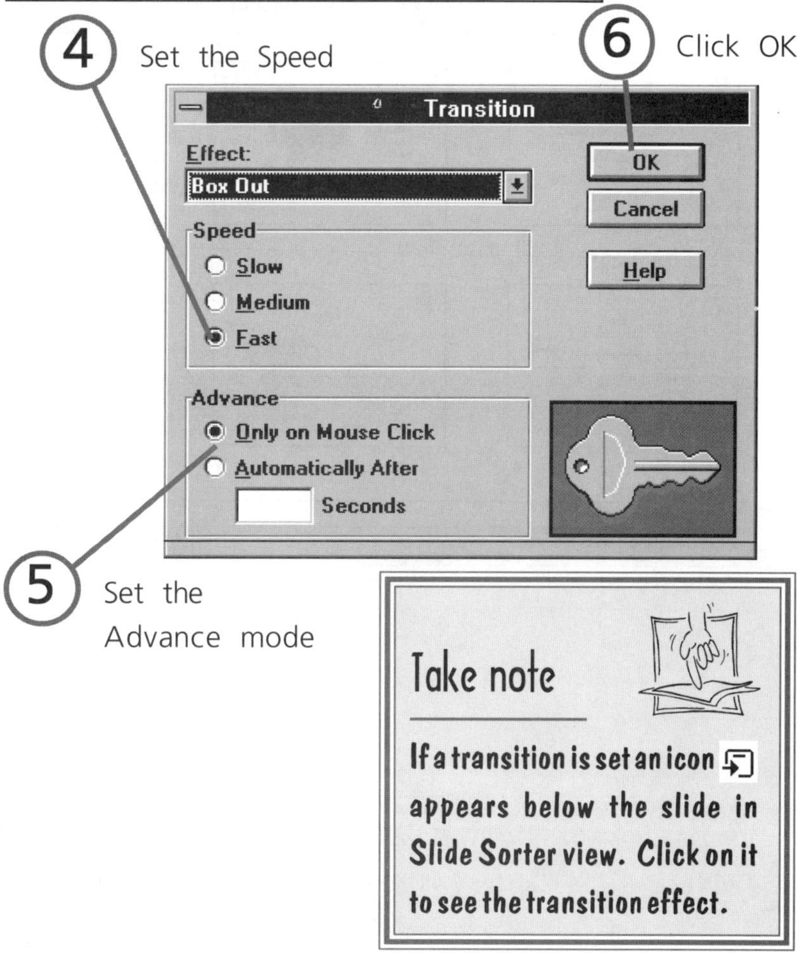

③ Choose an Effect

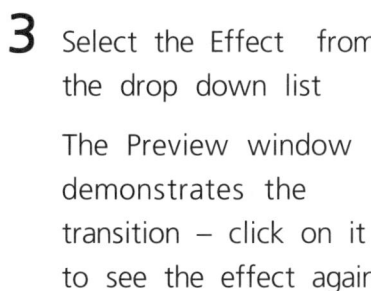

Preview window

④ Set the Speed

⑥ Click OK

⑤ Set the Advance mode

Take note

You can set slide timings manually (rather than through Rehearse Timings, see page 126) if you wish. Key in the number of seconds after which the slide should advance in the Automatically After XX Seconds field.

Take note

If a transition is set an icon appears below the slide in Slide Sorter view. Click on it to see the transition effect.

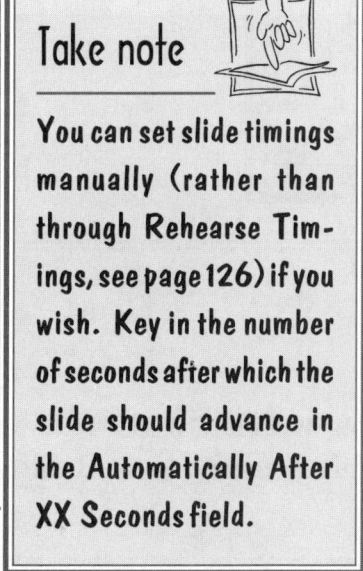

123

Build

If you have several points listed in the body text of your slide, you could try "building" the slide up during the presentation, rather than presenting the whole list at once. Experiment with the Build options and effects until you find the ones you prefer.

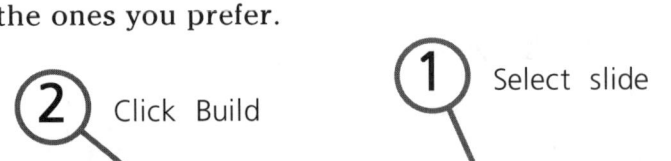

② Click Build

① Select slide

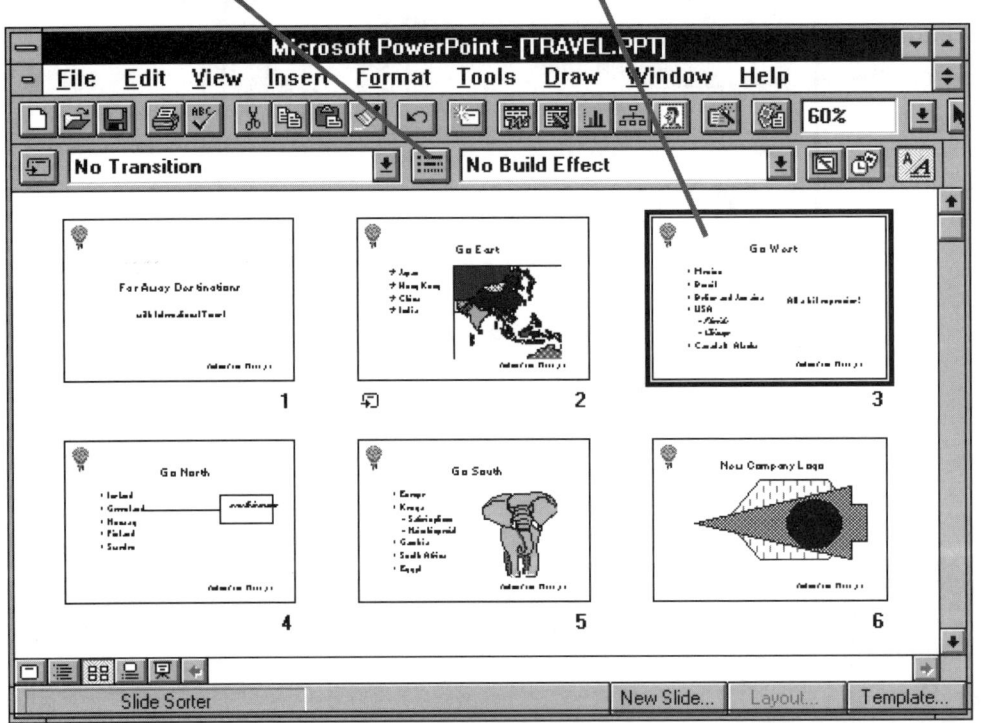

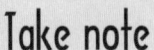

Take note

You can choose a Build effect from the Build Effects field on the Slide Sorter Toolbar if the default settings in the Build dialog box are acceptable.

4 To dim points as you go, check **Dim Previous Points**

5 Pick a colour for the dimmed text

6 Drop down the Effects list and choose one

7 Click **OK**

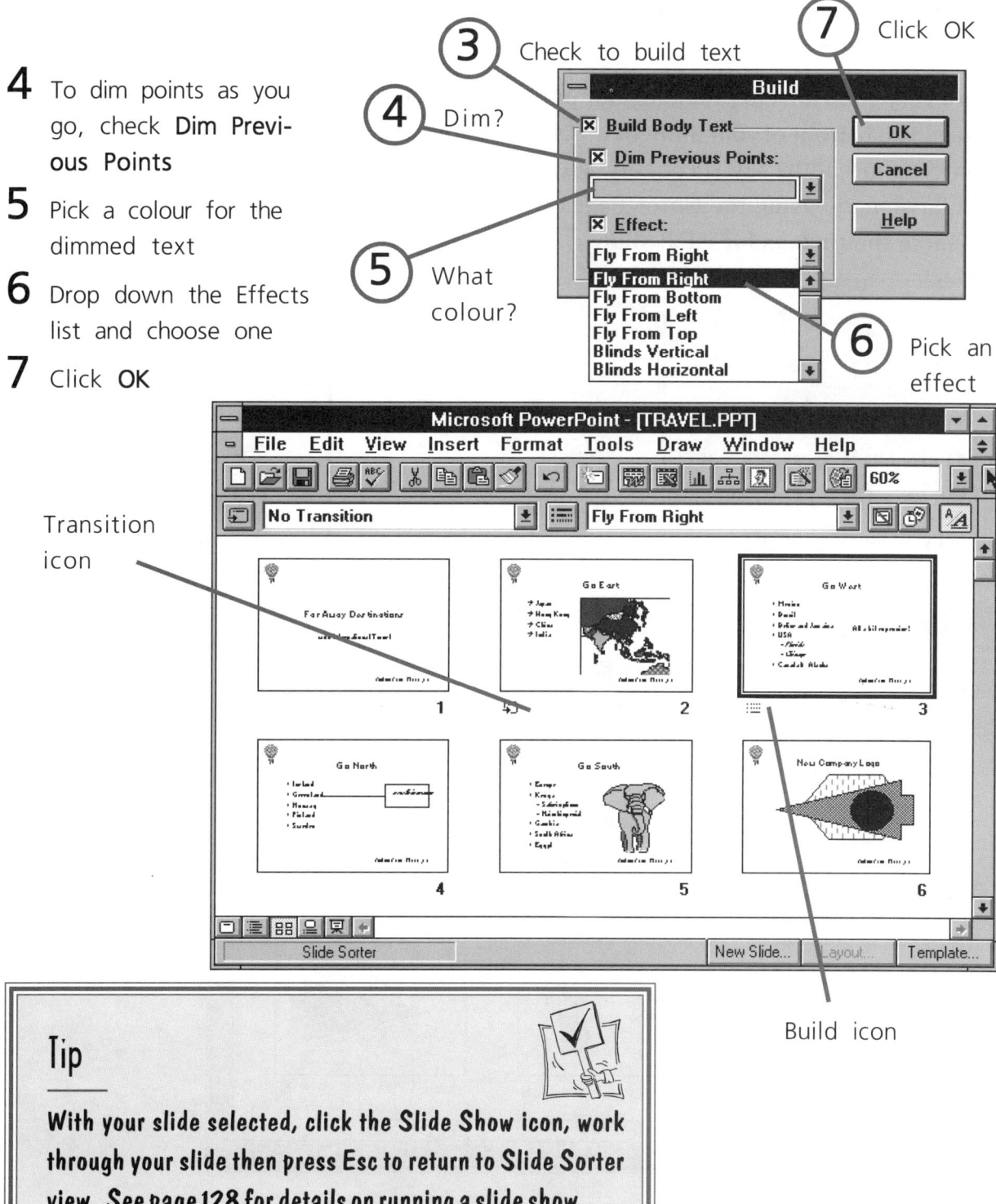

③ Check to build text

④ Dim?

⑤ What colour?

⑦ Click OK

⑥ Pick an effect

Transition icon

Build icon

Tip

With your slide selected, click the Slide Show icon, work through your slide then press Esc to return to Slide Sorter view. See page 128 for details on running a slide show.

125

Rehearse Timings

It is a very good idea to practise your presentation before you end up in front of your audience. As well as practising what you intend to say (probably with the aid of notes you have made using the Notes Pages feature), you can rehearse the timings for each slide.

Take note

You can rehearse your timings as often as is necessary, until you've got the pace right to get your message across.

Basic steps

1 Click the **Rehearse Timings** tool to go into your slide show for a practise run!

2 Go over what you intend to say while the slide is displayed

3 Click the left mouse button to move to the next slide when ready

4 Repeat steps 2 and 3 until you reach the end of the presentation

(1) Click Rehearse

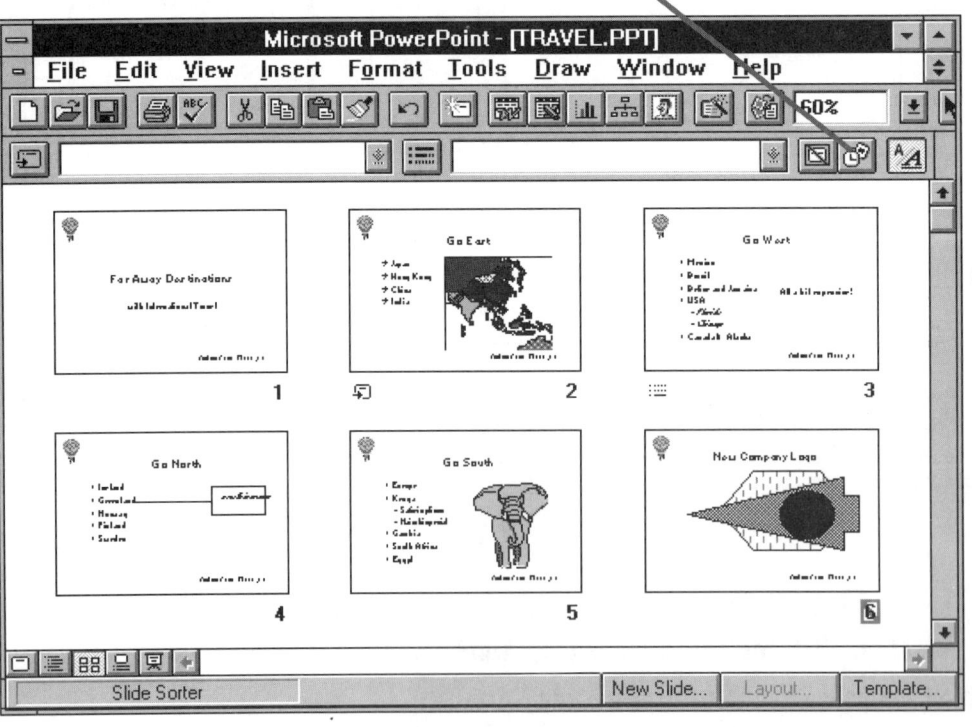

(3) Click left button for next slide

Displaying timings

A dialog box displays the total length of time your presentation took and asks if you want the individual slide times recorded under each slide in Slide Sorter view. If you choose yes, the timings are displayed under the slides.

Take note

You can set your timings manually in the Transition dialog box. See page 123.

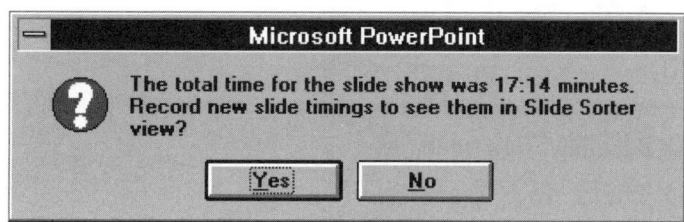

Timings

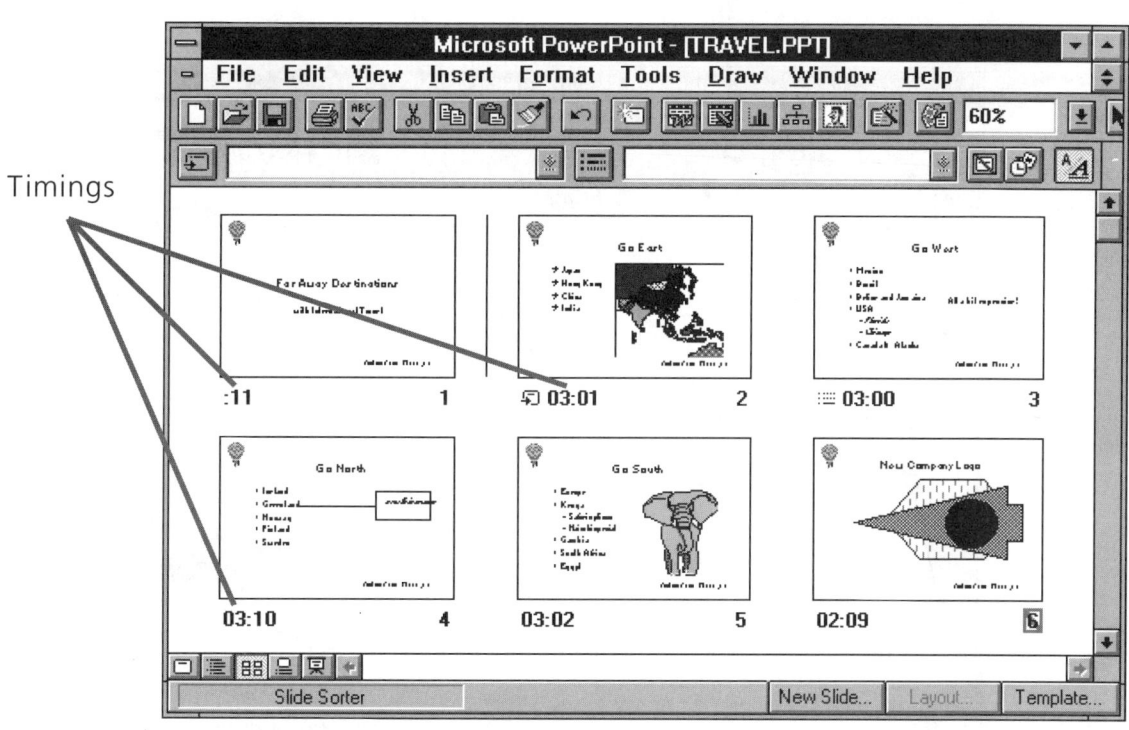

Slide Show

You can run your slide show at any time to check how your presentation is progressing. Each slide fills the computer screen. After the last, you are returned to the view you were in when you clicked the Slide Show tool

Tip

Use the Slide Show when testing Build and Transition effects to see if your options are having the desired effect.

Basic steps

1 Select the slide you want to start, usually the first

2 Click the Slide Show tool 🖳 to the left of the scroll bar

3 Click the **left** mouse button to show the next slide

4 Click the **right** button to show the previous slide if necessary

(1) Set start slide

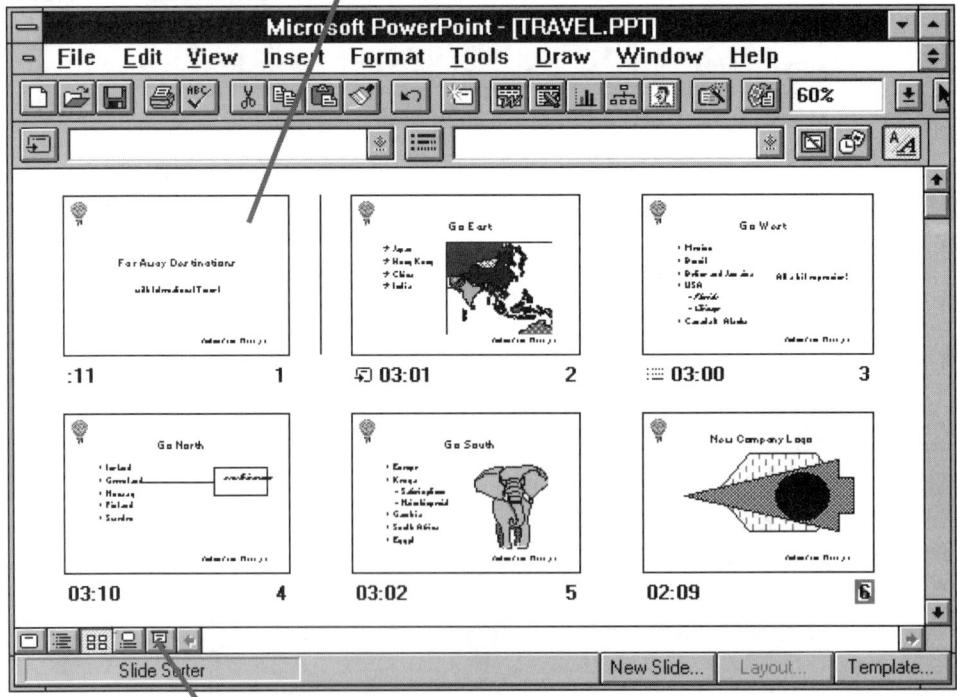

(2) Start the show

Basic steps

1 With your slide displayed in your slide show, move your mouse pointer. A pencil icon 🖉 will appear at the bottom right of your screen

2 Click on the pencil to "pick it up". The mouse pointer changes 🖉, and the icon at the bottom right of the screen changes to 🔖

3 Click and drag on your slide to "draw" your image

4 Click on the 🔖 icon to get your usual pointer shape back

Drawing on your slides

There are several other features you might want to experiment with when preparing your slide show. If you want to point items out as the show progresses, try using the "pencil and mouse" rather then your pen or finger!

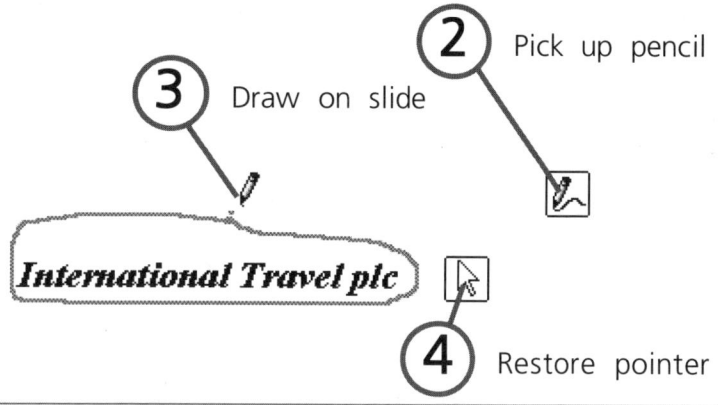

Slide Show key controls

[PageUp] [Page Down] to move from slide to slide
Enter the number to move to a particular slide
[Esc] to exit at any time
[E] to erase your drawing
[B] to Blackout your screen
[W] to Whiteout your screen
[B] or [W] again to restore the slide view.

Take note

To get more help on the options available to you while running your slide show, press [F1]. The slide show Help dialog box lists other options you might want to experiment with.

Slide Show options

Presenting your slide show using the Slide Show tool displays **all** the slides in your presentation (except hidden ones, unless you opt to show them). Each slide is displayed until your tell the computer to move on to the next slide using your mouse or keyboard – this is called a Manual Advance. You can choose to show a specified range of slides if you wish, or set up your presentation to run continuously (at an exhibition perhaps).

These options are specified in the Slide Show dialog box.

1 Choose **Slide Show** from the **View** menu

2 Specify the range of slides if necessary

3 Specify the **Advance** method required

4 Select the **Run Continuously Until "Esc"** checkbox if you want your presentation to run continuously once you've started it going

5 Click **Show**

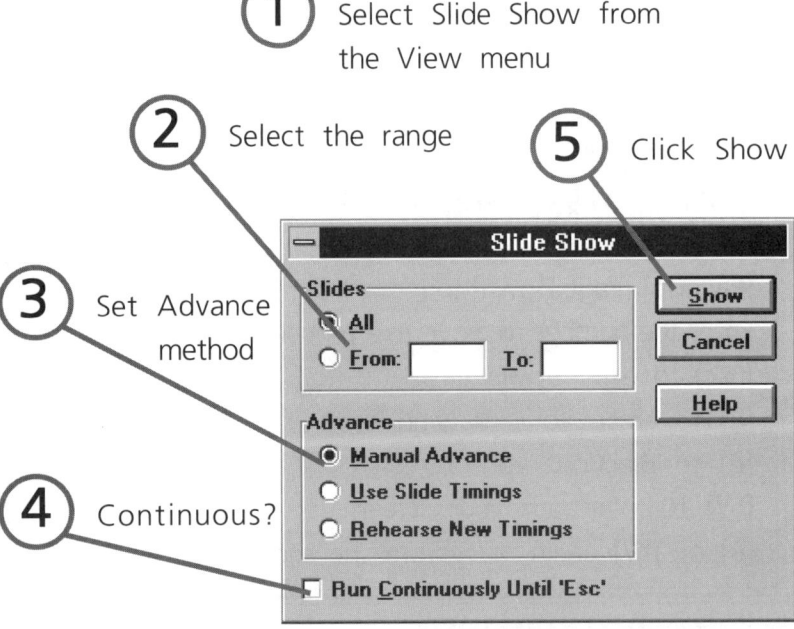

1 Select Slide Show from the View menu

2 Select the range

5 Click Show

3 Set Advance method

4 Continuous?

Slide Show

Slides
○ All
○ From: [ ] To: [ ]

Show
Cancel
Help

Advance
● Manual Advance
○ Use Slide Timings
○ Rehearse New Timings

☐ Run Continuously Until 'Esc'

Tip

If you set the Run Continuously Until "Esc" option to run your presentation at a demonstration or an exhibition, remove the keyboard and mouse once things are running.

Take note

Hold [Shift] down when you click the Slide Show tool to access the Slide Show dialog box

Basic steps

1 Add a New Slide, with the blank AutoLayout, to the end of your presentation

2 Choose **Slide Background** from the **Format** menu

3 Ensure the **Display Objects On This Slide** box is not checked

4 Under **Shade Styles**, select **None**

5 Set the background colour to Black

6 Click **OK**

7 Click [**Apply**]
(NOT [**Apply To All**] !!)

And finally...

Try adding a black slide as the last one in your presentation. The arrival of the black slide will indicate the end of your presentation (rather than being returned to the pre-show view, which is what normally happens).

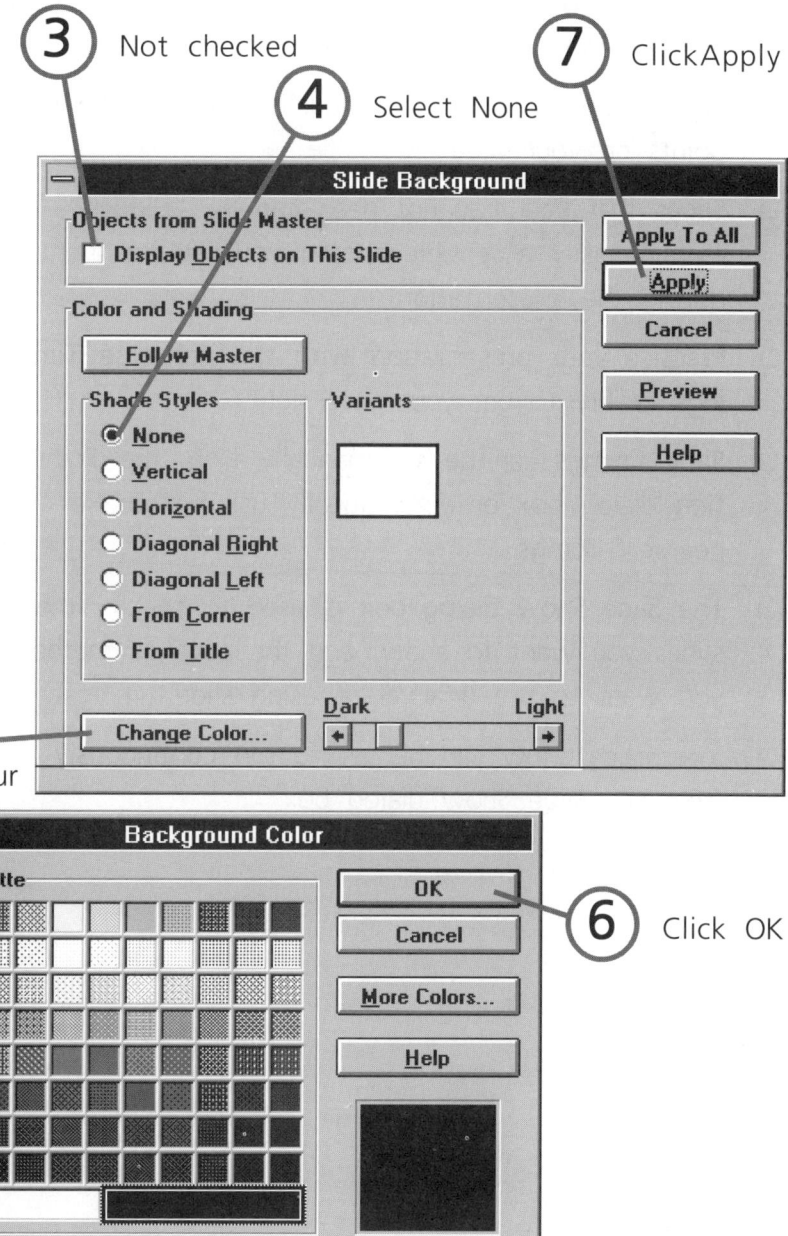

③ Not checked

④ Select None

⑦ ClickApply

⑤ Change colour

⑥ Click OK

131

Summary

❑ Use the **Transition** feature to modify the way your slides advance during the presentation

❑ The **Transition speed** is usually best set to Fast – this way your audience's attention remains on your presentation and not on your transition method

❑ Try the **Build** feature to gradually build up the main points on your slide

❑ Slides that you may not need can be "**Hidden**", but remain easily accessible should you require them during the presentation

❑ Practise your presentation with the **Rehearse Timings** facility to get your pace right

❑ **Slide timings** can be set manually from the Transition dialog box or automatically using from Rehearse Timings

❑ The **Slide Show dialog box** is used to specify the slides you want to show, and the advance method you want to use (manual or using slide timings)

❑ Your slide show can be set to **run continuously** from the Slide Show dialog box

12 Printing Presentations

Slide format

You can print your whole presentation in PowerPoint - the slides, speaker's notes pages, audience handouts and outline view.

You can print copies of your slides onto paper or onto overhead transparencies, or you can create slides using a desktop film recorder, or get a bureau to create the slides for you.

The first stage to printing your presentation is to set up the slide format.

1 Choose **Slide Setup** from the **File** menu

2 Select the size from the **Slides Sized for** field

3 Specify the orientation required for the **Slides**

4 Specify the orientation required for the **Notes, Handouts , Outline**

5 Click **OK**

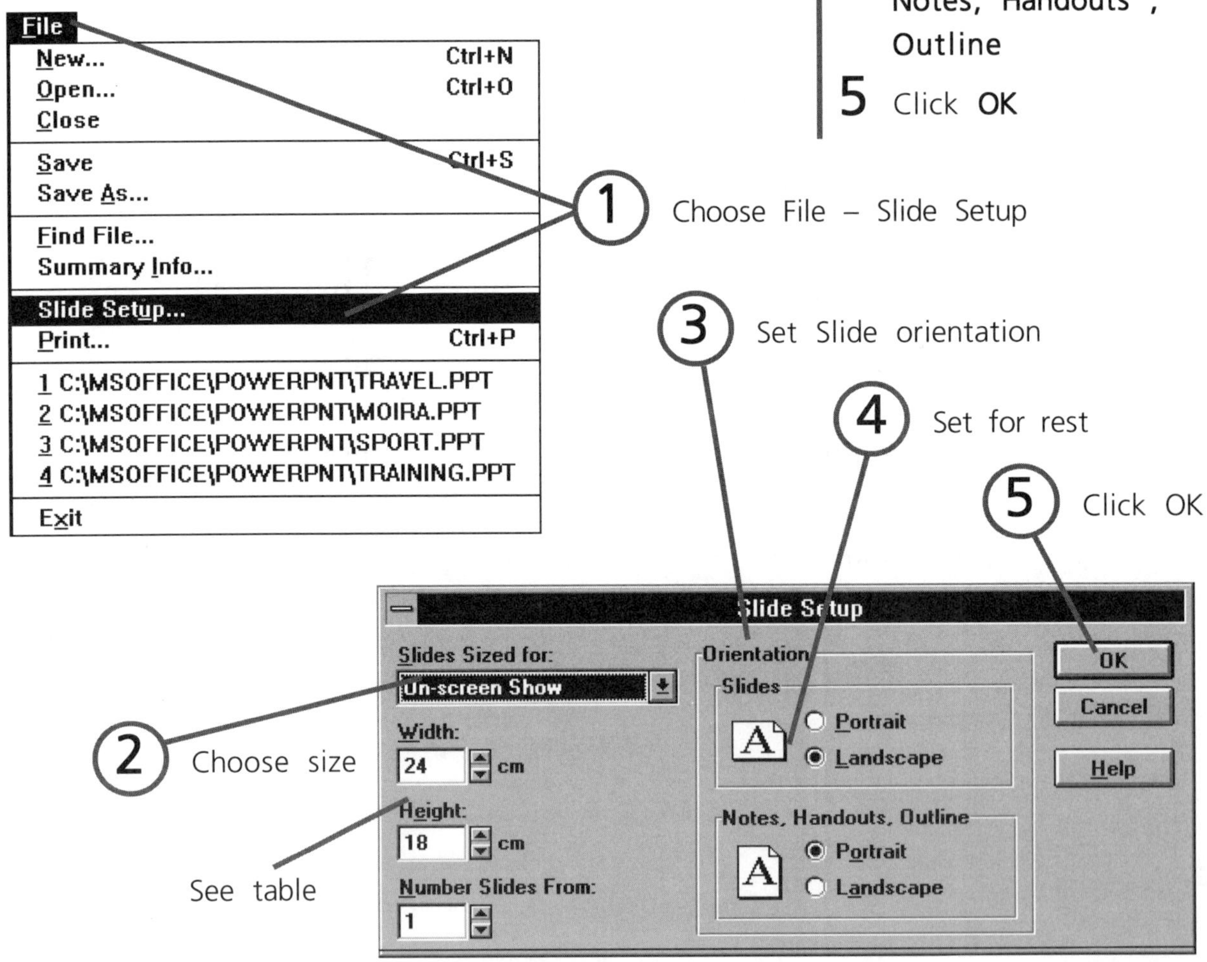

File	
New...	Ctrl+N
Open...	Ctrl+O
Close	
Save	Ctrl+S
Save As...	
Find File...	
Summary Info...	
Slide Setup...	
Print...	Ctrl+P
1 C:\MSOFFICE\POWERPNT\TRAVEL.PPT	
2 C:\MSOFFICE\POWERPNT\MOIRA.PPT	
3 C:\MSOFFICE\POWERPNT\SPORT.PPT	
4 C:\MSOFFICE\POWERPNT\TRAINING.PPT	
Exit	

(1) Choose File – Slide Setup

(3) Set Slide orientation

(4) Set for rest

(5) Click OK

Slide Setup

Slides Sized for:
Un-screen Show

Width:
24 cm

Height:
18 cm

Number Slides From:
1

Orientation
Slides
A ○ Portrait ● Landscape

Notes, Handouts, Outline
A ● Portrait ○ Landscape

OK
Cancel
Help

(2) Choose size

See table

Slide Size for:

Type	Width	Height	Notes
On-screen show	10"	7.5"	Orientation to Landscape, 3:4 aspect ratio
Letter Paper	8.5"	11"	select for overhead transparencies, 3:4 aspect ratio
A4 Paper	10.83"	7.5"	Aspect ratio between that of on-screen and 35 mm slides
35mm Slides	11.25"	7.5"	so content will fill the slide in landscape orientation 2:3 aspect ratio
Custom			Set own measurements required

Take note

The Aspect ratio is the relationship between the vertical and the horizontal co-ordinates. As pixels (screen dots) are higher than they are wide, an Aspect ratio of 3:4 on-screen produces round circles. Other ratios will make circles into ovals and squares into rectangles.

Printing slides

With the Slide Setup details specified to give the output required, you can go ahead and print your slides.

File	
<u>N</u>ew...	Ctrl+N
<u>O</u>pen...	Ctrl+O
<u>C</u>lose	
<u>S</u>ave	Ctrl+S
Save <u>A</u>s...	
<u>F</u>ind File...	
Summary <u>I</u>nfo...	
Slide Set<u>u</u>p...	
<u>P</u>rint...	Ctrl+P
<u>1</u> C:\MSOFFICE\POWERPNT\TRAVEL.PPT	
<u>2</u> C:\MSOFFICE\POWERPNT\MOIRA.PPT	
<u>3</u> C:\MSOFFICE\POWERPNT\SPORT.PPT	
<u>4</u> C:\MSOFFICE\POWERPNT\TRAINING.PPT	
E<u>x</u>it	

(**1**) Choose File – Print

(**2**) Print What type?

(**4**) Click OK

Print

Printer: Star LC24-10 on LPT1:

Print <u>W</u>hat: **Slides** ▼   OK

<u>C</u>opies: **1** ⬍   Cancel

(**3**) Set the Range

Slide Range
- ⦿ <u>A</u>ll   Printer...
- ○ <u>C</u>urrent Slide   ○ Sele<u>c</u>tion   Help
- ○ <u>S</u>lides: 1-9

Enter slide numbers and/or slide ranges separated by commas. For example, 1,3,5-12

- ☐ Print to <u>F</u>ile
- ☐ Print Hi<u>d</u>den Slides
- ☒ <u>B</u>lack & White
- ☒ Co<u>l</u>late Copies
- ☒ Scale to Fit <u>P</u>aper
- ☐ Pure Bl<u>a</u>ck & White

Print What:

Slides
Prints your slides on paper or overhead transparencies, one slide per page. This option is only available when there are no build slides in your presentation.

Slides (with Builds)
Prints each step of a build slide, one image per page, starting with the Slide Title, then each major bullet item in the text.

Slides (without Builds)
Prints one page per build slide, with all items included on it. This option is only available when there are build slides in   your presentation.

Tip

You can specify your print range in Slide Sorter view. Select the slides you wish to print from slide sorter view (click on the first one, then shift-click on each additional slide), then in the print range options of the Print dialog box, choose Selection.

Take note

If you are going to send your slides to a service bureau to be turned into 35 mm slides or other materials, choose the Print to File option. This "prints" the slides to a PostScript® file.

For additional information read the On-line Help "Preparing a file for a service bureau", or contact the bureau you will be sending the files to.

Printing notes pages

It is useful to print out your notes pages to help ensure you cover all the relevant points during your presentation. When your notes pages are printed, a copy of the slide is placed at the top of the page and your notes appear below it.

(1) Choose File – Print

(2) Select Notes Pages

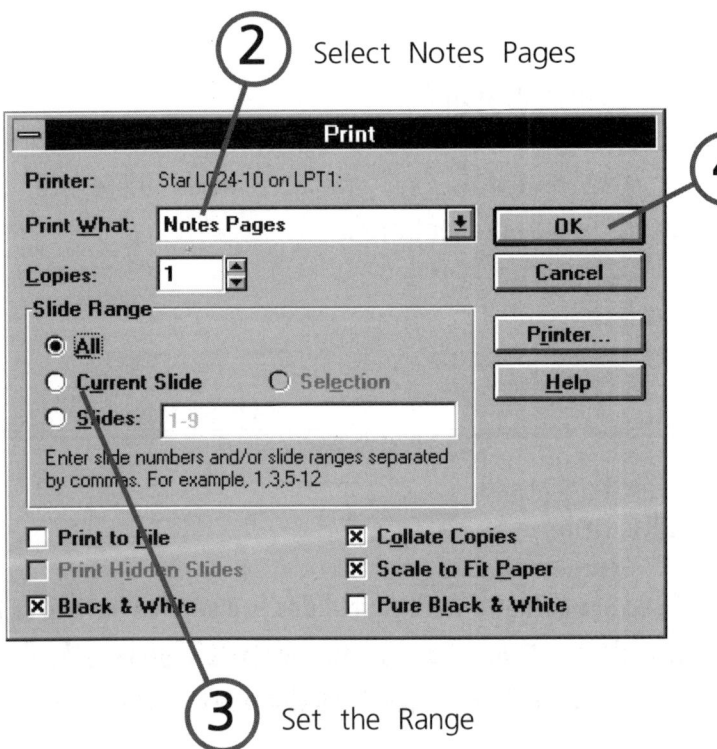

(4) Click OK

(3) Set the Range

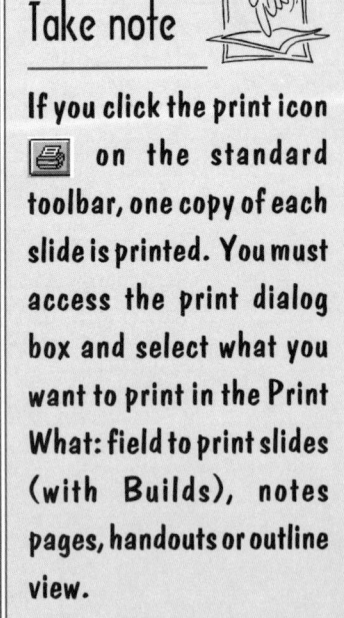

Take note

If you click the print icon 🖨 on the standard toolbar, one copy of each slide is printed. You must access the print dialog box and select what you want to print in the Print What: field to print slides (with Builds), notes pages, handouts or outline view.

Sample printouts of notes pages.

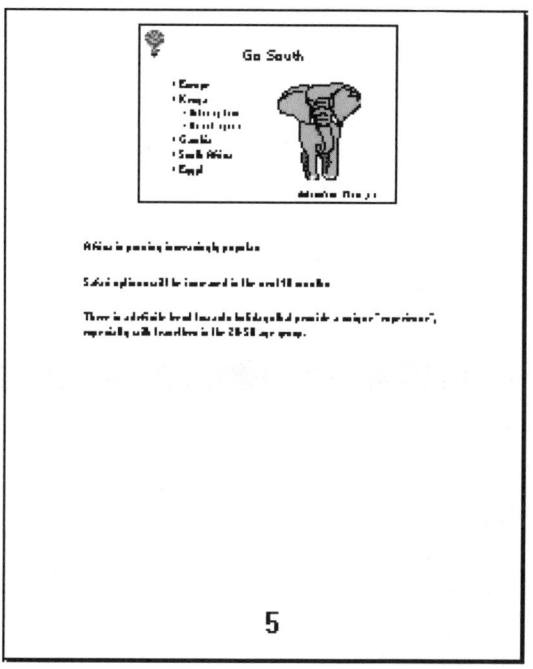

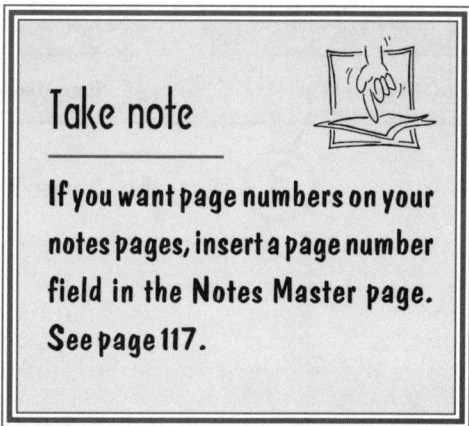

Take note

If you want page numbers on your notes pages, insert a page number field in the Notes Master page. See page 117.

Printing handouts

You can print copies of your slides to issue as audience handouts. The format of the handout can be set up to include 2, 3 or 6 slides to the page.

If you want to add text, page numbers, date or time to your handouts you must edit the Handouts Master page.

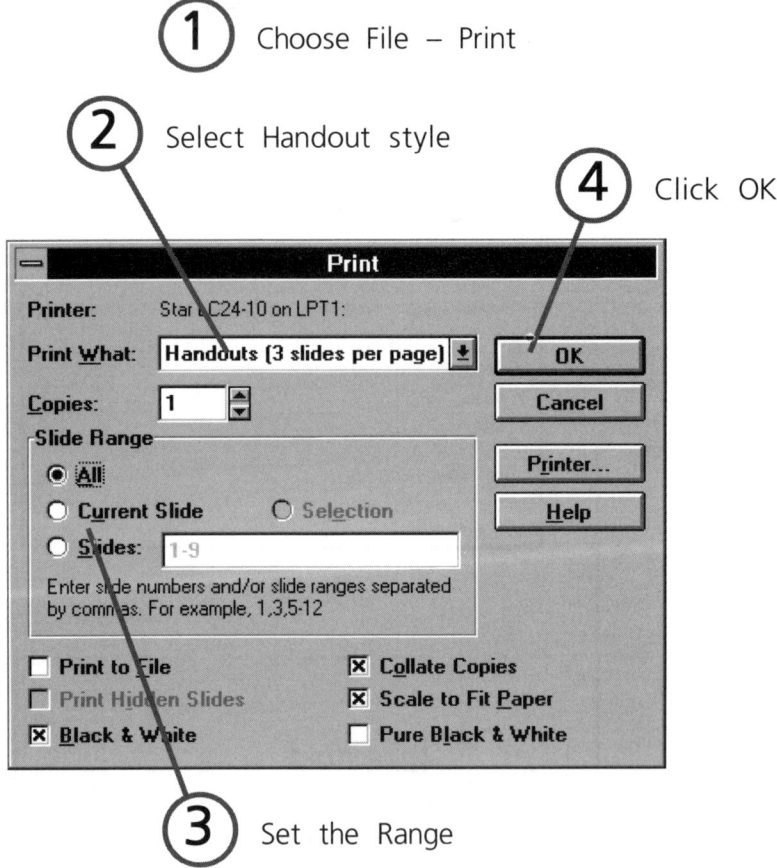

① Choose File – Print

② Select Handout style

④ Click OK

③ Set the Range

1 Choose **Print** from the **File** menu

2 Select **Handouts** (2 slides, 3 slides or 6 slides per page as required)

3 Specify the **Slide Range** to print

4 Click OK

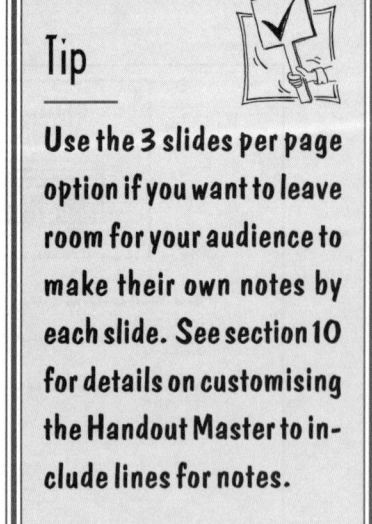

Tip

Use the 3 slides per page option if you want to leave room for your audience to make their own notes by each slide. See section 10 for details on customising the Handout Master to include lines for notes.

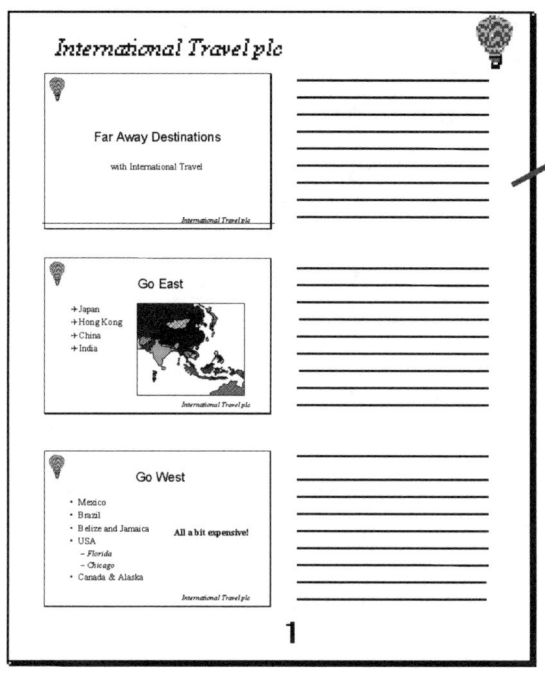

Handout printed 3 slides per page with space for audience notes. (See page 116)

Handout printed 2 slides per page

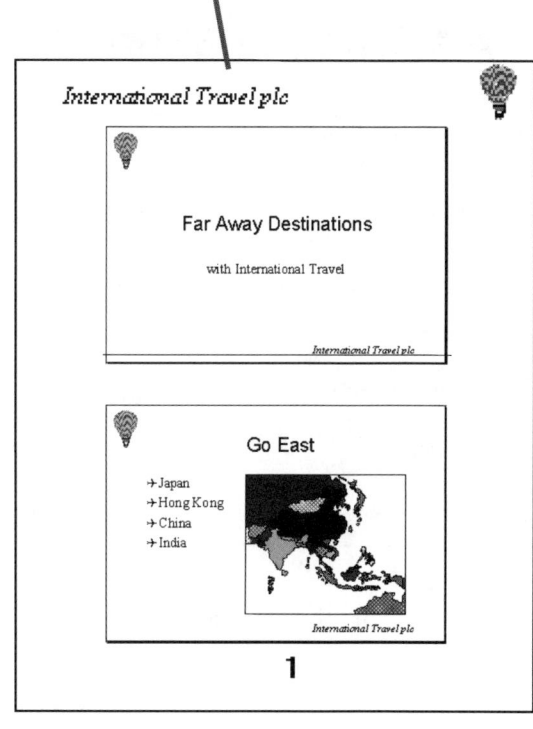

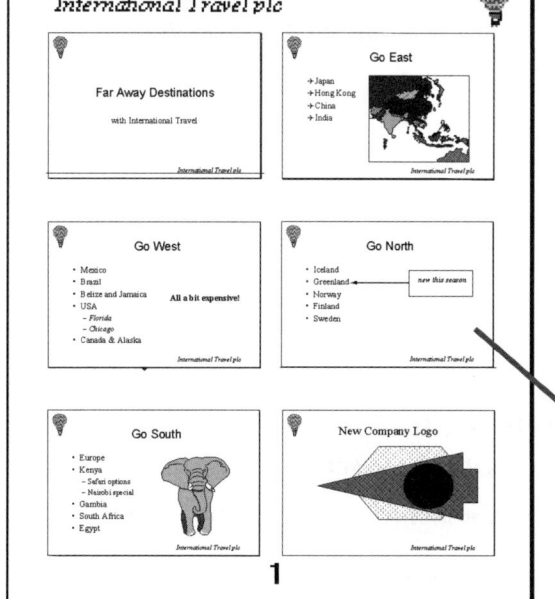

Handout printed 6 slides per page

Printing outline view

If you wish to print out a copy of the Outline view of your presentation, the same basic techniques are used. Your print will contain details of each slide title and the main points listed on each slide.

Basic steps

1 Choose **Print** from the **File** menu

2 Select **Outline View**

3 Specify the **Slide Range** to print

4 Click OK

① Choose File – Print

② Select Outline view

④ Click OK

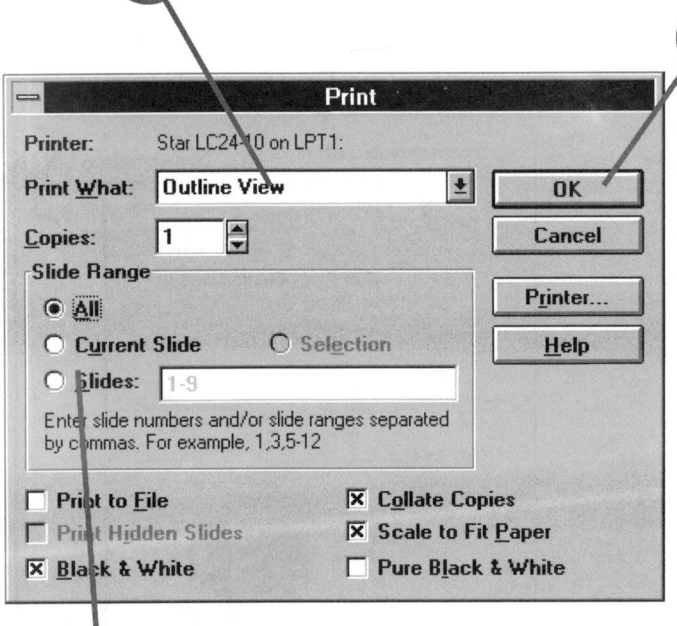

③ Set the Range

Tip

A printed outline can be very useful in that it lets you see an overview of the whole presentation.

Take note

Your outline is printed as it appears on screen in Outline view. You can expand or collapse your outline as required, or have the text formatted or unformatted. See Section 4 for details.

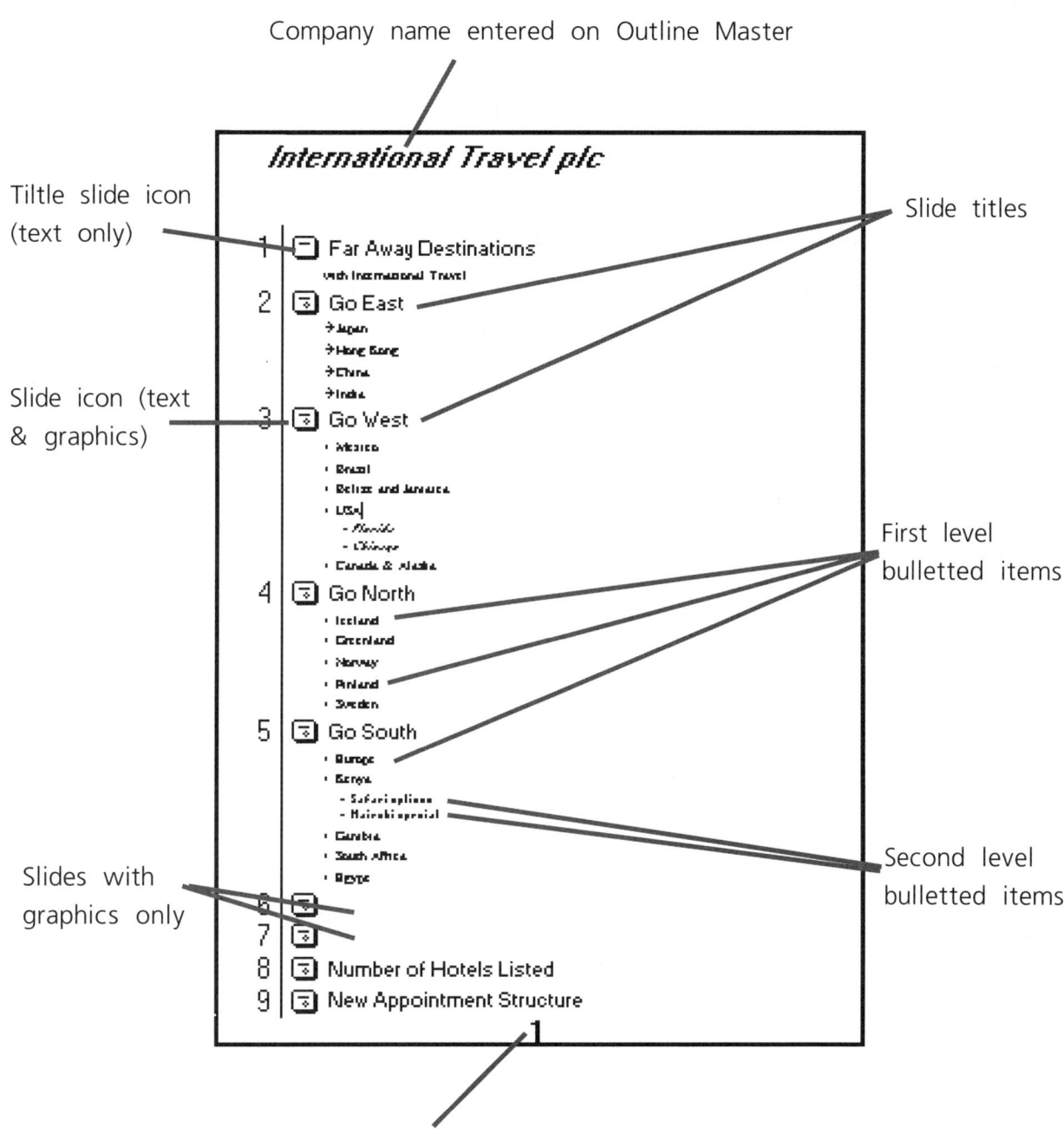

Company name entered on Outline Master

Tiltle slide icon (text only)

Slide icon (text & graphics)

Slides with graphics only

Slide titles

First level bulletted items

Second level bulletted items

Page number field added to Outline Master

International Travel plc

1 Far Away Destinations
   with International Travel
2 Go East
   → Japan
   → Hong Kong
   → China
   → India
3 Go West
   • Mexico
   • Brazil
   • Belize and Jamaica
   • USA
     – Florida
     – Chicago
   • Canada & Alaska
4 Go North
   • Iceland
   • Greenland
   • Norway
   • Finland
   • Sweden
5 Go South
   • Europe
   • Kenya
     – Safari options
     – Nairobi special
   • Gambia
   • South Africa
   • Egypt
6
7
8 Number of Hotels Listed
9 New Appointment Structure

1

Summary

❏ Specify your **Slide format** before printing your presentation

❏ You can choose to print your slides with or without **builds**

❏ It is often easier to specify your **print range** (if you don't want to print all of your slides) in slide sorter view

❏ Print the **Notes pages** to act as prompts while you give your presentation

❏ Take a print of **Outline view** if you want a summary of your complete presentation

Index